Magazine Movements

Magazine Movements

Women's Culture, Feminisms and Media Form

Laurel Forster

Bloomsbury Academic
An imprint of Bloomsbury Publishing Inc

B L O O M S B U R Y
NEW YORK · LONDON · NEW DELHI · SYDNEY

Bloomsbury Academic

An imprint of Bloomsbury Publishing Inc

1385 Broadway
New York
NY 10018
USA

50 Bedford Square
London
WC1B 3DP
UK

www.bloomsbury.com

BLOOMSBURY and the Diana logo are trademarks of Bloomsbury Publishing Plc

First published 2015

© Laurel Forster, 2015

Library of Congress Cataloging-in-Publication Data
Forster, Laurel, 1962-
Magazine movements: women's culture, feminisms and media form / Laurel Forster.
pages cm
Includes bibliographical references and index.
ISBN 978-1-4411-7263-1 (hardback) – ISBN 978-1-4411-7745-2 (pb) –
ISBN 97814411106018 (ePub) – ISBN 978-1-4411-1781-6 (ePDF)
1. Women's studies. 2. Feminism. 3. Women in mass media. I. Title.
HQ1180.F677 2015
305.42–dc23
2014037449

ISBN: HB: 978-1-4411-7263-1
PB: 978-1-4411-7745-2
ePub: 978-1-4411-0601-8
ePDF: 978-1-4411-1781-6

Typeset by Integra Software Services Pvt. Ltd.
Printed and bound in the United States of America

For Nick, Florine, Eden and Pierre.

Contents

List of Illustrations   viii

Acknowledgements   x

1   Introduction   1

2   Modernity and the Unstable *Housewife*   17

3   Producing a Magazine for Television: *Houseparty*   51

4   'Improving the Public Image of the Lesbian' in *Arena Three*   79

5   'Our Culture in a Racist Society': *Mukti*   111

6   A Magazine of Letters, CCC   147

7   'Make the Women Feel That They Are Important':
Developing the Radio Magazine   177

8   Magazines Working for the Feminist Cause   207

Afterword   239

Notes   242

Bibliography   268

Index   279

List of Illustrations

2.1 Master of Ceremonies: 'Christopher Stone introduces *Housewife*'.
© IPC Media. 25

2.2 Front cover of first issue, *Housewife* February 1939.
© IPC Media. 27

2.3 Teaching mistress and maid together: 'Laying the Table'.
© IPC Media. 29

2.4 Advertising Ovaltine: 'What are her War aims on the Home Front this Winter?'
© IPC Media. 40

2.5 Demanding post-war equality: 'Women, second-class citizens'.
© IPC Media. 48

3.1 Lucy Morgan shows off her recycled dress round the kitchen table.
© Wessex Film and Sound Archive. 58

3.2 Dressmaking item: From paper pattern to fashion show with Anne Ladbury and 'Marshie'.
© Wessex Film and Sound Archive. 60

3.3 The *Houseparty* set at Southern Television.
© Wessex Film and Sound Archive. 64

3.4 Marian Shuttleworth demonstrates traditional crafts.
© Wessex Film and Sound Archive. 67

3.5 Cherry Marshall and 'Marshie': Friends baking a cake.
© Wessex Film and Sound Archive. 71

4.1 Esmé Langley's editorial.
© Estate of Esmé Langley. 89

4.2 Esmé Langley and the MRG in the *News of the World*: 'Women Only' by Ron Mount.
© News of the World/News Syndication. 91

4.3 Early 'roneoed' first issues of *Arena Three*.
© Estate of Esmé Langley. 92

4.4 'Scouting for ... THE CURE' by Hilary Benno.
© Estate of Esmé Langley. 96

4.5 Running the magazine and opening up channels of communication.
© Estate of Esmé Langley. 100

5.1 *Mukti*'s defiant first cover, printed in six languages.
© Mukti collective. 120

5.2 Varied approaches to the subject of the dowry.
© Mukti collective. 126

5.3 Fighting immigration laws: 'Our Right to be Here Challenged'.
© Mukti collective. 132

5.4 Supporting the Brent Campaign against the police bill.
© Mukti collective. 135

6.1 A selection of embroidered and card covers for the *CCC* magazine.
© Trustees of the Mass Observation Archive, University of Sussex. 154

6.2 The construction and editorship of the *CCC* magazine.
© Trustees of the Mass Observation Archive, University of Sussex. 155

6.3 Illustrating tales of working-class life: Moving house by a
wheelbarrow chain.
© Trustees of the Mass Observation Archive, University of Sussex. 164

6.4 Travel pages of the *CCC*: Writing about travel to Tunisia (a) and
New York (b).
© The Hacker family, Rose Hacker Archive, Mass Observation
Archive, University of Sussex. 167

6.5 Snippets of local news: 'Our Railway', The Dengie Peninsula Line.
© Trustees of the Mass Observation Archive, University of Sussex. 168

6.6 The systems of reader response to letter-articles.
© Trustees of the Mass Observation Archive, University of Sussex. 170

7.1 Writing up the recipes: 'Marmalade Talks' BBC memo.
© BBC Written Archives Centre. 185

7.2 Producing talks in print: BBC 'Household Talks' leaflet.
© Estate of John Northcote Nash, Bridgeman Images. 187

7.3 Complementing radio talks: 'The Wise Penny' and 'Shopping and
Cooking' leaflets.
© BBC Written Archives Centre. 188

7.4 Shifting modes of radio address to women: 'Women at War' BBC
memo. © BBC Written Archives Centre. 196

8.1 The front cover of the first issue of *Votes for Women*. 224

8.2 Suffragettes and second-wave feminism, on the cover of *Spare Rib*.
© *Spare Rib* collective; permission kindly given by the
Fawcett Society. 233

Acknowledgements

My heartfelt thanks must go to Janet Floyd for her constant support, encouragement and insightful comments at all stages in the development of this book. Without her enthusiasm, advice and much-valued friendship, little would have been achieved. I am also grateful to Sue Harper for her very helpful input at the early stages of this project, and for kindly introducing me to Jean Orba. Chapter 3 on *Houseparty* owes a huge debt to Jean Orba, who generously granted a very long interview and also provided further responses at later stages. As always, I remain truly grateful for the love and support I receive from Nick, Florine, Eden and Pierre, and I dedicate this book to them.

A research grant from Portsmouth University CCI Faculty very helpfully enabled some teaching relief and gave financial assistance towards travel to archives to unearth the primary material at the heart of the book. I would like to thank my colleagues at Portsmouth University for their support and the students at Portsmouth University for their comments and observations.

Very helpful feedback has been received as a result of papers given at conferences, seminars and public lectures, including British Culture and Society in the 1970s, University of Portsmouth, July 2008; Blowing the Cover: Sex and Gender in Magazines, The Women's Library, March 2009; Designing the Decades: The 1970s, Victoria and Albert Museum, February 2012; Women in Media, Queen's University, Belfast, March 2012; Women in Magazines, Kingston University, June 2012; Television for Women, University of Warwick, May 2013; One World Forum: Feminism Panel, University of Warwick, January 2014; History Seminar on 1970s Feminism, Southampton University, February 2014; Situating Women's Liberation: Historicizing a Movement, University of Portsmouth, July 2014.

The dependence upon a good deal of primary material in *Magazine Movements* has led to research in numerous archives and libraries, where I have been greatly assisted by archivists and librarians who have often gone out of their way to locate and even suggest materials. I have encountered a number of commercial organisations who have also been very helpful and interested in this project. I am very grateful for the kind permission granted by IPC media to reproduce images from *Housewife* magazine, assisted by David Abbott. The British Film Institute archives were the source of much background information for the *Houseparty* chapter, and I am indebted to Nathalie Morris and Jonny Davies at the BFI National Archive, Berkhamsted, for permitting an early viewing of letters from the Southern Television Written Archives. The Wessex Film and Sound Archive, Winchester, kindly granted me access to archived *Houseparty* footage and, with Heather Needham's help, arranged permission to reproduce images from the programme. I am most grateful to the Wessex Film and Sound Archive for this permission. I would also like to thank Ed Thomas, technical assistant, who produced the images for the *Houseparty* chapter.

All staff at the Women's Library Glasgow, perhaps the friendliest archive in the world, including Wendy Kirk and Gabrielle MacBeth, must be thanked for all their help with information and materials for the *Arena Three* chapter. I would also like to thank Maureen Duffy for her advice and interest in the *Arena Three* images and chapter. Martin Gibbs of News Syndication, News UK, kindly supplied the *News of the World* image and I am grateful to *News of the World/* News Syndication for permission to reproduce this image. I remain indebted to the very well-informed staff at the Women's Library, London, now housed at the LSE, for their general assistance and in particular for first bringing *Mukti* to my attention.

I would like to express my thanks to all the staff at the Mass Observation Archive, The Keep, Sussex, for their assistance in working through the Rose Hacker Small Collection folders and other sections of the archive. Karen Watson and Rose Lock of the MOA were particularly helpful regarding the illustrations, and Jenny Geering produced the fine images for Chapter 6. I am grateful to Richard Pike of Curtis Brown and the MOA trustees for their permissions to reproduce from the MOA. I would also like to thank the Hacker family for their very kind permission to reproduce images from the Rose Hacker Archive. Monica Thapar at the BBC Written Archives Centre, Caversham, not only retrieved endless files for me but also made helpful suggestions of further programmes. Kate O'Brien, Samantha Blake and James Codd facilitated the use of the images for the chapter on the radio magazine, and I would like to thank the BBC WAC for their permission to reproduce those images. Thanks also go to Bridgeman Images for the use of the John Nash illustration. Frances Rankine and Margaret Timmers, from the Victoria and Albert Museum, expertly identified the artist, John Nash, and this was tremendously helpful. I am very grateful to the *Spare Rib* collective for their kind permission to use their front cover in Chapter 7 on feminist magazines. I was greatly assisted by Polly Russell of the British Library in gaining permission from the collective. I would also like to thank the Fawcett Society for their kind permission to reproduce the Paget illustration, with help from Miranda Seymour-Smith.

Assistance has been received from archivists and librarians at the London School of Economics Hall-Carpenter Archive, Sussex University Library and the British Library Sound Archive all of whom have helped in the development of this book. The staff at the British Library must also be thanked for the consistent and reliable work they perform. Jovita Callueng, Jackie Brown and Anna Vernon were all extremely helpful in securing and facilitating the images for *Magazine Movements*. Greta Friggens, University of Portsmouth Library, dealt helpfully and patiently with all my late Friday afternoon requests, and Justin Vaughan demonstrated tremendous technical skill in enhancing fragile 1970s televisual images, ensuring their inclusion. I am pleased to also thank Katie Gallof and Mary Al-Sayed of Bloomsbury Academic for their support in bringing this book to publication.

Introduction

Magazines are rich texts to study: of variable presentation and layered meaning, with multiple authorship and elusive target audience, they present endless challenges of interpretation and critique. However, their influence, authority, popularity and cultural competence make them significant objects of critical enquiry, be they print periodicals or broadcast programmes. A magazine can offer a whole 'world' to its readers in terms of outlook and instruction, apparently embracing every aspect of life, nurturing body and mind, teaching lifestyle, encouraging success at home, in the workplace and in all manner of relationships, and so seemingly leading the way to a more fulfilled existence. Magazines are perhaps the ultimate zeitgeist media form. It is precisely this expansive authority, dealing in the detail of lives that draws both readers and critics. Any media form that purports to guide its target audience to a better version of themselves, through direct and intimate communication styles, is a media form with a political agenda. The political intention may be overtly stated or latently enfolded between the lines of articles and advertisements. It may be the impetus of capitalism in the pursuit of profit and corporate competition or it may be gender politics or an anti-hegemonic stance that provides the imperative. The magazine form lends itself to opinionated expression.

Magazines are rich texts, but they are also hugely diverse and intricately complex. Their varied content opens up numerous avenues for critical investigation, and their real and imagined target audiences lead to a considerable range of cultural and social modes of understanding. Consequently meaning, reception and cultural competence can remain fascinating, but elusive. Further analysis, it seems, is always possible of magazines. Their depth in years, volumes, issues or programmes, their breadth across a vast array of subjects and their interconnectedness through publishing house and associated industries such as advertising, present rather daunting objects of study. Not only do some magazines last for decades, but studying their reach can be extensive work, encompassing changes in society, reflecting diverse engagements with issues of gender and class, exposing industrial processes and functions, showcasing the talents of writers and editors and demonstrating a remarkable cultural embeddedness. Meaning and communication, meanwhile, are conveyed variably and often unknowably between writer and reader, and there are endless permutations in the format, content, tone and appearance of magazines. Moreover, the very term 'magazine' has lent itself to multiple interpretations and uses and is used to indicate any media genre with mixed content: a television programme, radio broadcast, web page, newspaper supplement, even a home-made scrapbook might call itself a magazine. The term is a capacious one.

In order to investigate the flexibility of the format we refer to as a magazine, each of the following chapters looks at an example that highlights a different way of understanding the context and function of the magazine. However, this is also a study of the work that magazines might do for women. Much critical work has been produced on the commercial, consumer-oriented print magazine for women and such magazines have long been understood to be important to women readers. From the very first, women's magazines have offered advice, information, companionship and inspiration and many have possibly concomitantly offered a persuasive image of a reactionary, conservative femininity into the bargain. Critical work in the field has discussed and revealed how such ideological constructions of women have potentially imposed or, at best, reflected, patriarchal restrictions on women's lives, in terms of a pervasive domesticity, an adherence to ideals of beauty, a slavishness to fashion, the establishment of constraining and conflicted modes of female feminine behaviour and so on. Work by feminist scholars in this field has been invaluable in both recognising the lure and potential persuasiveness of magazine editorials and images, and understanding the compellingly intimate personal dimension of this form of media communication. Some of the major writings are briefly outlined later in this chapter.

However there is a paradox here. Much of the existing body of work on women's magazines, engaging with aspects of the 'cult of femininity' in its various insidious guises and pointing to the contradictions inherent in ideological constructs within magazines, concentrates on examples of commercial, capitalist production of the service magazine, or the glossy domestic or celebrity publication. This focus can lead to readings of women's magazines as characteristically closed texts that urge a predominant meaning or mode of consumption.[1] This study does not take issue with those readings.

Such studies have paved the way to penetrating these complex texts we call magazines: they have drawn on different aspects of magazine content and political interpretation, reflected on reader interpretations and industry practices, and generally and convincingly demonstrated the significance and influence of the form. My argument is not with the conclusions of such studies, but with the exclusivity of their choice of magazines. Whilst there have been good reasons for studying mainstream commercial magazines with mass circulations and therefore mass influence, this study opens up for consideration a range of examples that moves away from the publications that have dominated critical commentary for so long. The aim of the following chapters, therefore, is to add breadth of media form, including radio and television broadcast and Internet formats to the usual print media genre. Further, *Magazine Movements* explores the homespun, the minority-specific, the little-remembered and the politically-oriented magazine for women. Many of the examples are out of the way, of limited circulation or of unusual presentation, stretching boundaries of form, suggesting new modes of presentation and meaning, and engaging in different ways with their audience.

Magazine Movements has two central modes of enquiry: firstly to investigate and consider the expansive form of magazines for women; and secondly to reflect upon how magazines simultaneously address, engage with and understand their female target audiences, that is, how magazine communication is staged. I investigate the structure and form of magazines across different media genres, and by extending my examples to include radio, television and the World Wide Web, as well as print, explore the pervasiveness and importance of this media form. My second aim is to employ a more varied set of critical frameworks to bear on these unusual magazines, frequently focusing on the initial stages of a magazine as the moment of start-up is crucial in establishing the manner of communication. Even commercial magazines, in the minority in this study, communicate variously. They are polysemic texts: on the one hand, they frequently represent the ideological strictures, gender norms and assumed subjectivity of the dominant classes, acting as a vehicle for the commercial requirements of producer and advertiser contributing to the capitalist system, yet on the other hand, this is a form which has been so enthusiastically embraced by women over a number of centuries, that the positive energies of aspects of the magazine format must be equally important. It is possible, perhaps, that women have been and continue to be duped into a blind observance of and adherence to the messages of the magazine, yet this seems unlikely for all of us who engage with and enjoy certain magazines at various times.[2] Commercial magazines, in their multi-layered construction of meaning, offer oppositional kinds of interest and entertainment, simultaneously providing practical advice and a fantasy world, giving authoritative instruction as well as passing on gossip, engaging with uncomfortable social realities on one page and dispensing aspirational discourses on another. In this way, different component parts of magazines produce different potential meanings and interpretations.

In response to the obvious question of how magazines achieve this and yet still retain their popularity amongst readers, this volume argues that changing, disjointed, even conflicting and contradictory communication is the norm for commercial magazines, and for some small and non-commercial magazines too. Such 'polyvocal' texts are not purveyors of harmonised or consistent messages, rather they embody difference, and divergence.[3] The very form of the magazine enables a breadth of views and participations.[4] Its conventions of articles, snippets, features, letters and so on should be viewed as hospitable to diverse opinion, as storehouse forms rather than necessarily cohesive texts. In discussing the processes of signification of a range of texts, all called magazines, this present volume hopes to approach an understanding of the diverse communicative strategies possible through this important media form.

Women's magazines have often reflected dominant, socially constructed images of womanhood, and yet have also engaged with issues of real concern to women; some, proving their diversity of address, seem to do both simultaneously. Furthermore, whilst some women's magazines may have remained seemingly impervious to changing social circumstances for women, others have reflected those developments. The relationship of the magazine to the prevailing historical, social and cultural situation for women is an important aspect of the magazines selected for discussion here. It is the particular way that magazines have alighted upon, or responded to, an issue for women – and there have been many across the long twentieth century – that has drawn my attention to the particular magazine. Whilst not all the magazines in this study could be labelled as overtly and politically 'feminist' in a narrow sense, in another broader sense, they all enter into a female discourse, identifying and attending to the particular needs of women.

From as early as the 1960s, feminist writers have criticised and discussed women's magazines. Yet it was to the magazine format, later in that same decade, that many women's liberation groups turned when they wanted to express themselves and reach out to potential new members, and in so doing were following a pattern established by many suffrage groups of the first wave of British feminism. Of course, different types of magazine communication obtain here: critics were condemning prevailing ideologies prominent in commercial domestic 'service' magazines,[5] whilst suffrage and liberation groups were producing official organs or newsletters to promote oppositional political ideas. Nonetheless, formats of the conventional magazines were copied by feminists, layouts were mimicked and contents reworked. Precisely because the magazine is a highly flexible form, it has been able to accommodate a varied representation of, and address to, a spectrum of women. Equally, if the magazine form has variously worked both for and against female politics, then the differences, dualities and similarities of magazines for women may be better understood by a close examination of their formal structure and approaches to readership communication.

Alongside a reflection upon the communication strategies adopted by magazines as they address and appeal to their target readerships, are observations concerning how those readers talk back. Studies in print media have demonstrated that magazines and periodicals express an exchange of ideas, not a static pronouncement. Ideas might be exchanged with society in general, with institutions, with other media forms, with particular groups of women (and men) and, not least, with individuals. The exchange and dialogism permitted by the magazine gives it its lifeblood: it refines its form and content; it keeps it current. The relevance of subject matter to the readership and the cultural moment, the adaptability to different modes, and the cultural competence of a magazine, offer up a complex set of discussions.

The social and political movement that lies at the heart of this study is feminism in its broadest sense, and the magazines I have chosen to discuss have an interest, at some level, in the social and individual progression of women. Feminism, with its history, diversities and contradictions, its promotion of gender equality and of female cultures, its variety, exclusivity and inclusiveness, has touched every magazine in this volume. All the magazines engage with aspects of female politics, and sometimes feminist politics, to some degree or other. That is, they take one or more aspects of women's lives and seek to develop understanding, consciousness and engagement through identity formation, sharpening of subjective consciousness, education or collective action. In each chapter, my aim has been to reach an understanding of the significance of the magazine in its address to the individual female reader, or viewer, and the broader female audience.

The critical field of women's magazines

A range of critical approaches have proved useful in this study in trying to understand the form and communication strategies of magazines that, in their different ways, address different arenas of female politics. To gain a sense of a magazine's communicative abilities is to assess how well it understands its audience, how it manages the delivery of its messages and information and how it deals with the target audience's responses. The chapters in this study draw on a full range of previous work in this field.

In the brief overview below, I have divided the major discussions of women's magazines into two overlapping groups: general and specific discussions of women's magazines. The general discussions have been useful in understanding the ideological imperative and potential reception of a range of mostly commercial magazines, for comprehending the historical sweep of the magazine and the influence of the magazine industry over the centuries. The specific discussions provide more focus on either historical period or particular audiences or particular magazines.

From at least as early as 1963, it has been clear just how important women's magazines have been in shaping and reflecting women's consciousness and identity. Betty Friedan's seminal *The Feminine Mystique* describes the 'happy housewife heroine' as a creation of American women's magazines of the post-war period:

> In the second half of the twentieth century in America, woman's world was confined to her own body and beauty, the charming of man, the bearing of babies, and the physical care and serving of husband, children, and home. And this was no anomaly of a single issue of a single women's magazine.[6]

Broadly, Friedan charts a history of women's magazines in which there is a withdrawal from female independence, ambition and engagement in the wider world in the 1930s to a female persona of child-like dependence, heroic only in childbirth, subsumed into a man's life in an ideology of 'togetherness', finding true happiness in the materiality and domesticity of being a housewife. Friedan laments the diminishment of the life of the mind within women's magazines and points to other concomitant factors such as the deterioration of the quality of fiction writing, and the commercial imperatives imposed on the editor. In particular, Friedan is critical of the way that women editors and fiction writers of the late 1940s and 1950s were replaced by male editors and 'Housewife

Writers' writing formulaically to a male perception of the new housewife. As an ex-editor of women's magazines herself, Friedan is in a position to point out that female writers and editors of the period were not themselves confined to a domesticated femininity. Writers may have been enjoying their domestic lives, but this was alongside their careers, and editors did 'not bow to the feminine mystique in their own lives'. The paradox of seeming equality in the workplace and yet the intense portrayal of the housewife-mother figure in women's magazines is not lost on Friedan, as she goes on to discuss the need for a new female identity other than femininity.[7] Although criticised for her dual position, Friedan's observations struck a chord and have remained important. In Chapter 2, I suggest that wartime circumstances pulled away from the purely feminine and women's identity was viewed changeably by one such domestic women's magazine.

The ideological power and prominence of the 'cult of femininity' and its magazine construction has been critically analysed and discussed in foundational texts such as *Forever Feminine* by Marjorie Fergusson (1983).[8] Some studies point to the contradictions and tensions in women's magazines, and *Women's Worlds*, for example, by Ros Ballaster, Margaret Beetham, Elizabeth Frazer and Sandra Hebron, argues that women's magazines present women's subjectivity as the problem and the various elements of the magazine as the solution. This winning formula, despite production changes and diversification, has been a fundamental means of survival of the genre across the centuries. Yet, as Ballaster et al. point out, the tensions between both creating and then addressing women's needs, and giving expression to women's lives whilst ideologically constraining them, remain unresolved.[9] In selecting a different range of magazines, the present study brings to light ways in which some magazines tried to address the existing needs of specific groups of women, rather than creating needs for all women.

In 1987, Janice Winship's *Inside Women's Magazines* problematised this important discussion. Winship faced the dichotomy of women's magazines head-on, approaching magazines both as a reader and as a feminist. Her book addresses the ways in which magazines contrive to appeal to women whilst also securing women's secondary status. She explains this in terms of ideological function:

> Women's magazines trade selectively in some ideologies and ignore others. Each magazine has its own ideological pattern offering knowledge, posing problems and providing solutions to capture its readers' hearts and minds. Such patterns

have not, however, appeared out of nowhere: they are the product of many historical developments and are constantly being reworked to make sense and deal, as best they can, with the changing experience of women's lives.[10]

Winship analyses the 'ideological patterns' of magazines of the 1980s, including *Woman's Own*, *Cosmopolitan* and *Spare Rib*, and demonstrates how 'inequalities between women and men continue to be reproduced'.[11] Whilst 'ideological patterns' remain, some of the magazines in the following discussion acknowledge women's secondary status as their starting point: their solution is to develop more positive identities for women.

The analysis of the ideologically-charged meanings relayed through women's magazines, and the recognition of their contradictory nature, has been a very significant area of study in women's magazines. However, fewer critics have undertaken the task of analysing how readers actually engage with magazines and derive meaning from them. Joke Hermes in *Reading Women's Magazines* has approached the study of magazines from an ethnographic point of view and has analysed the ways in which readers read and relate to their magazines of choice.[12] Her findings have led her to believe that readers tend not to engage overly deeply with their mostly commercial magazines:

> I wanted to know how women's magazines became meaningful for readers and readers told me that women's magazines have hardly any meaning at all. They are convenient, my informants said, easy to put down when other things need to be done, but of little cultural value and therefore not very meaningful.[13]

Alternatively, other critics such as Brita Ytre-Arne have considered how women's magazines operate within the context of the 'public sphere', where magazines might provide information about political issues or be seen as, 'resources for learning about the lives of others and for – vaguely and indirectly – relating one's private lives to a greater community'.[14] Rebecca Feasey has written about another potential use of women's magazines from findings arising out of a focus group set up to discuss the everyday use of celebrity magazines.[15] Feasey argues that these magazines are useful within a secondary function of providing non-contentious material for subject matter within daily conversational patterns.

Whilst on the whole the majority of criticism of women's magazines has remained within a fairly tight spectrum of commercial glossy and weekly print publications for women, nonetheless, even within this limited range, critics have in fact argued variously about these magazines' significance. Some have seen them from the textual perspective, as monolithic meaning makers expounding ideologically-bound instruction; others have seen these magazines as having little cultural meaning from the reader's point of view. In choosing, in this study, to look more closely at the format, construction and work of very particular magazines, and how this has been engineered to create significant and often innovative meanings between producer, audience and society, this study opens up new types of magazine and new approaches to understanding their function. The close readings of content, and the social implications of the following magazine examples within their varied contexts, will help to unravel some generalised arguments about magazines and point to more particularised arguments.

Another group of media historians and commentators have provided histories of magazines and their production issues. A crucial text is Cynthia White's *Women's Magazines 1693–1968*, a most useful history and sourcebook that spans four centuries.[16] White discusses an extensive array of magazines, but helpfully positions her encyclopaedic list within periods of change in magazine production or shifts in publication objectives. White's detailed historical research, her collection of much useful industry information and her sociological background enable this history of the form to be specific in example, critical in discussion and contextual in overview. Brian Braithwaite's *Women's Magazines: The First 300 Years* also offers an historical sweep, but this time mostly from the perspective of the magazine industry, pointing to differences between magazine companies. Illuminating aspects here are the links and mergers between magazine titles, the rationale for new magazines and for closures and the company-level decisions that had an impact upon the history of women's magazines.[17] Braithwaite writes from the position of a magazine professional who has been associated with a number of high-profile titles in his career such as *Harpers and Queen* and *Cosmopolitan*. His co-authored books, with Joan Barrell, such as *The Business of Women's Magazines* help to open up the industry of women's magazines to academics.[18] Anna Gough-Yates's *Understanding Women's Magazines* also provides a detailed and specific focus on production, practitioners and industry organisation of women's magazines in the 1980s and 1990s.[19]

One particular partner industry, advertising, has been the focus of much discussion. The important role of advertising in magazines, at once essential for many magazines' survival and often integral to the content and flow of meaning of the whole magazine, has been singled out as an aspect of women's magazines worthy of study in isolation. In addition, many studies of advertising make extensive use of examples from women's magazines. *Images of Woman* by Trevor Millum brought this important and influential aspect to critical attention in 1975, analysing the process, the construction and the communicative effect of this genre of advertising.[20] Judith Williamson's *Decoding Advertisements* remains an important text for unlocking meaning in commercial magazine advertising.[21] Ellen McCracken, drawing attention to the magazine's component parts in *Decoding Women's Magazines*, argues that both advertising and editorial aspects of magazines exist, in fact, on the same continuum in commercial magazines for women in the United States.[22]

What is clear from examining these different strands of critical writing about magazines is that magazines for women remain important areas for study and illustration across many disciplines such as sociology, cultural studies, ethnography, media studies and others. Books on specific female roles such as Johnson and Lloyd's *Sentenced to Everyday Life: Feminism and the Housewife* draw extensively on women's magazines to illustrate the complexities underlying the construction of female identities,[23] whilst more general studies such as Rosalind Gill's *Gender and the Media* devote whole chapters to representations within magazines.[24]

It is these approaches to magazines, specific, detailed and with an intense focus on a particular readership group that are extending the boundaries of discussions about magazines. Specific histories of women's magazines have been written, allowing the range of examples to broaden and the level of analysis to deepen. Margaret Beetham's *A Magazine of Her Own* takes a very detailed look at the ways in which domesticity was structured in magazines for women in the long nineteenth century.[25] Beetham's study investigates layers of meaning in the development of femininity in that most formative period. Class, social position and emerging female politics within women's periodicals are all shown to play a crucial part in the onslaught of domestic ideology. Commodity culture, the influence of royalty as well as progressive ideas are all argued to have had an important influence on the development of a female subjectivity in the rising middle classes in nineteenth-century Britain. Examples of excerpts from the magazines in question in Beetham's volume have been compiled into an anthology by Beetham and Kay Boardman.[26] An important historical study, *Feminist Media History* by Maria DiCenzo with Lucy Delap and Leila Ryan, with its employment of wider discursive contexts and inclusion of primary material, helpfully situates feminist and suffrage periodicals of the early twentieth century within the public sphere and a history of the print media industry of the time.[27] The present study is confined to women's magazines from the mid-twentieth century onwards as a period of important social change for women. Earlier periods of magazine studies, such as the Victorian or Modernist periods, have been received specific academic focus.[28]

Other writers have opened up thinking about magazines produced for particular audiences. Angela McRobbie has written extensively on the influence of magazines on girls, *Jackie*, in particular. McRobbie has seen magazines as powerful influences on developing female minds, if not so much as direct influence, then as ways of girls coming to terms with their own sexuality and providing some answers to teenage questions.[29] Penny Tinkler's (1995) *Constructing Girlhood* takes a detailed look at popular magazines in the period 1920–1950 targeted at adolescent girls.[30] It discusses ways in which magazine editors addressed girls' needs for independence but balanced these within capitalism, patriarchy and domestic work as either unpaid housewife or paid domestic servant. This age-specific study considers young women from a range of social classes and reflects on the magazines' engagement with the changes in girls' lives at this time in their life and at this era in history.

Discussions of magazines for audiences beyond the mainstream have also emerged. Noliwe Rooks' *Ladies' Pages* focuses on a previously unexamined readership group, bringing African American women's magazines to the fore, and investigates the modes of cultural representation of African American women in the magazines intended for them.[31] Issues of ethnicity and rhetoric are evaluated in the context of a magazine-encouraged emerging middle class status with statements about fashion and consumption practices. Erin A. Smith's *Hard-Boiled: Working Class Readers and Pulp Magazines* looks at the working-class cultures surrounding pulp magazines and how their stories and advertising reveal much about the men and women who read them.[32]

There has been much discussion about the influence and meaning of mass-circulation commercial magazines, often with quite oppositional critical points of view, on the journey to understanding these complex texts. There have also been extremely helpful studies of magazine histories and the capitalist imperative behind most women's magazines. But the study of women's magazines also needs to move away from the mainstream in order to reflect the diversity of the form and to consider the multifariousness of the term 'magazine'. Whilst mainstream magazines may always be seen through the commercial imperative/gender construction lens, more marginal magazines, less dependent upon advertising, can be evaluated differently. They may borrow from the mainstream, but their political premise is different. They are set apart by being formulated in different ways for different groups of people. Successful or not, the magazines in this study offer a different take on the magazine, stretching its boundaries, experimenting with form and content and appealing to particular groups of women.

Magazine Movements

The magazines selected for this study span a time period from the mid-twentieth century to the present. This was a period of great change for women and also an expansive moment in the development of what we refer to as the magazine. Emerging at various moments of heightened awareness, often politicised or politically related, each magazine in this volume focuses on a different issue for a different group of women. The mid-twentieth to early twenty-first century is a fascinating period for women's history, with both change and stasis in women's position in society. Whilst there has been official advancement towards equality, actual equality in women's daily lives has been frustratingly slow. Meanwhile, there has also been debate and dispute about feminist goals through first-, second-, third- and fourth-wave feminisms. At times this has involved a nuanced understanding and development of cross-generational engagement with different kinds of feminism. It should be noticed that the magazine form has continued to serve feminists in their pursuit of various feminist goals, and that women new to feminism have also recognised the powerful communication properties of the magazine, a point to which I will return in the final chapter.

The process and output of magazines across different modes of production have much to teach us about the appeal and usefulness of the magazine format, and this is the rationale for venturing, in this study, across more than one genre. The magazine may have started in the medium of print, but even in the printed form there are different subgenres of magazines to consider. Newspapers from early on, for instance, keen to encourage a female readership, produced women's pages not too dissimilar from magazine content from as early as 1896.[33] Print magazines have been intended as public and politically oriented organs of women's organisations such as the suffrage movement, and also hand-produced for private, even secret, circulation. They all use the medium of print, but in different ways, resulting in quite different publication outputs. The magazine format, following its success in print, has been adopted by broadcast media too. Radio programmes for women have followed the notion of a woman's magazine in both content and form as well as programme title: from as early as the 1920s the BBC has broadcast radio programmes giving advice to women about subjects deemed to be primarily of women's concern: housekeeping and childrearing. Early *Woman's Hour* for instance, adopted the magazine's mode of making sense of a woman's world by including a variety of items in a structured sequence. This magazine style of programming is a format choice that now lies behind much daytime televisual broadcast material. The continued use of magazine characteristics in the plethora of new offerings on the Internet must give us pause to think about the reasons for survival of this enduring form.

In choosing the magazines for discussion in this study, I have looked for examples that add something new to our understanding. Some magazines have had a role to play in effecting or encouraging or reflecting social change. *Magazine Movements* starts with two such examples. The 'housewife', whoever she may be, is the target audience for the magazines in Chapters 2 and 3. We may discern this at the superficial level through the very title of the print magazine *Housewife* (1939–1968), and the daytime scheduling of the television magazine *Houseparty* (1972–1981). Both these magazine products emerged at different times of increased social and political focus on women, one just before the Second World War, and the other at the moment of the Women's Liberation Movement. These were also moments when the notion of the housewife, in particular, was under considerable pressure, and magazines responded in different ways. In the case of *Housewife*, anxieties about the expression of class identity in the domestic sphere segue into wartime and then expectations of peacetime roles for the housewife. In the case of *Houseparty* both domestic fulfilment and domestic isolation are explored in a model of television companionship made possible through televisual negotiations of the magazine form. *Housewife*, a commercial magazine for an emerging sector of the middle class, lost interest in class-related issues when it started to guide women through the Second World War, reflecting, as the war years passed, on changes to women's roles as well as to their sense of themselves. *Houseparty*, a new television magazine programme of the 1970s, navigated, in a turbulent decade, a participatory path for its female viewers by reflecting back a more positive and less constrained mode of domesticity.

Both *Housewife* and *Houseparty* address a mainstream audience and were concerned with ways in which magazines might imagine, reconceptualise and reconstruct an already existing and understood mode of womanhood: the housewife. The following discussions in Chapters 4 and 5 examine magazines for women who were considered and who considered themselves, to be not merely minority groups, but barely recognisable in broader British society at the time of the magazines' inception. These two magazines are intent upon identity determination through community formation, and they work to construct, articulate and recognise women within those communities: *Arena Three* (1964–1971) was the first openly lesbian magazine in Britain, and *Mukti* (1983–1987) was formed to support 'Asian' women living in Britain. *Arena Three* announced itself as a magazine for lesbian women in Britain at a time when 'homosexuality' (for men at least) was illegal, and when few lesbian women in Britain had access to a subcultural scene in the 1960s. Mobilising the resources of a Social Movement Organisation, *Arena Three* sought to generate change through openness and research enquiry. This magazine, and its associated groups, can be seen as central to the growing lesbian social movement. By contrast, in the 1980s when the plight of British women of colour was seen to be worsening, *Mukti* emerged out of regular meetings in Camden, London, and was intended for 'Asian' women, in this context and at this time, meaning women from the Indian subcontinent, who were living in London in the 1980s and subjected to an increasingly marginalised and racially oppressed existence. *Mukti* offered information and guidance, news and information, and raised and connected issues of race and identity formation at a time when prejudice was widespread. Created for a specific group of women, identified by their ethnicity and immigrant status, this magazine functioned at multiple levels in trying to draw this disparate group together. *Mukti*, in only a few issues, disseminated important and essential information, but it had a wider function too. It also attempted to encourage personal political awareness, by bravely celebrating, defining and naming a subject position and sense of self, on behalf of this oppressed minority. Both these magazines set themselves the difficult task of speaking to women who were hard to reach, for respective reasons of secrecy and language, and both these magazines were battling against media stereotypes and societal prejudice.

Where Chapters 2 and 3 look at how different forms of majority magazines reinterpreted the traditional and conservative role of housewife, Chapters 4 and 5 consider ways that minority magazines identified and worked for less visible female communities. Chapters 6 and 7 also deal with identifiable, but very different audiences: one a private club, the other a growing national radio audience. Such disparate media forms and target groups serve to challenge our understanding of the format possibilities for the magazine. In order to understand both the pervasiveness and the significance of what we call the magazine, these two chapters examine a private magazine constructed purely of letters, the *Co-operative Correspondence Club* (1935–1990); and, in the radio magazine context, the precursors to the current BBC Radio 4 *Woman's Hour*. The *Co-operative Correspondence Club* circulated letter-articles to a self-selected group of women. Discernible in these letters, however, is a distillation of the deep involvement with women's lives and intimacy of address, often attributed to, but not always earned by, more mainstream commercial published magazine offerings. Significantly different in format to many other magazines, this was nonetheless read with an enthusiasm that sustained its readership group through thick and thin for the majority of their adult lives. In contrast, the iconic radio magazine, *Woman's Hour*, perhaps the longest running radio magazine programme ever, is widely and rightly respected for its quality, variety and engagement with the world of women. However, its predecessors travelled a long learning curve with much criticism and development, before learning how to assemble a successful broadcast magazine. This chapter looks at the less-than-successful early beginnings of the radio magazine programme for women in the 1920s and at subsequent prototypes of radio magazines engaged in experimenting in format and making necessary adaptations in order to garner a national female audience.

Many of the magazines discussed in Chapters 2–7 have supported women's cultures and groups, offered identities for women and experimented with the form of the magazine to find new modes of media communication that can support, engage and address women in positive ways. Most magazines discussed in the following chapters engaged with feminism directly or indirectly, intersecting ideals of raised consciousness and women's politics from different starting points. Others have existed alongside more strident feminisms, offering various interpretations and representations. The last chapter of *Magazine Movements* approaches a different set of magazines: those actively engaged in feminist politics and in protesting against patriarchy. This chapter does not attempt a history of the feminist magazine, nor does it attempt to summarise the extent of the work that feminist magazines have achieved for the feminist cause. It does, however, discuss recognisable similarities in the ways they use the magazine format to convey their feminism. Through defining three consistent attributes of the feminist magazine – engagement with the magazine as a political act, a dynamic relationship with other print media and an emphasis on feminist history – it becomes possible to discern the ways in which feminist magazines, even when supporting very different types of feminist causes or adopting different media forms, ranging from newspapers to websites, nevertheless share similar attributes. Despite changes of all kinds, the magazine has remained a powerful political tool, working for feminism.

Modernity and the Unstable *Housewife*

It is axiomatic to say that the housewife has loomed large in mass-circulation women's magazines, and sometimes it seems that the breadth of womanhood has been distilled to the imagined identity and role of housewife in their pages. Betty Friedan, from her dual position as magazine editor then feminist critic of magazines, explains this dominance:

> You could sometimes get away with writing about a woman who was not really a housewife, if you made her *sound* like a housewife, if you left out her commitment to the world outside the home, or the private vision of mind or spirit that she pursued. [...] When you wrote about an actress for a women's magazine, you wrote about her as a housewife. You never showed her doing or enjoying her work as an actress, unless she eventually paid for it by losing her husband or her child, or otherwise admitting failure as a woman.[1]

She blames male editors and writers in the post-Second World War period, idealising home and a 'cosy domestic life' so that the housewife, according to Friedan, became a 'formula' for magazine copy and advertising.[2] This formula has been extremely important in magazine configurations: the figure of the housewife has provided a mode of addressing the target reader and a focus for the content of articles, acted as a channel for aspirations and needs subsequently identified and fulfilled by advertiser's products and, more didactically, simplified the conundrum of how to live a successful life as a woman. Almost any topic may qualify for inclusion in a woman's magazine as long as it relates to the housewife and her domain, and such incorporation of difference and diversity as has taken place has only served to reinforce the social centrality of the housewife. Surprisingly, whether or not the reader is married, has children, works outside the home or even runs that all-important home, has been largely irrelevant to this phenomenally successful magazine formula for communication with women.[3] The explosion of magazines focused on the domestic in the late nineteenth and twentieth centuries, and the impressive sales figures of many titles are both testament to this success and also, surely, to readers' willingness to be identified in this way and participation in this vehicle for communication with women.

Critical feminist discussions about the portrayal of the housewife in magazines have been clear about the ways in which women's containment within domestic confines and their restriction to the strictures of domesticated femininity are signs of patriarchal oppression.[4] This chapter does not argue politically with this overall position, but it does ask whether the housewife can really be understood as such a stable entity. As I argue later, the consistency of nomenclature in the magazine shorthand of housewife need not be interpreted as an unvarying subject position for women. While Friedan and those whose arguments have followed her imply that the housewife offers a single unchanging focus for communication, I suggest that the flexibility of the magazine format has permitted a layered, malleable and variable interpretation of that formulaic address.

This chapter deals with the only capitalist magazine example in this volume, *Housewife*. The mode of address of the magazine not only encompasses, but actually embraces, an engagement with change in the period before and during the Second World War, permitting the housewife to be understood as an ambiguous figure inhabiting diverse and modern identities. This is reflected in dialogic processes within the magazine: we can glimpse the housewife, not just as a creature of the domestic, but also as an agent of a female modernity.

Of course, the housewife herself is far from a modern phenomenon. Historians of housework have long made evident how the work of the housewife has always been subject to dramatic change. As Catherine Hall has argued, the medieval housewife had a broader remit as part of the pre-industrial family's 'self-sufficient family unit', with the result that 'domestic work had a much wider definition that it does now': 'It might involve brewing, dairy work, the care of poultry and pigs, the production of vegetables and fruit, the spinning of flax and wool and also medical care – nursing and doctoring.'[5] Hall goes on to discuss the close relationship between 'the position of women at work and at home – in a pre-capitalist society, because there is no split between the two, being a housewife means being engaged in a whole range of productive activities centred in both domestic activity for private consumption and in domestic activity which would be marketable'.[6] The housewife's range of skills has a place and a potential economic agency beyond the home, and, 'Being a housewife, then, is a condition which is socially defined and its definition changes at different historical moments.'[7] In this way, over the centuries, the role of the housewife might have been viewed both positively and negatively by both the women who fulfilled that role and others whose lives intersected with the housewife.

Hall, in drawing an important distinction between this fourteenth-century housewife with her various skills and consequent economic and professional status recognised within the village, and the 'hidden condition' of the housewife in contemporary modern capitalism, creates a context for the discussion that follows.[8] Since the nineteenth century, the housewife has been largely without political agency or independent economic power. She has been placed in a position of gender-related weakness and subservience in the home, and her 'condition' has been the subject of 'constant cultural review'.[9]

As early as the mid-nineteenth century, when mass-circulation magazines emerged for the middle classes, women's engagement with domestic concerns and the running of a home, either as the lady of the house or 'domestic woman', was a mainstay of magazine content.[10] Magazines diversified and specialised to reach new readerships from different classes or with different belief systems or prominent interests and ideas, but through all this diversification, domesticated femininity remained the dominant mode of understanding a gendered role for women. Cynthia White has discussed the post-First World War return to housewifeliness in women's magazines by means of the professionalism of household management. Moreover, women's magazines at this time encouraged women to 'spend more time than ever in the discharge of their household duties, to the exclusion of external interests and activities, thereby narrowing their outlook and contributing to the revival of an insular feminine role'.[11]

Subsequently, during the interwar years, the British cultural imagination elevated the idea of home and the housewifely role to such an extent that the home came to be publicly seen and imagined as the only proper sphere for women.[12] Alison Light has drawn attention to the interwar period when the very idea of the housewife had become prominent, with an upper middle-class version of a pleasurable and reassuring domestic life popularised in *The Times* through the 'Mrs Miniver' column, invented by Jan Struther. This fictitious housewife, with an array of servants and society connections to mark her status, captured the imagination of the country. As Light argues, the domestic and private life was viewed by many as of paramount significance to conservative notions of privacy, domesticity and even nationhood.[13] For many middle-class women, to be married was to gain power as opposed to remaining single without a household to run. The housewife then had become a figure of national importance in the 1930s, and there was national interest in how she lived her life.

However, not all scholars have seen the role of the housewife as a focus for reactionary cultural politics (or a site of patriarchal oppression). They have discussed the private sphere as itself 'radically implicated in patterns of modernization and processes of social change'.[14] Rita Felski, for example, sees the modern as a 'category of cultural consciousness' with mobile and shifting meanings.[15] In *The Gender of Modernity*, she argues against the exclusion of women's agency from discussions of modernity and questions the reduction of modernity 'to a single meaning and historical logic'.[16] Felski argues that it is not only in high modernist writing with its formal experimentation where 'authentically resistive practice' is to be found, and that theories of women's exclusion are 'unable to illuminate women's complex and changing relationships to the diverse political, philosophical and cultural legacies of modernity'.[17] Martin Pumphrey has also discussed how women's links to modernity were problematic and partial, but that women were just as likely to experience the public freedoms of modernity through discourses of consumption and fashion as through visions of skyscrapers in modernist cityscapes.[18]

Felski goes on to suggest that 'a central aspect of feminist scholarship has been its concern with the everyday and the mundane, and its consequent recuperation of those areas of women's lives often dismissed as trivial or insignificant'.[19] Judy Giles in *The Parlour and the Suburb*[20] interprets modernity as a concept 'which foregrounds experience and cultural negotiation', as a 'structure of feeling that enables women and men to make sense of the social processes of modernisation in the light of the responses, visions and ideas generated by these processes'.[21] Giles regards domestic modernity in terms of 'the ways in which women negotiated and understood experience and identities in terms of the complex changes that modernisation provoked in the so-called private sphere'.[22] She articulates the competing discourses surrounding women and domesticity where, 'On the one hand they were encouraged to see themselves as agents of modernisation and scientific rationalism in their domestic roles, while on the other hand they remained caught up in conceptions of home that valued it precisely because it was constructed as the antithesis of modernity'.[23]

It is precisely this engagement with ideas and processes of modernity and yet a concomitant duality of the sense of the housewife's role that is apparent in *Housewife* magazine. The flexibility of the format in its collection and collation of different pieces permits, without prior announcement or total commitment, the inclusion of such nuanced and seemingly contradictory and temporally attuned discourses.

Housewife (1939–1968) is a little remarked upon women's monthly magazine, with initial editors Bernard E. Jones and Margot Jones, that took its name directly from its intended audience and assumed reader, and augmented the range of magazines owned by the Hulton Press which had already enjoyed great success with *Lilliput* (1937–1960), *Picture Post* (1938–1957), *Eagle* (1950–1969) and *Girl* (1951–1964). In a pocket size format and targeted at lower-middle and middle-class readers, *Housewife* came out in February 1939, and grew in popularity, even outselling *Good Housekeeping* and *Homes and Gardens* in the post-Second World War period. It was taken over by Odhams Press and in 1968 subsumed into *Ideal Home*. Many magazines, including *Woman* and *Good Housekeeping* to name but two best sellers, developed the role of the housewife into a capable figure, fighting the home front for king, country and family over the period of immense social upheaval and uncertainty of the Second World War. However, in *Housewife* there exists a layer of additional tension in actually trying to define who the housewife really is, and even more complexly, who she might become. In this, *Housewife* broadly reflects Adrian Bingham's observations about the interwar period when he suggests that there was a 'multiplicity of different voices and images' in the popular press, with policies not dictated by proprietors and editors, resulting in a 'variety of divergent gender visions'.[24] This lack of clarity in a woman's magazine is a perfect scenario for the process of giving contradictory advice. Moreover, in the detailed engagement with the persona of the housewife, her social situation and her class position at this transitional stage in the twentieth century, a range of direct and practical responses to the social changes affecting women in the 1930s and 1940s, may be given. As a domestic magazine, *Housewife* certainly continues the 'work of femininity' importantly discussed and argued by Ballaster et al.[25] However, in other ways it proffers solutions to the complexities of a changing way of living for middle-class women. Indeed, a complex set of class assumptions configure any comprehension of the 1930s housewife. Class differentials and gradations across the British middle classes at this time were complex and detailed. David Cannadine has argued that as the middle classes in Britain expanded in the 1930s, there were many whose family income, mostly the husband's income, did not match the cost of maintaining a middle-class standard of living. These households, where extremely careful budgeting and household management was required to maintain appearances, were categorised as the middle-class 'new poor'.[26] The housewife addressed within *Housewife* is far from consistent and the changing tone, uncertain mode of address and hugely varied article content of this magazine leave numerous undetermined spaces for the reader to occupy. Ironically, this magazine, with its unequivocal title, goes on to offer its readers attainable visions of life beyond the confines of the domestic.

Housewife magazine started just before the war and at the end of a decade of class redistribution in Britain during which the middle classes had developed new classification strata as well as overall growth in sheer numbers. Cynthia White positions it as one of a group of magazine publications of the 1920s and 1930s 'intended for middle and lower-middle class consumption', and as one of 'three titles for a slightly higher class of readership', suggesting the middle rather than the lower-middle-class bracket. A number of magazines already on the market featured some aspect of homemaking in their titles: *Good Housekeeping* (UK) came out in 1922; *Woman and Home* in 1926; *My Home* and *Modern Home* in 1928 and *Wife and Home* in 1929. Also, two long-standing weeklies started in the 1930s: *Woman's Own* in 1932 and *Woman* in 1936. White argues that the 'prime function of these magazines was to render the woman reader "intimate personal service", with a secondary emphasis on entertainment'. This 'trend', White suggests, 'was associated with the reorientation of women's journalism away from the servant-keeping leisured classes, and towards the middle ranks'.[27] This kind of magazine was associated with changes in social class in Britain, contributing to and reflecting back the shifting 'cultural consciousness' of women's modernity. It was part of the expansion of interwar publishing for women, and a 'growing middle-class orientation of the women's press'.[28]

Housewife, targeted at both the 'new poor' and the slightly wealthier middle classes, promoted, through the very detail of its advice, a practical rather than leisurely mode of housewifery. (Undoubtedly this practical element was influenced by Bernard E. Jones, one of the original editors who was already a well-published author of various books on woodwork and other practical skills.)[29] The magazine is interesting in its frequent address to the reader as if she belongs to the professional or higher middle classes and yet, in fact, giving practical advice as though her budget falls in the lower income levels, a duality that may account for the magazine's popularity. *Housewife* when it first appeared had a diverse appeal, suggesting more than just a publishing house casting around for the right market, but an intelligent editorship that understood that the middle-class housewife was not a rigid entity, but a role oscillating between careful budgeting and aspirational living, hard work and leisured appearances, as well as intelligent capability and yet a need for advice. Accordingly, *Housewife* devoted space in its articles to the persona of the housewife, addressing her directly and intimately and always at some level evaluating her role.

Housewife magazine, unusually, recognised that this role still needed to be negotiated, and against the backdrop of shifting class definitions the magazine responded to social changes. It maintained a practical focus – other magazines were less practical, such as *Woman's Journal* which offered more generalised advice in decorative homecare – but offered its readers a more esoteric dimension too, ranging from social etiquette to philosophical leanings, so that instruction and advice was provided not just in running a home, but in how to live a life. What follows is an analysis of *Housewife's* response to social change, the shifting world of the housewife and her varying cultural meaning at three critical moments: during the pre-war late 1930s, at the start of the war and from 1943 onwards, when expectations of life for women in Britain after the war started to be anticipated.

'*Housewife* will be a good friend to you'

Housewife sets its stall at housewives who, while privileged in having a good home of their own to look after, must nonetheless stretch the household income imaginatively in order to maintain appearances. This is a magazine that from the outset claims to help the housewife weave her way through middle-class expectations and economies; there are few upper-middle-class assumptions of the Mrs Miniver model. *Housewife*, understanding its reader's predicament, purports to teach her how to achieve certain outward standards of living such as dress style, home decoration and entertaining whilst not easily affording them, through learnt techniques of careful and close budget management.[30] *Housewife* suggests itself as not only an arbiter of taste, but also as an advisory interface between the housewife and her consumption practices, thus offering its services as a negotiator of class determination.

With special mention of houses along dual carriageways or on housing estates in the opening address, there can be little doubt that *Housewife* targeted itself at women in the suburbs, working a distinctive appeal to middle-class allegiances, and from the very first issue carving a particular niche, perhaps amongst women who were not as class-confident as they could be. The lower-middle-class suburban woman might have been diagnosed with 'Suburban Neurosis',[31] or scorned in the 1930s by writers such as George Orwell and Vera Brittain. Further, Roger Silverstone, discussing suburban culture, has remarked: 'The suburban home has been built around an ideology and a reality of women's domestication, oppressed by the insistent demands of the household.'[32] Yet for other critics, suburbanisation has been seen as a more positive outcome for women, with the prospect of citizenship and improved health and living conditions.[33] Most significantly for this discussion, suburbanisation positioned the housewife as a crucial consumer, making purchasing decisions for the home and family, and as such a perfect target for commercial magazines. However, unravelling precisely which class of suburban woman the magazine addresses reveals the many contradictory messages within the magazine. Whilst in some ways this points to a failure of communication, in other ways it could seem a strength in not only attempting to encompass a range of middle classes through a broad appeal, but also as a way of understanding the magazine's pursuit of active engagement for women: a way of glimpsing its modernity.

The introductory address of *Housewife* to its readers is by Christopher Stone (1882–1965), who adopts the role of 'Master of Ceremonies' (Figure 2.1). Stone was a very well-known early radio disc jockey who also wrote a regular column for *The Listener* and so was already a participant within the world of modern mass communication. Stone's celebrity as well as his evident knowledge of his radio audience, which he implies and anticipates will correspond with the readership of *Housewife*, permits him to make imaginary links between himself and those two audiences in this piece of positioning journalism:

> My best friends of all, I believe, are the people who live in modern medium-sized houses with electric light, water from the mains, radio, local cinema and so on, in housing estates or along by-passes—or wherever you, who read this, are living.
>
> That is why I'm venturing to call on you now and pulling a copy of HOUSEWIFE out of my pocket to say: 'Here's something new that I think you will enjoy. The editors are friends of mine and if they can't make a success of it, it won't be because they don't know their subject.'[34]

The crossover between his radio listeners and the magazine target readership lies in women occupying suburban homes. The magazine readership and middle-class status are defined here by home ownership and

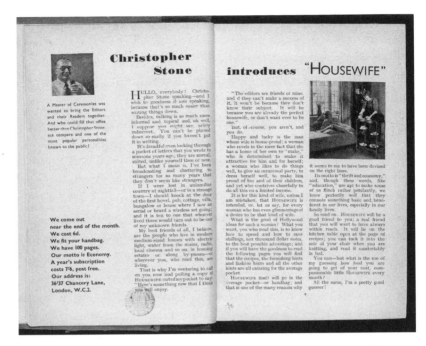

Figure 2.1 Master of Ceremonies: 'Christopher Stone introduces *Housewife*', *Housewife*, February 1939, pp. 4–5.
© *IPC Media.*

by modern facilities, making the type of home significant. This was an astute conflation of two media forms particularly as the isolated suburban housewife had become dependent upon the radio.[35] The radio had also become an integral aspect of her consumption practices, and as Maggie Andrews has argued, 'Women were both consumers of radio (which was in itself a new domestic consumer item) and were also seen as consumers of many of the products advertised on commercial radio.'[36] In appealing to the suburban housewife, perhaps new to her role, Stone targets not only a ready media audience, but a ready consumer too. It is just this domesticated woman, ready to receive instruction on how to maintain her household, who will be the ideal reader for *Housewife*. The target reader emerges with greater clarity as the introductory address continues:

> Happy and lucky is the man whose wife is house-proud; a woman who revels in the mere fact that she has a home of her own to 'make', who is determined to make it attractive for him and for herself; a woman who likes to do things well, to give an occasional party, to dress herself well, to make him proud of her and of their children, and yet who contrives cheerfully to do all this on a limited income.

Stone defines this British female reader further: 'What is the good of Hollywood ideas for such a woman? What you want, you who read this, is to know how to spend and how to save shillings, not thousand dollar notes.' In eschewing imagined American extravagance, Stone claims that the recipes, furnishing and fashion hints 'are all catering for the average pocket', and with its motto of 'thrift and economy' *Housewife*, he promises, 'will be a good friend to you; a real friend that you will want to have always within reach'.[37]

The all-important front covers are a case in point.[38] On the very first cover a mother is toasting crumpets by a fireside alongside her small boy playing trains on a deep-pile rug (Figure 2.2). The fabric-covered armchair and highly polished occasional table speak of a comfortable, but not grand home, and the cosy maternal affection speaks of emotional warmth too. So far so conventional, yet juxtaposed with this epitome of middle-class comfort is the subtitle: 'And here's to the housewife that's thrifty.' The rather jarring juxtaposition of words and image implies that it is women's active participation in household economies that will enable domestic pleasures and comforts: it is her engagement in necessary modern processes that will produce the middle-class home to which she aspires. Other cover illustrations always in full colour depict women, children and occasionally men in husbandly or fatherly roles in middle-class domestic or everyday leisure activities such as flower arranging, feeding the ducks or baking with mother. All the covers speak of the daily round and pleasures of the housewife and mother, frequently effacing her entirely to make room for her children. These images exude wholesomeness and contentedness with an inward happiness evident not necessarily through smiling faces, but through simple traditional pleasures, and well-dressed, well-behaved, healthy-looking children usefully occupied or supervised by their parents. Such values of a middle-class life are prioritised, orchestrated by the frequently absent housewife, with attention directed, not to the notion of female glamour, but to modest class confidence, stability and security. This, the magazine seems to say, will be the reader's reward for following the advice contained within its pages: the cover represents the 'personality' of the magazine.[39] Some slight typographical changes such as a plainer font against a solid black masthead from January 1941 may have updated the covers, but importantly, the appearance always remained glossy.

However, whilst the cover of *Housewife* depicts the comforts and privileges of an idealised middle-class life, inside things are less certain: class differentiation, social change and various types of engagement with

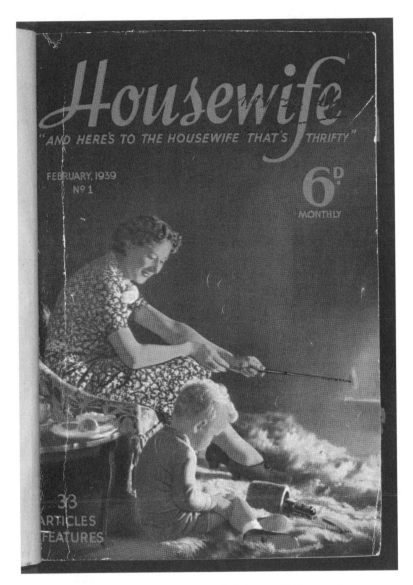

Figure 2.2 Front cover of first issue, *Housewife* February 1939.
© *IPC Media.*

modernity become apparent. Middle-class variation becomes evident when the socially complex 'problem' of domestic help is dealt with head-on. After the First World War, working-class women were especially reluctant to go into domestic service as they started to have other options in clerical or factory or shop work. Judy Giles has described how the demise of 'servant keeping' was of immense importance to the status and domestic organisation of middle-class women and how the decline of domestic service threatened middle-class identity.[40] As a signifier of middle-class status a maid was a key indicator, but there were stratifications too, existing within a continuum of arrangements from a full staff with specialist skills who exercised a layered authority within the household, to a single maid-of-all-work. Live-in servants were to be preferred to live-out 'help'.

Ideas of modernity are frequently explored through the different types of narrative available within the mixed content of *Housewife*. 'Narrative', as John Corner puts it, 'exerts a pull on the imagination',[41] and those narratives that help the reader to establish a sense of herself in the rapidly changing social climate perform crucial work within *Housewife* magazine. On the one hand, narratives that offer a path through the minefield of class adhesion help the reader to understand her position and to play her part, and on the other hand, narratives that are open-ended in their imaginative reach extend the potential readership for the magazine. The opening item, 'My Maid and Me', is a hybrid piece of writing, ostensibly a short story but employing the device of an interview that offers advice to the young wife by outlining the potential pitfalls in the delicate operation of hiring and, crucially, retaining domestic help.[42] Light in tone, recollecting a comedy of manners, the humour extends to the reader address too: 'If you have a maid, you'll enjoy this article. If you haven't, you'll enjoy it more.' Thus through a formal device of direct address, the editorial note extends the appeal to include those who need the advice, whilst also indulging the conceit that those who cannot afford a maid, perhaps from the lower-middle classes, have saved themselves an amount of 'servant trouble'. This careful positioning cleverly softens the class distinctions so that, for the reader, the difference between aspiration and actuality may not seem so great. In its multiple perspectives, the 'narrativised understanding' promoted by the story may be flexibly applied by the reader to her own circumstances.[43] Further monthly episodes continue to guide the reader through delicate scenarios of: managing and timetabling the maid's duties (with the lady of the house doing a fair amount herself); avoiding the disaster of the maid handing her notice in because of the master's insensitivity regarding her time off; and integrating additional staff once the first baby of the house is born. In short, these are lessons in coping with the modern servant, whose rights to free time and a social life must now be respected, and whose work ethic has to be encouraged rather than assumed. Yet whilst the article is instructive of the modern world and class-inclusive in its scope, it also harks back to an earlier era in teaching the new housewife how to maintain appropriate class differentials between mistress and maid.

Through such class-related articles particularly at the magazine's outset, *Housewife* both positions its readership and offers instruction in class behaviour, sometimes giving cross-class instruction simultaneously. For instance, 'Laying the Table' gives practical rather than 'highfalutin' advice to the housewife at the same time as she might be teaching her maid, retaining the magazine's position as the purveyor of middle-class mores (Figure 2.3).[44] Modes of entertaining are understood as obvious indicators of class and *Housewife* takes the rules of such outwardly visible ventures seriously. The suggestion for a 'Bridge Afternoon' comes complete with careful notes that whilst furniture might be borrowed, 'The hostess, however, makes […] her own bridge cloths to cover the table top, matching the colour of her drawing room.' Fiona Hackney has argued that magazine-led home sewing and craft were re-cast as modern activities in commercial magazines and the housewife imagined as an agent of modernity in her performance and consumption of them.[45] Whilst a bridge party may recall gentility it is a class-located activity, and painstaking instructions for the timing

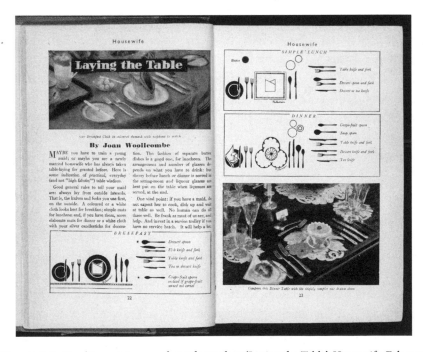

Figure 2.3 Teaching mistress and maid together: 'Laying the Table', *Housewife*, February 1939, pp. 22–23.
© IPC Media.

of the party, the sequencing of introductions and even the wording of the 'At home' card, all point to an inexperienced hostess without the necessary bridge cloths, offering, again, a range of class positions for the reader. Her autonomy and creativity in her home, however, make assumptions about her intelligence, adaptability and modernity.[46] This focus on the niceties of social etiquette needs to be contrasted with other instructional articles such as the one which sees the lady of the house mending her own electrical fuses in order to save money on calling out an electrician, to fully comprehend how middle-class display is funded by behind-the-scenes economies.[47]

Perhaps nowhere is public display and private economy more obvious than in the fashion editor's advice about a woman's wardrobe. One month the reader is guided through the purchase of the fur coat, an expensive but seemingly class-essential investment, and the next month behind-the-scenes economy is advised with suggestions for dressmaking and tips on extending the life of existing clothes.[48] The tightest budgetary controls, however, are exercised over the family food provision, an aspect of household management which may be kept largely hidden: 'Keeping the Food Bill Down' has a number of sections such as shopping lists with prices, menus and recipes, and its content operates to very specific budgets for varying family sizes.[49] The subject of money and expenditure is made explicit through lists, calculations and columns of figures. Furthermore, hints about cheaper cuts and avoiding false economies make these articles the epitome of no-nonsense instruction from a former teacher of domestic economy at a technical college. A more direct or controlled approach to the family food budget is hard to imagine.

Understood in the circulation of meaning between reader and magazine writer is the premise that the housewife's time and domestic skills are spent in place of any earnings or monetary contribution to the household, and that this represents the hidden economic exchange of the role of the housewife. Advice and discussions about motherhood, crafts, home furnishing, gardening, basic beauty and fashion as well as etiquette, home management and general interest fill *Housewife*, but they also fulfil the requirement for 'thrift'. Thrift here means economical living as a private matter undertaken in order to maintain quite specific rules of middle-class or upper-middle-class presentation and engagement. It is not parsimony but a modern and necessary attitude. It has played its part in traditional magazine advice for women for decades. According to Leonora Eyles (1889–1960) novelist, feminist and magazine agony aunt, 'it is a wholesome respect for time and material' and it needs to be part of our routine.[50]

However, Eyles also argued that thrift could not be learnt from snippets in the women's press,[51] the implication being that it needed to be felt from the inside as an attitude to life, that is, an approach, perhaps even a social process of modernity.

For this class of woman and the target reader of *Housewife*, femininity is her trademark, but thrift is her expertise. *Housewife* projects an image of a woman, not disempowered by a lack of independent economic status, but empowered by her determination to maintain a rigid class adherence. Yet *Housewife* harbours no illusions about a wife's economic status in the eyes of the law, as 'The Money Side of Marriage' demonstrates: a woman who has squirrelled savings for herself through thrifty management of the housekeeping allowance has been forced, on divorce, to return this to her husband.[52] Women's agency, in this project of maintaining middle-class appearances, is to perform her role as efficient manager of the household budget. With the help of *Housewife*, readers are encouraged to assume responsibility for the successful production of self, family and the domestic domain, no matter the limitations of a husband's income. This is directed as women's modernity; it is her way of embracing and coping with the modern world, and is seen as empowering and class reassuring. Domestic economy and management remains a guiding principle in *Housewife*, achieved through careful editorial control and direction, detailed articulation of different class expectations and, most interestingly, an open acceptance of the contradictions inherent in being a middle-class housewife. These contradictions did not disappear with the onset of war; if anything what it meant to be a middle-class housewife became even more complex and varied than before. The relative newness of *Housewife* as well as its focus on thrift meant that the magazine easily adapted to the concept of the wartime housewife. War was announced on the front cover of the November 1939 issue with the picture of a mother cheerfully dressed in a coral blouse and jewellery, tenderly leaning over her bonnie young daughter, and the strap line: 'Happy and Healthy – in spite of Hitler.'

Housewife at war

Many monthly women's magazines, including *Housewife*, due to two-month lead times, did not even mention the war until the November issue.[53] The war brought a number of changes to magazine production: publishing companies, short of paper and staff, had to decide which magazines would survive, which would reduce in size or frequency and which would have to fold. There were implications for distribution with transport reductions and implications for the safety of editorial teams. *Good Housekeeping*, for instance, moved its entire editorial team from London to Wales for the duration of the war.[54]

Meanwhile, changes to women's lives as a result of wartime conditions were numerous and contradictory, and not just limited to coping with rationing of food and other goods. As Sonya Rose has discussed, women, in order to comply with the idea of 'good citizenship', were encouraged and then directed into war work, sometimes male gender-specific work, although not necessarily for equal pay, and yet this often conflicted with what was regarded as women's morally responsible 'civic virtue'. Further contradictions were experienced in the expectations of a feminine appearance, and even though war work might be arduous, standards of hygiene, beauty and feminine aspirations of homemaking and motherhood were still expected of those same women.[55] Different discourses played their part in negotiating women's roles, and empowering as well as oppressive perspectives might be understood regarding the part women were expected to play in the war.[56]

Expectations of the role the housewife was to take in the Second World War were announced at the very highest levels. On 11 November 1939, only a little more than two months after the start of war, Queen Elizabeth, consort to King George VI, broadcast a Remembrance Day speech directed towards the nation's women. She pays due tribute to the women of Poland, France and the Commonwealth, and to those who 'have the privilege of national service', but also draws attention to those other women who play the 'humbler part', those women who do not have the 'novelty', 'excitement' and even 'exhilaration' of new duties in the war. The Queen addresses the nation's housewives directly:

> Be assured that in carrying on your home duties, and meeting all these worries cheerfully, you are giving real service to the country. You are taking your part in keeping the Home Front, which will have dangers of its own, stable and strong. It is after all for our homes and for their security that we are fighting. And we must see to it that, despite all the difficulty of these days, our homes do not lose those very qualities which make them the background, as well as the joy, of our lives.[57]

The conflation of 'Home Front' with 'home' implies that the domestic space too is a war zone which has 'dangers of its own'. Britain's housewives then are given royal permission to prioritise the upkeep of their homes and households as their own personal battleground, upon whose familiar terrain their war might be fought.

The home and, by extension, the women and children who occupied this space were raised in status, becoming the very reason men were prepared to fight in a war: 'It is after all for our homes [...] that we are fighting' said the Queen. The implication was that these homes would be maintained more or less as they were, bomb damage notwithstanding, for the soldiers' return. The successful running of a home, despite the difficult privations of war and without a man in the household, was thus elevated as one form of war work for women, and the housewife became a prominent figure in both popular and governmental discourses about the war effort. Her supposed cheerfulness and spirit, her selflessness and household management skills became symbols of national pride as well as conduits for the implementation of new codes of citizenship.[58] At the same time, the accomplishments of the housewife had to stretch to accommodate other changes brought about by the circumstances of war, and some retraining was necessary in new methods and new skill sets, including those domestic skills which had become professionalised over decades (or even centuries) into trades, and consequently 'taken over by men'.[59] These returned once more to the housewife's domain, and she had to learn to be her own painter, plumber and handyman. In these circumstances, the wartime housewife's world produced an intricate and nuanced web of social delineations, which still illustrated the delicate yet firmly differentiated textures of the British middle classes.[60]

Housewife magazine, perhaps more than most, took every opportunity to respond to those domestic battles; it engaged fully with the sense of female domestic modernity brought about by the war. If the disparate attributes of an increasingly indefinable middle class were taxing the editors, the Second World War provided a focus so clear and definite that *Housewife* articles, one way or another, could now employ this as a primary focus neatly sidestepping convolutions in articulating class differentials. Thrift and luxury according to income stratification and the minefield of domestic help could now be subsumed, within the magazine if not in actual social experience beyond the home, into an altogether worthier, class-immune, wartime economy. The war, and how best to survive it, quickly became the dominant theme of advice and instructional articles of all kinds. Furthermore, as the popularity of *Housewife* grew, so did advertising within the magazine, including a fair amount of government advertising, probably attracted by circulation numbers and the magazine's no-nonsense advice to a large section of the middle classes. The Ministry of Information was concerned to communicate women's role in the war and women's magazines were central to this communication, with women's magazine editors being invited to 'serve on a government committee which helped to ensure that particular messages were conveyed to women about issues such as dress and appearance'.[61] War Departments made use of women's magazines to communicate strategies and directives for dealing with the inevitable and sometimes prescribed changes to domestic living during wartime. Government policies for women as well as direct communication through the Ministry of Food and the Ministry of Fuel and Power were communicated through magazines' advertising pages. Additionally, communication about rationing and advice on make do and mend strategies filtered through both editorial and advertisements, as all parties adapted to the new conditions and strictures of war. In this way, government directives were repeated and explained in detailed and often ingenious ways through writers' explications in numerous war-related articles. The cascading of governmental advice through women's magazines has been noted by Waller and Vaughan-Rees who raise questions around the role of women's magazines as tools of the government, in supporting official campaigns and chivvying women into doing their bit.[62]

Housewife retained its highly practical approach, giving copious amounts of advice concerning all manner of things. The change in tone of *Housewife* magazine at the outbreak of the Second World War can be understood as a shift to participation in wartime processes and propaganda, where governmental instruction and advice was interpreted by magazine editors and writers, and subsequently passed on to the reader. This adapted governmental advice was turned to fit the usual personalised and intimate communication of *Housewife* to its reader, who in turn, was expected to interpret the advice and put it into practice for herself and her household. A process of 'cultural transmission' took place of wartime advice and instruction through the early wartime issues.[63] In this way, magazine writers and commercial advertisers in *Housewife* acted as cultural mediators between the government and the housewife and *Housewife* was particularly dynamic in giving up-to-the-minute advice on new ways of coping with increased privations of a deepening war. Whereas other magazine editors saw the role of their magazines to inspire and enliven women, to maintain morale and boost spirits,[64] *Housewife* was, in addition to those aspects, also practical and realistic, mediating the new wartime housewife culture.

Housewife had already laid the ground for middle-class thrifty housewifery from its very first issue and from November 1939 onwards began to slant its articles towards the daily and long-term challenges faced by British women during the war. There was no pretence that reader's lives could remain unaffected by war, but there was not a trace of defeatism either. Readers were depicted as capable women who were already contributing on a number of fronts: maintaining a home, and the idea of home for others, dealing in practical ways with hardships, as well as trying to uphold themselves physically and emotionally, and in addition doing something, however small, towards the war effort. Little wonder that the various governmental war ministries chose to advertise heavily in this magazine.

Given the pre-war emphasis in *Housewife* magazine on thrift, household budgeting, childcare and maintaining a good appearance in terms of the self and the home, when the war started it seemed that in some ways, whilst everything changed, everything also stayed the same. Some articles merely nodded to the war, as though it were an editorial thematic directive, drawing on the practicalities of wartime living in a matter-of-fact way and incorporating the war into daily living. The interior design editor, Roger Smithells,[65] when considering the faults of many hallways, comments that hall tables are 'littered with gloves, bags, circulars, gas masks and visiting cards',[66] thus bringing his usual editorial up to date by incorporating the everyday paraphernalia of war, including the gas mask amongst other more regular hallway clutter, and diverting attention away from the war to the more practical task of giving the hall a facelift. The fashion editor, questioning whether war work is sufficient excuse, asks: 'Should Women Wear Trousers?': 'Since last September we have learnt to bear with a certain fortitude a great number of somewhat surprising by-products of the War, from Unmentionable Things on the Drawing-room Walls – introduced by favourite evacuees – to no bacon with our breakfast eggs.'[67] The gist is that given these already existing problems, why would any woman indulge in the 'voluntary self-sabotage' of wearing trousers? The jolly tone, where culottes are definitely the answer to the problem of wartime efficiency, is available to be mimicked, proffering a mode of discourse of humour and practicality for housewives to emulate as they position themselves in the war. This tone could be adopted regardless of class status, household income or housewifely aspirations; it could provide an outward-facing version of the modern housewife regardless of her internalised concerns.

The perennial topic of food in women's magazines is similarly made relevant to war, and subtle adjustments in class behaviour may still be communicated whilst simultaneously fulfilling the role magazines were encouraged to play as partial mouthpieces for the government. In asking: 'Can it Do?' with the pun in the title seeking to persuade the housewife that canned food is no longer to be despised, the housewife is reassured that: 'there's plenty of food in Britain's larder – thanks to our Government's precautions – to keep us alive for months to come. Part of this larder is made up of canned foods'.[68] Similar adjustments arise in the regular family meal budgeting series now renamed, 'Catering in Wartime': 'Housewives can do their bit towards winning the war on the Home Front by keeping their families well and happy, even under war conditions.' For instance, as to be expected in a November issue, there is a 'Preparing for Christmas' article, this time acknowledging shortages in foodstuffs such as sugar, flour and fats, and so gives modified recipes to accommodate those shortages.[69] At the same time the larger, national issue of changes in food distribution is referenced: 'There is no shortage of food in this country, remember! The whole idea of the rationing scheme is to regulate distribution and to ensure that each person receives a fair share.' Implied is a prevailing common-sense attitude: 'Just imagine some of the difficulties which might arise if there were no rationing system', and gives the whole system of rationing royal approval, 'Now, even the King and Queen will be entitled to no larger rations than you can obtain,'[70] thus implying an equality of sacrifice.[71]

Changes in the circulation of meaning within the magazine were inevitably brought about by the privations of war, women's reconsidered roles and governmental intervention. Margaret Beetham has identified a number of power structures at play within women's magazines, and the most important for the discussion here is the triangle of communication and power between readers, writers and editors in the production and reception of women's magazines:

> Readers may be relatively less powerful than writers but they can still accept or resist meanings the writer produces. Writers are powerful in relation to language and the reader but less so in relation to the editor, the publisher or the advertiser. Editorial power is itself limited, discursively and economically, by pressure from advertisers and from readers.[72]

This triangle of readers, writers and editors provides a flexible model for understanding both the power relationships at play, and the processes in place, for the production of meaning within magazines. During the Second World War, however, the impact of the overarching authority of governmental communication through the vehicle of magazines disrupts this triangular dynamic. The government intervened in women's magazines in a number of ways besides the rationing of paper: it bought advertising; it introduced systems and policies which specifically and directly affected women; it determined new working roles for women and perhaps most intriguingly, the government and its associated public speaking agencies introduced a tone which demanded a certain mode of behaviour and conduct from the housewife.

Housewife, which was a magazine of high cultural competence at this time, carried a wide range of instructional articles suggesting how to appropriately and creatively accommodate the demands and changes brought about by war. Managing on less was a recurring imperative and as the months of war went on, and scarcities increased, so planning, resourcefulness and adaptability became increasingly important skills. Food, clothing, household items, books and more, all became the subject of many articles which devised ways to accommodate shortages, suggested ways of sharing or advised on simply how to do without. The idea of economic household management became a 'patriotic duty', elevated to the status of war work: 'Every housewife who economises strictly and sensibly is playing her part in defending her country'.[73] And this could be achieved through holidaying at home, converting the back garden to a vegetable plot, making blackout curtains or using luminous paint. Accompanying this, advice on new skills abounded with independent practicality being vital for the woman running her household single-handedly: 'How to put out an incendiary bomb' offers an extreme example of this. It was even suggested that disrupting the household might be a necessity: letting rooms was seen as a way of earning an income from the home if husbands had gone to war leaving wives with no money.

This advice performs interesting work within the context of a woman's magazine; it fills the pages and meets the need to engage with war, but the take-up of this advice is hard to calculate or imagine. Its function therefore might be more esoteric: to inform of what might come, or to let *Housewife* readers know of the hardships of other women less fortunate than themselves, thus bolstering the morale of the reader who has not yet had to resort to letting rooms in her home. Such articles not only work at reinterpreting the rules of middle-class acceptable behaviour, they even suggest crossing those crucial boundaries into working-class necessity.

The war had an impact not just on the content, but also on the formal properties and structure of the magazine. The contents pages, for instance, indicated the impact of wartime economies and processes by splitting its list into two with part one entitled 'The housewife at War', and part two, 'Life goes on ... '.[74] However, in such a division, we also might note that the magazine gives the housewife permission to be apart from the war too, to try and maintain a sense of self. In another formal change, obvious by the mid-1940s, there were nearly forty pages of advertisements before some contents pages of *Housewife*, including a number of government adverts, such as the message to 'Eat plenty of salads. They are home-grown' from the Ministry of Food.[75]

However, as the war deepened and it became clear it would not end as quickly as initially anticipated, a different mode of advice emerged in *Housewife*. The regular advice continued of course, on childrearing, napkin folding, home furnishing and so on, but besides practical, decorative or necessary skills, *Housewife*'s advice broadened: fortitude and solidarity became important themes. Readers were instructed in various ways: 'How to be brave' urged readers not to ignore fear, but to combat it by 'eating correctly and comfortably'. Calmness whilst eating, regular meals and chewing thoroughly were all proffered as ways of dealing with fear.[76] *Housewife* was full of praise for the fortitude of its readers. In 'On Putting up With Things' by Margaret Munro, the housewife's difficulties are listed, but her elevated status is also noted:

> And meanwhile we know that all these restrictions have brought the woman of the house into her own. No one can ignore her or do without her. She is home ruler and administrator. She is the only one who has the right to 'grumble to win'.[77]

As the impact of the war became clearer, *Housewife* magazine charged its readers with the challenge and duty of finding and maintaining an inner strength. Managing the self, controlling emotions and displaying appropriate conduct were all dealt with in *Housewife* as part of the modern wartime construction of their reader; in the absence of consumption, these qualities became the necessary contemporary outlook on life. 'Flying off the Handle' is about keeping one's temper and encourages serenity and self-control.[78] The inner housewife, so to speak, started to be addressed and catered for with advice on how to cope with the poor manners of evacuee children and how not to mind if your best things were broken, within the new context of a country at war. *Housewife* proved its competence in offering advice on coping with external hardships, but it also addressed the more complex issue of inner battles too, and different ways of appealing to the inner housewife became evident. Images of serenity were offered, making esoteric reference to the wartime challenges faced by women readers, such as the black and white close-up photograph of an icicled plant foregrounded against a backdrop of clear sky and snowy, pine tree-covered mountain slopes, with the caption, 'There is still peace and beauty on earth.'[79] In this image, picture and words combine to structure an idea of stillness and serenity; the war is acknowledged, but displaced. Unlike much else in the magazine, this image does not seek to construct the reader into her different roles; rather, its emptiness introduces a space for contemplation. Being able to manage nervous behaviour, and instead drawing upon calmness, and inner strength, in addition to dealing with the changing outer world, were presented in the magazine as an integral part of the reader's developing engagement with modernity.

Advertisements too started to change their approach; a prominent theme had been the housewife fighting on the home front. Some manufacturers with no products to sell were forced to produce advertising copy that kept their brand names in front of the consumer, others were in short supply and so suggested rationing or giving to the sick and needy first. However, many moved towards a theme of interior or psychological strength. An advertisement for Ovaltine, a malt drink, imagines the inner thoughts of the housewife with its title line, possibly taking a lead from the War Aims Committee: 'The housewife – What are her War aims on the Home Front this Winter?' (Figure 2.4). Like many others, this advert appropriates the circumstances of war directly and reinterprets them for the housewife; her involvement in the war is not questioned, but it is carefully positioned. There is no choice but to participate, however this is structured: she must protect her family, build her own 'Strong Nerves', maintain energy and ensure proper sleep. The advert uses the phraseology which became standardised as short cuts to other meanings: 'nerves' was a frequent wartime code word for anxiety; and restorative sleep was a regular term which obliquely referred to nights disrupted by air raids, sirens and other night-time disturbances, such code words acknowledge the psychological responses to war without labelling them as such. Similarly almost absent is the product, barely visible in the basket, and with a nod to shortages of other foodstuffs, this serves the advertisement well. Also concealed is any outward evidence of the housewife's

The Housewife – **What are her War aims** *on the Home Front? this Winter!*

To Safeguard the Family against Ills and Chills

To Build up Strong Nerves

To maintain Energy for Work

To ensure Restorative Sleep every night

That is why she buys

Ovaltine

P.509A

The Nation's Protective & Nerve-restoring Food Beverage

Figure 2.4 Advertising Ovaltine: 'What are her War aims on the Home Front this Winter?', *Housewife* January 1940, p. 2.
© *IPC Media.*

war worries; the happy appearance of both woman and child, their cheerfulness in the face of difficulty, is an essential part of her wartime contribution and an important propaganda message. The association with the product is powerful and the advert carries an abstract authority in demonstrating approved models of behaviour, continued within *Housewife* magazine. Fear and anxiety are acknowledged, but latently, paralleled by the almost-hidden product as the cure for these ails; however, what remains manifest is correct conduct and evident capability. The power of Horlicks, the preferred meaning of the advert tells us, may be understood as the housewife's silent helper.

The housewife is addressed on a number of different levels in *Housewife* as the war progresses, and as an assemblage of items with various editorial voices, the magazine demonstrates flexibility in the face of changing wartime circumstances. The overt encouragement of readers to define themselves in terms of class recedes and the new mark of distinction, no longer concerned with disguising domestic hardships and frugalities because the war has affected all the middle classes to some degree or other, is the ability to cope with fear and worry whilst maintaining a cheerful capable demeanour. Personal satisfaction for the housewife is to be found less in retaining her maid and matching her bridge cloths to her décor, but in maintaining a comforting home and a positive outlook, no matter what the war might throw at her. Her modernity can no longer be focused on consumption practices, but by attuning to the zeitgeist of war citizenship and on the inner resources on which she might draw to make her contribution to society.

The progressive *Housewife*

Predictions of the end of the war started very early in *Housewife*, from as early as 1943 the magazine started to think beyond the war. Meanwhile, as the war had become a reality to all households, it brought challenges for women in their homes, not just in stretching food rations and employing a 'make do and mend' attitude, but to the very meaning of the housewife role and her occupation of the spaces of her home. Lesley Johnson has argued that the middle-class suburban home might be seen not just as the passive and limiting other to the dynamic and active spaces of the city but also, at the end of the war, as a place for the housewife to engage with modernity in actively 'creating a place called home'.[80] This female agency relating to place[81] can be discerned within the pages of *Housewife* where home was subjected to newly competing discourses as a result of the war: it should be maintained as the imagined static idealised peaceful haven for husbands and sons fighting away from home, and yet in total war it was part of the war zone itself. Middle-class notions of home were fracturing in the magazine: what was private became more public as the occupants of home were likely to be fewer family members and more strangers; what was decorative became productive as 'Dig for Victory' campaigns instructed people to turn gardens into vegetable plots and what was unpaid labour became part of the wartime economic system as the spaces of home had earning potential.

Housewife's conception of the war home was a changing entity, reinvented, re-imagined and re-inhabited, in many ways it became even more important as it was elevated to the status of a business to be managed and in some cases became pivotal to the housewife's survival. There was, of course, the necessary compliance with war regimes such as blackout regulations, the provision of some form of air-raid shelter and 'make do and mend' campaigns. The magazine provided detailed engagement with all of these. However, there were also many articles that encouraged the reader of *Housewife* to think about how her home might be managed differently in order to contribute to the war effort, to utilise the actual spaces of the home to serve and provide safety to others and to provide a source of income for herself. Articles no longer discussed home as a sanctuary of domestic privacy and renewal, with negotiated duties with servants and fashionable redecoration projects as a main concern. In her role as manager of a wartime resource, the housewife might extend some generosity to others and put a sign up outside offering hot baths to soldiers,[82] or she might make her war contribution by offering her home as a billet.[83] Billeting, providing lodging for a member of the forces or a war worker, was one way in which the war affected the territory of the private home with its spaces now occupied by paying strangers. The housewife might take in evacuated children, sent from heavily targeted industrial cities to live in areas less likely to be bombed and the merging across social classes that this implied was a frequent subject within the magazine, with concerns expressed in one reader's letter about needing medical training to look after evacuees.[84] However, the magazine tried to present evacuees in a positive light, for example, a letter from one evacuee hostess with two children from Plumstead has little sympathy for those who complain about the government's allowance of eight and a half shillings per child, as she expresses her gratitude that her evacuees enable her to make some wartime contribution, 'however infinitesimal'.[85] Such articles altered the notion of home from a place of middle-class privacy, a protected space removed from the vagaries and harshness of working life, to somewhere that might be opened up to unknown children, war workers or even the homeless. In this new role, the middle-class home had the potential to be less insular, less bound by limited social codes of privacy and less stable.

The Blitz meant that for some, the home that they had come to rely upon as a permanent basis in a changing world also became a transient entity. 'A home made with hands' shows the ingenuity of a young couple whose home has been bombed and who have made a new home for themselves by refurbishing junk shop finds.[86] Still speaking to issues of class, but also resilience and determination, this article demonstrates that a home is quite literally what you make it.[87] Permission is therefore given to all middle classes to think more creatively about how to furnish without needing to buy new, especially given that both goods and money were often short. A caravan became the war home of choice for one family: 'We lost our nice town flat through enemy action, and in order to keep our cherished independence, settled down in a caravan in a field.'[88] The home in *Housewife* became less about traditional class indicators, and more about an association with people and safety, an affective attachment. War displaces people and *Housewife* acknowledged this in various ways, sometimes humorously as in Antonia White's 'M-Day', where sharp ironic observations offer a way of dealing with the inevitable frustrations of moving house during the war,[89] and this light touch regarding the housewife's most treasured place is a far cry from previous intensities.

More seriously, as many housewives were left on their own to cope without a wage earner *Housewife* explored how the home might become a source of income, giving information in bite-sized chunks about income, rent and other money matters. For those readers without enough money to live on there were suggestions to supplement incomes and discover 'The Advantages of Sharing House' by sub-letting or taking in lodgers made homeless by the war.[90] This was a way for the stay-at-home housewife to be rewarded with a wage for doing precisely what she had always done for no wage: keeping house for others. By 1942, it was long understood that the *Housewife* reader would be without a maid, she would indeed be doing all the work herself.[91] *Housewife* gave permission for its middle-class readers to use their greatest asset, their home, to enter into the fiscal economy. A more realistic and less selfish middle-class attitude emerged in the magazine as the war progressed and having a home, and the opportunity to make some money from it, was something for which middle-class readers learnt to be grateful. Poor housing and bombed-out homes featured frequently in the magazine, so that whilst for some a home was a site of financial security, for others it had been destroyed as truly part of the war zone.[92] The housewife who still had a home should not be too proud, the magazine urged, to use that asset to help herself, her family and others to survive the war: the housewife and the space she occupied was compelled to move with the times and function as part of the war.

Part of the progressiveness of *Housewife* during this wartime period can be seen in the introduction of an international element to the magazine, challenging the reader to think beyond her own experience, and was in contrast to many weekly magazines for women at the time.[93] In these articles gratitude, not class distinction was the implied message behind investigations into the plight of other women suffering under at this time of national emergency. Women who married foreign nationals, living in Britain, were now classified as 'Aliens' Wives', with reduced status and monitored activity, even requiring a police permit to travel to see their evacuated children. Such injustice for 'English women who have lost their Birthright' leads to a call to action and readers are urged to write to their Member of Parliament (MP) or local paper or to organise a speaker from the Nationality of Married Women Committee.[94] Other articles look further afield, at Russian orphanages or abandoned women in Africa and in seeing the world as a smaller place, mothers might consider evacuating their children abroad, perhaps to Canada, America or the Bahamas, where a good 'outdoorsy and useful' life will lead to 'a sound common-sense training in a trade or career by which to earn a living'.[95] This internationalism, brought about by *Housewife*'s extensive engagement with the impact of war and enabled by the mixed content and varied voices within a magazine, was one way in which readers were offered a view of the changing world; however, in being encouraged to actively use domestic skills outside the home, readers were also offered a stake in the life of nation.

The home in *Housewife* became less of a total world for the domesticated woman and more of a stable base from which these same women of immense capability might participate in other ways. There was an expansion beyond the domestic as the terrain of the housewife as the magazine actively encouraged external deployment of her skills. Cynthia White has suggested that during the war, 'The enforced containment of spending and the consequent limitation of the scope for advertising left magazine Editors free to concentrate on meeting the needs of their women readers unhampered by commercial considerations.'[96] Although *Housewife* did carry a fair amount of wartime advertising, I suggest that editors used any freedoms they may have had to encourage the middle-class housewife, albeit gently, to change her social behaviour: readers were urged not to suffer in solitude, but to join in the war effort. She should ask herself, 'What Can I Do?' and reflect on her contribution, with the clear suggestion it was no longer enough to remain stolidly isolated, adhering to a now-imagined and perhaps outdated class requirement of defensive domestic privacy, and that it was important for the housewife, perhaps with no husband or children at home, to have social contact. Moreover, she should think of others and try to have a positive impact on them through her efforts: her engagement with modernity was not just about bringing the world to her home, but it was also to take her domesticity to effect the outside world.

Housewife felt its way beyond the confines of home, even for the most resolutely house-bound housewife. The magazine carefully demonstrated and explained in detail how to extend home-making skills, management and crafts to the world beyond home: knitting for soldiers, cooking in communal kitchens and domestic budgeting to make wartime donations were all potential ways the housewife could use her household skills to participate in the war effort. As part of this new communication, and aligned with government initiatives for women's war work, readers' experiences were reported: 'The initiation of a voluntary worker' describes how a housewife reader became, by accident, a voluntary helper with London's homeless. The reader is reminded of the value of the human touch and the joy of giving when a child's jumper, hand-knitted and sent over from America, is handed out: 'if she could have seen the delight on the face of the mother ... she would have known just how much her work and kind thought were appreciated.'[97] This personalised incident, tiny in the scheme of war, reminds readers of the satisfaction of contribution; a gleaming home must now be a secondary consideration. A gift born of domestic craft, donated with thoughtfulness, administered by a voluntary worker to a grateful, needy mother, connects women and war work across the Atlantic.

Most significantly, class was no longer seen as a barrier to work, whether paid or unpaid, or even to the type of work undertaken. For a magazine called *Housewife*, paid work started to feature strongly, demonstrating its engagement with a changing world. In suggesting 'Twenty things a woman can do ... alone or with others, to help win the war' *Housewife* outlines war work ranging from joining the W.V.S Housewives' Services, to taking in refugees, to knitting socks.[98] As early as January 1940, readers were writing in with their experiences of wartime jobs and these acted not only to connect the middle-class housewife to other women who had made decisions to work on the land, in the canteen, driving, nursing and munitions making, but crucially, to encourage her to do the same.[99] *Housewife* acknowledges that war work is not for everyone, but goes to some lengths to find ways in which every woman can 'do her bit'. Penny Summerfield has discussed the tensions that arose out of 'the construction of the mother as a non-worker and the wartime social reality of extreme labour shortages' and that *Woman's Own* magazine 'kept up a stream of advice to women on how to cut down on housework' in order to make time for war work.[100] *Housewife* too made it clear that the role of the housewife was seen as perfectly compatible with a working life for a woman.

Following competent participation in the world of work, *Housewife* anticipated a broadening of women's horizons after the war. Women's war experiences featured strongly, with well-known writers such as Monica Dickens, Vita Sackville-West and journalist Alison Settle reiterating the successful and difficult jobs completed by women.[101] Women prominent in their professions were heralded as role models of female achievement, and interesting careers for women were regularly spotlighted, such as 'Women on Air', which suggested radio broadcasting.[102] Women were also urged to make a greater contribution to their local community or council. In short, the magazine tried to collapse the difference between professional women and their readers, devoting much space to considering what women might now go on to do, beyond being a housewife.

Housewife expressed a belief in women's capabilities, and demonstrated their ability to contribute to the workplace, to form part of the labour economy and to contribute to society and the wider world.[103] And although in some ways, being guardians of democracy might restrict women,[104] readers were positively encouraged to become more involved in the wider society and community with suggestions to participate in local council and local affairs,[105] to embrace the town planning debate asking: 'What is Wrong with our Towns?'[106] or to become a magistrate,[107] join Parent Teachers Associations or become involved in youth groups. Tom Driberg, an independent MP, wrote an article, 'Women at Westminster', rallying for more women in parliament.[108] This sense of participation led *Housewife* to assume a significant role for women in building the post-war world (emulating *Picture Post*, another magazine from the Hulton Press, in this regard).[109] Elizabeth Denby, Housing Consultant, discussing working-class living conditions in British towns, explains the money trap of using loan sharks,[110] and advocates converting large empty houses to accommodate several families.[111] Such social transformation was a powerful trope.[112] European relief was also a concern and needed careful planning[113] many such articles appeal to the reader to 'give a hand' and offer practical help. Women were encouraged to think about using their wartime service skills in different ways in peacetime: 'ATS girls will make modern teachers!'[114] Dreams and plans for the future were listed in 1943 in 'What I hope for in the post-war world' and ranged from 'a zest for living' to the more practically based, such as slum clearance, to the more esoteric 'a general improvement in our knowledge of each other' anticipating sexual equality and an end to Britain's insularity.[115]

Even more than this, an emergent feminist consciousness can be detected as *Housewife* joined in with ongoing discussions of necessary social changes, and potential concomitant difficulties, which would come to light at the end of the war. Articles on men returning from the war and the difficulties that might ensue, anticipated social changes such as the increase in the number of stepfathers.[116] The future role of women remained prominent, with some lamentation that women's talents are rendered redundant in married life, and it was a consistent theme that, having shown their abilities, women would be able to enter the workplace and occupy a more prominent position in society: 'We must fight ceaselessly for the kind of lives we wish to lead. Now is our chance.'[117] One plea was for women, doing factory work alongside men, no longer to be seen as second-class citizens and to achieve true equality (Figure 2.5),[118] while another was by Mavis Tate MP discussing equal pay.[119] Equality, working prospects and future careers for women all featured in *Housewife* at this time, as did the need for childcare and birth control.[120] Interestingly, also required was help to run a home, but this time around, when the thorny subject of having a maid returns, it is as a confessional of previous class inequalities, 'I remember, not too happily, that I myself have caused my fellow woman to call me "madam" and wear a hated and ridiculous piece of starched muslin precariously perched on their pretty hair.'[121] Whilst the problem of who was going to do the housework had not gone away, some things had changed and at the very least consciousness had been raised. As one article puts it, 'The new mother's help is – father!' and this was followed up with a plea begging 'mothers of small boys not to bring them up to despise housework'.[122]

Housewife, in its progressive ideas, was ahead of the competitors that White describes as looking beyond the home only after the war.[123] The broadening of the role and interests of the wartime housewife owes a debt to the remaining female editor Margot Jones, who commissioned national experts to write regular editorial sections, and well-known writers and media personalities to make significant feature contributions. The feminist forays of *Housewife* at the end of the war into notions of equal status, paid work for women with equal pay,

Men and women work side by side to forge a fighter

WOMEN,
second-class citizens

A plea for true equality. By Rebecca D. Sieff

Most people will still remember the three years campaign which had to be waged both inside and outside Parliament to establish the principle of equal compensation for civilian war injuries. The traditional position of women in Great Britain was vividly illuminated by the various Bills put forward by His Majesty's Government to deal with this question. These Bills exposed in an almost naïve manner the usual male attitude towards the housewife and mother in particular and to women in general. The housewife and mother emerged as persons of no economic value whatever, either to her husband, her family or the community, and females generally, whatever their job

33

Figure 2.5 Demanding post-war equality: 'Women, second-class citizens', *Housewife*, December 1943, pp. 33–35.

equality within the home as well as greater participation in society at large are discernible in editorial copy and named journalism as a natural progression of women's fortitude and capability regarding their war work.

***

Housewife presented a flexible formula for the housewife: one that adapted to the circumstances of the Second World War, but one that also encouraged women to deploy their domestic skill base, resources and resourcefulness, not only in order to survive the war and help others do the same but also to be confident in those skills and consider life beyond the personal, private middle-class home. It built on women's increased contact with the public and working world during the war and tried to develop their confidence in this domain, stepping beyond the natural boundaries of the housewife-at-home reader. *Housewife*'s consistent messages of housewifely competence looked to encourage women to move beyond the confines of the home to war work, both paid and voluntary, and long before the end of the war, as a natural extension of that belief, the *Housewife* reader was being encouraged to think in feminist terms of interesting jobs with equal status and equal pay to men, and of childcare and domestic help to enable those careers. The magazine used a range of experts in their fields, established writers and well-known figures to give authority to their suggestions for a life beyond the home. It offered rationale and role models aplenty in the cause of a new modernity for women: a progression into the public arenas of social decision-making and community work. The notion of what a housewife's role might encompass changed in *Housewife* magazine from a class-bound idea, to a more diverse range of identities, capable and participatory.

The cultural competence of the magazine is evidenced through its discernment of important shifts in the visibility of the housewife at this time. *Housewife*'s flexible sense of femininity, based on community rather than the domestic, started to question, deeply and directly, women's role and place in society as a result of having imagined the housewife differently.

Producing a Magazine for Television: *Houseparty*

A Poem to Houseparty

Mary, with her spice and herbs turns plain cooking into fancy dish.

Cherie, with her eye for style, brings glamour to the table place.

Ann, stitching, giving hints, sure in her dreams she must do this.

Sylvia, horoscopes, tea leaves, reading palms, and what her grandmother said!, her quike wit often makes me laugh. Can you guess what star sign is 'me'.?

Jean, with lovely long dark hair, I often feel (though I am fair.) that she and I would happy be talking of ghosts, poems, music, art, children, animals, and wearing long medieval gowns, would see the hours flit away, with little housework done all day. [sic][1]

The friendly, light-hearted tone of this viewer's self-interpolated poem to the presenters of *Houseparty* (STV 1972–1981) is completely at odds with the events of the decade itself. The 1970s Britain was a conflicted decade and indeed a decade of conflict: conflicted because of competing cultural discourses and immersed in conflicts in terms of politics and social movements. There were frequent changes in the dominant political party, strikes over pay and working conditions, racial tensions, arguments about education and contention over the role of women in the home and in society. Whilst women came to social and political attention in various ways, there were competing discourses in play. Few images in the media directly represented or addressed the difficulties women faced in the 1970s. The Women's Liberation Movement had demanded more from society for women – sexual freedoms and rejection of domesticity were two of the highly contested areas – and yet the restrictive forces of both sex discrimination and social prejudice continued to be felt by many women in their daily lives. In the face of widely disparate conceptions of feminism and femininity, women were left with difficult decisions to make: acceptance of the status quo could mean the double burden of lowly paid work as a secondary member of society, alongside running a home and bringing up children; but the alternative of a feminist stance of resistance, politicisation and freedom from domestic constraints could lead to the breaking up of homes and social isolation.

One way of responding to the prospect of isolation in the home was to turn to the television, an important mass media form in the 1970s. There were many amusing television series in a decade that saw an improved provision generally, and that has since been described as a 'golden age'.[2] Reflecting concerns of the era, domestic dilemmas were inflected in various ways in popular series such as *The Good Life* (BBC, 1975–1977), *Fawlty Towers* (BBC, 1975–1979) and *Love Thy Neighbour* (Thames, 1972–1976), and often masked with humour. Historical television, with an emphasis on the Edwardian thematic, transported the viewer to a different era, where women were portrayed as occupying predetermined social positions. Most realism was to be found in the hugely popular and never-ending narratives of soap opera,[3] and perhaps most diversity and even the most controversial representation of women appeared in one-off dramas such as *Play for Today* (BBC 1970–1984). In a decade famous for memorable advertising campaigns, much advertising depicted women as either hyper-feminine domesticated subjects or overtly sexualised objects of the male gaze.[4] Women could also be viewed working on television as presenters of children's programmes, as professional or home cooks such as Fanny Craddock and Delia Smith and even occasionally as reporters on serious programmes such as Valerie Singleton on *Nationwide* (BBC1, 1969–1983) and Joan Bakewell on *Reports Action* (Granada, 1976–1981), although, as television professionals, such women often enjoyed a celebrity or career status quite alien to many of their viewers.

Into this mixed response to women on television and in a contentious decade of struggle, Southern Television brought *Houseparty*: a regional magazine programme for women in the afternoon slot that had become an established spot for television magazines.[5] The programme's success as perhaps 'the most popular daytime programme there's ever been',[6] led to it being networked to Anglia, London Weekend Television, HTV and Yorkshire, and so achieving wider coverage.[7]

This chapter, against the backdrop of a different period of social disruption for women, and another moment when the woman in her home became culturally visible, investigates what this magazine programme offered its viewers at this unsettled time. It does so by examining the formal magazine properties of *Houseparty*, in terms of structure, content and performance style. Through reflecting on presenters as editors, on televisual direction and content as a magazine house style, and on how communication is effected between presenter, director and viewer, the chapter considers how, in a decade when women were discussing their isolation in the home, the *Houseparty* formula and style directly addressed that isolation and attempted to forge a televisual companionship. *Houseparty*'s popularity and viewers' letters are testament to its success.

The task of defining *Houseparty* generically raises several interesting points about the programme. In essence this is a magazine programme and yet it lacks the current event discussions, interviews or commentary seen as fundamental to this televisual genre. Unlike highly formulaic magazine programmes such as *This Morning* (ITV 1988–ongoing), originally hosted by Richard Madeley and Judy Finnigan, *Houseparty* had none of the stylistic qualities associated with the magazine such as anchoring presenters, an on-screen time-specific running order or introductory/round-up presentation moments. In contrast, on *Houseparty*, no one welcomes the viewer to the programme or says goodbye, and the viewer does not know who will enter by ringing the famous doorbell, or what items will come up for discussion. The set was a convincing and detailed domestic space and the camera never left that environment. As such, it is a visualisation of female companionship, women getting together in someone's home, sharing, showing, conversing, though in this instance on television.[8] As daytime television for women, which overlaps with the older category of light entertainment, *Houseparty* was the sort of programme Frances Bonner defined as 'ordinary television'. Bonner is concerned with 'the ways in which the content of television calls on ordinary, everyday concerns and patterns of behaviour, using them not just as topics, but as guides to style, appearance and behaviour'.[9] And yet *Houseparty*, in its total commitment to reflecting back the domestic ritual of women's conversation, disturbs other generic categories of ordinary television. It cannot be defined as a talk show because it had no live audience, or, in the absence of a host or celebrities, as a chat show. However, it does intersect with talk television.[10] It was not a lifestyle programme, as the genre is currently understood, there being no particular directive being pursued, and no full team of professional presenters; nor did the presenters see themselves as intermediaries.[11] Although some of the main presenters had worked in various capacities in front of a camera, many of the presenters had no prior experience of working on television and only learnt once invited onto the programme. Rather, they were interesting women, with talents, skills or unusual lives to talk about, who were mostly living in the Southern Television region along the south coast, and they either knew each other or became friends while developing the skill of 'being themselves' in one another's company, albeit on a studio set in front of television cameras.[12] Through their familiarity and open conversational style, the presenters developed and engendered interest, trust and even consciousness-raising, leaving some viewers wanting more: 'Each subject is immensely interesting, but not dealt with thoroughly enough.'[13]

However, while *Houseparty* stepped outside some of the more formal structures of the magazine programme, it adroitly mimicked some of the constructs of a print magazine, adapted them for television and, in consequence was able to offer a strong sense of companionship to its loyal viewers: 'The thing I like most is the air of informality about it all, and all of them looking "quite at home," ' said one viewer.[14] As a magazine programme, *Houseparty* formed an assemblage of items that ranged across the domestic sphere into the full spectrum of items of interest to its listeners, from non-stick pans to women's role in the newly joined Common Market (EEC). If it was not formulaic, it was at least produced to a familiar pattern with three or four main sections.[15] Like sections of a printed domestic magazine, viewers could, without knowing the actual content, look forward to a cookery slot, a craft or sewing feature or two, some chat about families and problems, a discussion of particular relevance to women or perhaps a book of interest. Viewers also responded to this magazine in their many letters: some requested recipes and advice just like a print magazine, whilst others commented on the novel format of *Houseparty*, revealing interest in and observations about the televisual processes. Most interestingly of all, some viewers wrote in and, in one way or another, expressed a sincere sense of friendship, companionship and connection with the presenters. Some viewers resisted the dominant 'encoded' messages of the programme, cake baking or dressmaking, and drew, or 'decoded' messages of female company.[16]

Houseparty, in the absence of any formal address-to-camera presentation, brought the magazine form and appeal to life on television. In any one programme half a dozen demurely dressed, apparently middle-class female presenters would cover a range of topics through a seemingly casual mix of conversation and demonstration. And yet *Houseparty* was more than a discussion programme: it was personal, familiar and most of all welcoming: it spoke to women.[17] Presenters talked about their own experiences of life as well as their careers and offered their personal views into the conversation, be they well-informed opinion or frivolous interjections. The unconstrained timbre and range of conversation topics as well as the naturalised format revealed the individual personalities of the presenters, and their familiarity with each other. Often sitting around a kitchen table, the *Houseparty* 'ladies' chatted, showed off their hobby projects and enjoyed each other's company (Figure 3.1). Above all, the programme was homely.[18] This mode of presentation captured the attention and heartfelt loyalty of a generation of female (and male) viewers, for *Houseparty* was immensely popular and is still very well remembered in the region and elsewhere, more than three decades after it finished.[19]

Although directed and produced for television, the apparent authenticity and sincerity of this television magazine is beguiling. Jack Hargreaves (1911– 1994), known for his pioneering work in addressing a television audience, oversaw the programme and brought innovative techniques of television presentation from America to *Houseparty*. He also made use of his earlier career experience of working on print magazines and advertising for the Hulton Press where he learnt to address the individual through a mass medium.[20] Later, at Southern Television he worked with the director George Egan, on a number of programmes. Under Hargreaves' guidance, Egan's direction of *Houseparty* undoubtedly contributed to the programme's appeal.

The relationship to the feminism of the time is multi-layered. *Houseparty* was set in a 'home' and cookery, craft and homemaking were mainstays, but rather than see this as anti-feminist, it should be remembered that early 1970s folk or utopian feminism engaged heavily with anti-capitalist and anti-consumerist ideals,[21] and that home-made was a political choice.[22] There was much discussion of domestic issues and family, yet there was also an engagement with the wider world with gender rarely off the agenda: women in the workplace, women being judged by appearances, men wearing make-up, abortion and other subjects both personal and political all found their way on to the programme. *Houseparty* may be seen as oscillating between a seeming complicity with the media-projected status quo of 1970s woman-at-home status, shying away from forthright feminist demands on the one hand, and a sophisticated engagement with a moderate feminism on the other. There was no attempt to adhere to any media-constructed or imagined sense of woman-at-home with little engagement with the outside world.[23] Equally, there was no attempt to hide previous or current careers. In fact, it was often those aspects of their lives that formed the focus of conversation. Perhaps in this sense, *Houseparty*'s presenters and participants really did represent the 1970s 'housewife' when few women truly had the economic luxury or the desire to live solely for and within the home. Many married women did perform some form of paid work inside or outside the home in the 1970s, and many struggled to combine home, children and job.[24]

Presenters as editors: 'Intelligent, interesting women'

The *Houseparty* presenters, as 'A Poem to Houseparty' attests, were well known for their skills and personalities on an individual basis by very loyal viewers. One viewer in praising a 'super programme' said:

> The fact that I can just relax and listen to a group of intelligent, interesting women discuss very interesting topics makes me drop everything at 2.30 and do just this![25]

Behind the televisual performance of perceived 'intelligence' lay women with particular professional skills who were able to reproduce their skill sets and subject knowledge in a way that was interesting and engaging for the medium of television and, most importantly, was targeted accurately and appropriately at their viewers. *Houseparty* soon came to be structured around four main presenters who brought their different skills to the programme, and frequently researched, managed and presented their different sections, acting, I would suggest, like features editors within a print magazine. They were Ann Ladbury, a home economics sewing expert; Cherry Marshall, an haute couture model who also ran her own modelling agency; Sylvia Marshall, or 'Marshie', who had worked for Cherry as an outsize model and whose husband was involved in the world of women's magazines on *Woman's Own*; and Mary Morris, a professional cook and demonstrator.

There were significant contrasts between these main four presenters. Ann Ladbury was a highly competent professional dressmaker and teacher, appearing on television in early sewing programmes such as *Clothes That Count* (BBC 1967), writing nearly forty books on sewing from the early *Batsford Book of Sewing* (1967), and presenting on radio. In 2010, Ladbury was still giving sewing classes, having had a very long and successful media career.[26]

Cherry Marshall was beautiful, glamorous and urbane, and unlike many of the others she lived in London and had moved in literary as well as fashion circles. Her autobiography *The Cat Walk* reveals the hard work involved in running her successful agency as well as bringing up her children as a single mother.[27] Sylvia Marshall, in contrast to Cherry, appears warm and vulnerable, full of humour and humanity and not afraid to offer advice; Jean Orba described her as a 'round the village well kind of person'. Marshie, as she was known, although well connected in the media world, came across on television as a down-to-earth type with a likeable common touch. Jean commented on how Marshie was a 'natural stylist' able to put together an outfit quite economically; she 'could buy something in British Home Stores [a high street chain], put it with something else and look as though she had just walked out of *Vogue*'. She was 'gifted but not educated', perhaps like many of the women watching her in the 1970s. Having visited her home however, Jean was surprised that Marshie was in fact very wealthy, and, with hindsight, reflected on how Marshie was really two people: 'she was as she was when she was younger on *Houseparty*; and then grew into this wealthy lifestyle.' Mary Morris, the trained chef, again in contrast to the others, has a televisual persona of more determined authority, and Jean explained this was indeed her personality in real life, and that her slightly grand manner and class-consciousness made it more difficult for her to fully integrate into the group.

Apart from these mainstays, there was a wider pool of about twenty-five women, chosen for their different interests, skills sets and general outlook on life. They may have been invited initially, from a network of acquaintances, because they had something of note to tell or a skill they could demonstrate, and been used as occasional freelance journalists, but if they worked well with the *Houseparty* style and offered something fresh to the mix, they were invited to stay. The presenters were not assigned roles but drew on their own personalities for their television persona, permitting a constancy and consistency in opinion and outlook that became extremely important to viewer identification. Marian Shuttleworth, for instance, appeared as a slightly unfashionable grandmotherly figure, not hesitating to state her disapproval if she felt it was warranted. Although she would 'keep us all in order', as Jean put it, she too was a very skilled craftswoman who 'lived and breathed for her craft'. Although of a similar age to the others, she nonetheless appealed to the older viewer (Figure 3.2). Lucy Morgan, by contrast, was 'such a lovely, pretty girl' full of creativity, who sadly died in her early forties of cancer: 'everyone loved Lucy' reminisced

Jean. Lucy frequently made glamorous creations out of junk shop discoveries, thus promoting an anti-consumerist mode of creativity, very different to the traditional crafts of Marian (Figure 3.1). Variety in the group was important: Avril Bell was an ex-Bluebell dancer; Lynne Inglis was a farmer's wife; Daphne Lee's interesting life led her at one time to live with a Romani and differently again, Sister Immaculate, from a St Joseph's Franciscan Convent in Littlehampton, was 'quite unshockable' having worked in the poorest of communities. Jean recalled how for the viewers at home 'You became their friends, a certain type would go for me, another one for Mary, another type for Cherry'.

Just like a print magazine then, there were different voices and different points of view presented, but contained within the overall format. No single personality carried the programme or was allowed to dominate proceedings, but individual interests and personalities remained constant. As a result, whilst the variety of presenters allowed viewers to relate to, or align themselves more closely with, some presenters than others, the consistency of the individuals, like the sections of a magazine, allowed readers to get to know and even anticipate the mode of presentation that each woman might make. If a clothes item was presented by Cherry it would likely deal with couture, whereas Marshie would talk about high street fashion. If Ann was demonstrating it might be needlework and if it were Lucy, she would be recycling something. Similarly, Marian would talk about traditional craft, but when it was Daphne's turn her

Figure 3.1 Lucy Morgan shows off her recycled dress round the kitchen table.
© *Wessex Film and Sound Archive.*

item would be more artistic and quirky. In this way, each presenter had her particular approach or preferred strain of fashion, craft or cookery but all were still presented in a manner that embraced the house style of *Houseparty* and contributed variety to the magazine assemblage. Significantly, as revealed in the poem, viewers came to know and anticipate these different frameworks in the same way that readers understand the differences between a print magazine article, say, that points to current fashion trends, and another that shows how to style a garment in numerous ways. Two such distinct articles in print would employ diversity in presentation through page layout, photographic styling and editorial commentary. Similarly, in the televisual magazine *Houseparty*, the presenters each carried their signature approach.

Some items required more preparation, specialist knowledge and staging than others, but personalities still emerged differently even in these specifically constructed magazine items. One discussion of the new trend for machine-knitted clothing, led by Cherry and Ann, would have involved a fair amount of preparation, Jean revealed, involving going to a London fashion show, selecting items of clothing with specific presenters in mind and through Cherry's fashion connections, buying the clothes or negotiating publicity for the manufacturers. The producer would have ensured the right presenters to be on that episode, selected because they would look particularly good in this type of knitwear, perhaps: 'Daphne because she was tall and slim, and Lucy because she was young and pretty,' suggested Jean, and having one older and one younger presenter accommodates a range of viewer's ages. This sort of presentation worked well because 'these women would have had years of experience'. Yet in front of the cameras it is a natural performance, artfully managed by the couture 'editor' and supportively staged by the other women. Preparatory work is hidden, women are at ease talking to each other, the camera just happens to be there; it is a typical *Houseparty* item.

A similar item is presented according to a different presenter's personality when Marshie models a dress that Ann Ladbury has sewn for her. In this item we see the professional model walk down the staircase with a graceful air and confident poise, adopting the model's side-on pose and finishing with an upturned flick of one hand towards the hat. This 'catwalk' performance is mesmerising. Yet even this is not distancing, the professional model is revealed as the skilful stylist: explaining colour selections of accessories: 'You should always match your bag to the background colour of the dress.' Here, in televisual terms, the 'footing' shifts in this sequence from Marshie the refined model to Marshie the authoritative stylist.[28] Ann Ladbury, standing at the bottom of the stairs, talks about the making of an under-slip rather than lining the dress; Marshie points to Ann's very neat sewing and Ann contributes some detailed input about how to adjust a pattern to fit an individual woman's shape and preferences. Rather than abstract advice in a print magazine, there is a genuine exchange over the dress that Ann really has made especially for Marshie. They share a joke when Ann reveals the picture on the dressmaker's paper pattern: Marshie would have refused the style as illustrated, 'I'd never have had it,' but this allows Ann to emphasise the importance of choosing the right material (Figure 3.2). Other observing presenters help to break down the formality of the item too by prompting questions, giving Marshie cues for viewer tips: a larger woman should roll back her sleeves if she has slim hands and wrists to draw attention to that attractive area. Sewing techniques and clever details, styling variations and dress sense are all proffered through conversation: *Houseparty*'s equivalent to 'how to' articles and hints and tips in a print magazine. Presenters have their particular approaches to fashion, their own background knowledge sets and, literally and metaphorically, their own 'voice'. This was part of the appeal of the programme and viewers got to know these well, but also part of the appeal was the format, and it is this aspect of

Figure 3.2 Dressmaking item: From paper pattern to fashion show with Anne Ladbury and 'Marshie'.
© *Wessex Film and Sound Archive.*

regularity of style, and the impact of the style itself, that helped to distinguish this particular magazine.

Whilst some items were more staged than others, there was great freedom in the programme's content, permitting presenter's interests to have free rein, and in this context, Jean diminished the aspects of script and rehearsal. Jean described the contents of *Houseparty* as 'true' in the sense that the presenters spoke about their real-life experiences, demonstrated the items that reflected their genuine interests, suggested discussion topics from their own observations and revealed their honest opinions in conversation. According to Jean, there were outline scripts, but only of topics not of conversations, and the scripts such as they were, were really lists of items to be covered which she would write each week merely indicating subject matter, presenters involved and seating set-up. The personal assistant (PA) and secretary would send these out a few days beforehand to the presenters requested for each programme so that they could think about their potential contributions and opinion on the subject, but apparently, only Mary Morris would actually do any homework. One presenter would get the main discussion point across, and others would respond, as Jean said, 'It might be something trivial or something deadly serious' and in her experience it was 'amazing how you could always come up with something you weren't desperately interested in'. The PA's job also entailed responding to some of the many letters viewers sent in – the record was perhaps 200 just for one muesli recipe!

With this light touch of scripting and rehearsals, even when it came to technical rehearsals, whilst the camera angle needed to be aligned and rehearsed for a technical run-through, the conversations did not take place prior to filming. The rehearsal would mention the topic, but generally it would go no further, they would 'start the item off, but did not talk about it'. When conversations were rehearsed, perhaps by a different director, they were invariably stilted or fell flat in front of the camera and Jean recalled that it was never the same as when the conversations were spontaneous, sometimes these were sufficiently heated to continue after the cameras had stopped. Shows were shot in one take and recorded as live, sometimes as many as three in one day, and were largely sent out as recorded. Noises off might justify a retake, but mostly presenters would ad lib to cover errors, they might say something silly, but someone else would help out and the conversation would recover and just carry on. Sometimes Jean intuitively moved away from the outline script to allow spontaneity, such as one very moving account of a stillbirth, where the item had been allocated only five minutes but Jean let it run on. Jean made all the decisions about who was invited on the second series and who stayed, and she rang the changes, with some great successes and some disasters. If there were disasters, such as an unexpected crash behind the scenes, an inexperienced presenter might stop talking, but the important thing was 'to always carry on until the director or floor manager says stop'. It does not come across as professional talk: presenters speak over each other, try and sometimes fail to interject, switch clumsily between topics, become a bit heated or lose focus, but it is all forgiven as part of the weft and weave of flawed, but friendly, conversation.

Just as a regular print magazine often mixes things up in order to remain fresh with guest editors, swapped roles and contributors interviewing each other, so the women of *Houseparty* also deviate sometimes from their main roles, breathing life into the format. Mixing up the roles occurred, for instance, in the cookery department, where Mary Morris' extravagant cookery style, featuring, as Jean said, 'the left-over bottle of sherry and half a pint of cream', was interspersed with other presenters' cookery and home-made items produced in the kitchen. But there were shifts that had deeper social meanings too: Jean remembered that on one occasion Marshie was persuaded to return after an absence to talk about her experience of depression, a barely understood and still taboo phenomenon in the 1970s. This 'personal' conversation was an early and rare televisual testimonial of female depression and Jean remembered this as an instance when the structure of the programme was consciously and spontaneously put aside and the cameras were just allowed to roll. Marshie's honesty and sincerity, Jean recalled, shone through the constructs of television production. Out of her usual role as stylist, she portrayed a different version of herself.[29] The feature touched the hearts of many viewers, just as a 'triumph over tragedy' style of print magazine article might inspire or reassure readers. Hundreds of letters were received from viewers who had also suffered from depression, grateful for the public acknowledgement and airing of this condition.[30] This is a way in which *Houseparty* might be considered to have had significant cultural impact. Maggie Andrews has remarked upon the way Lucy Morgan's 'do-it-yourself divorce' did much to 'undermine the taboo about divorce'.[31] At such moments, the viewer sees the presenters shift from demonstrators to individuals with real-life problems and concerns, with the freedom to present what they wanted, including their own stories.

Jean Orba's shift from presenter to organiser-editor revealed to her some of the difficulties in having a male director produce a female-centred programme. Egan's directing experience was invaluable, as discussed earlier, but Jean sensed that he did not fully understand how instinctively and spontaneously the women responded to issues and on-set conversations. If his production of the programme was unsympathetic, it was probably because he was not part of the friendship circle that so many of the presenters had formed, and so was not party to other conversations held in each other's homes. Egan was professionally demanding and exacting in technical rehearsals, repeating technical items to his satisfaction, often to the dismay of the presenters. Egan fully understood the significance of *Houseparty* to its viewers, but was less conscious of how carefully the seeming female reality was balanced by its presenters and organiser. As a consequence, Egan was happy to let others research and develop topics, and to let others direct and manage the programme, but as Jean concluded, this meant there were great freedoms in content choices by the women, and in what they said. Jean's prior experience as a presenter on *Houseparty* meant that when she took the organiser's role, her dual perception from both sides of the camera enabled her to make decisions that reshaped the programme slightly, introducing new people, and managing with a light touch. 'You usually came down and said that was a great programme. I would sometimes say "you didn't mention so and so as we discussed, but it doesn't matter." As long as it was interesting it didn't matter. You had to let go. I realised you could become very possessive.'

One area of difficulty was over advertising. Of course, advertising is essential for the survival of many women's magazines, especially the glossy variety, with economic dependence straining or even dominating editorial impartiality; in a similar vein, it posed a particular set of difficulties for *Houseparty* too. As *Houseparty* increased in popularity, companies were keen to attempt to have their products placed on the programme and the many letters from manufacturers of fashion and household goods testify to this. Jean had to be careful of companies trying to get free advertising, labels had to be turned away and stores could not be mentioned, Marshie's use of the term 'Orrods' for Harrods was a bit too close, and 'because it was ITV we had to be even more careful than the BBC' stated Jean. Money was made for the broadcast company though, and Jean was very well aware that whilst *Houseparty* had the feeling of being the Cinderella of the programme schedule, in fact it made a lot of money for the Southern Television company.

All these aspects, whether presenters were presenting to their specialist skill sets or whether the items had been mixed up, whether particular products were being discussed or new people were involved, all presentation items had to become integrated into the performance values of the programme: the 'House Style'.

House style: 'No inadvertent glance at the camera'

The house style of *Houseparty*, the appearance of the set and the dynamics and use of space, the direction and organising of the programme format all combined to achieve a seemingly 'natural' performance on television. In its emulation of an afternoon social gathering for a regular group of friendly and interesting women in a large and spacious home, *Houseparty* managed, through its format and style, to construct the premise that viewers were invited to enter the spaces of that home and to participate in the conversations. From her lectures at village halls, Jean recalled that viewers were frequently completely taken in by the construct of the studio set at Southern Television and assumed it was a real home (Figure 3.3). However, originally as a temporary set, struck each time after filming and so requiring continuity work, but later as a permanent set, it was

Figure 3.3 The *Houseparty* set at Southern Television.
© *Wessex Film and Sound Archive.*

a vital setting for the programme. Each episode, always located in this same domestic space, had a sense of comfortable familiarity about it. If the Southern Television compass point logo was this magazine's 'front cover', the set was the backdrop for all the 'articles'.

The set imitated three spaces of a home: the kitchen, the dining area with the all-important table and, more variably, another space for standing demonstrations, a window seat or fire side snug. It followed a contemporary open-plan design, with a staircase leading up to another exit, referred to as the bedroom, and was furnished of its time, with an eye-level oven and Formica worktops in the kitchen, and light wood furniture and hessian wallpaper in the living areas; it reflected an aspirational version of a viewer's home. The fashioning of the domestic space, and the imaginative processes of the audience in reframing their homes, is an important aspect of the appeal of women's domestic magazines. At one time the set underwent redecoration, causing disruption for weeks, an experience that viewers might recognise, but the home decorations featured in the conversations and the presenters, in true 1970s Do-It-Yourself fashion, would join in and do a bit of decorating themselves on the show. In this way, the presenters were very much linked to the spaces of the home set, as well as using this opportunity to demonstrate decorating skills. Anna Gough-Yates has commented upon a later shift in print magazines in the 1980s when editors started to imagine themselves as the readers of their magazines with this level of authentic interest in the magazine content enabling a shift in approach.[32] *Houseparty* always projected this genuine levelling of its 'editorial team' with the magazine items.

In order to emulate a home successfully, the programme's movement dynamics had to be orchestrated to fit the house style needed, but concealed from the viewer, to make her feel as though she shared the same space as the presenters. Arrivals of women not already at the table would be heralded by another signature feature: the doorbell. The doorbell would sound, and another familiar face would appear in the dining room, be greeted by her friends and she would join in the conversation or bring new objects or crafts to the table. Such was the intensity with which many viewers watched and joined in this 'at home' event, that one viewer at least clearly lost herself in the *Houseparty* world:

> I do get annoyed when that doorbell rings sometimes in the middle of the programme as the tone of my doorbell is exactly the same and so I often mistake the House-Party doorbell for my own and vice-versa.[33]

The spaces were used to reflect the way the housewife might use her own home; however, movement between the limited spaces was largely dictated by the requirements of the scheduled 'item'. Movement, Jean remembered, had to be gracious and controlled, and required careful direction in order to avoid any unruly scenes such as 'six women leaving the table at once', consequently, cameras would usually follow one person at a time moving between zones. Ways of ending one item and starting another without breaking up the flow of conversation needed to be devised, and sometimes sequencing was orchestrated by a voice off calling for help in the kitchen, avoiding overt cutting between scenes with movement heralding a shift to another item, a new section. Similar to the turning of a printed page, the regular viewer comes to recognise the techniques and anticipate the next section without actually knowing precisely what is coming. One device Jean employed was to thread something through the programme sections, such as a birthday card to be signed, facilitating the movement of presenters, cameras and viewers, with purpose, from one space and magazine item, to another. The arrival of the tea tray, carried through from the kitchen, is the regular indicator of the close of the programme as all come together at the dining table. The tea cups, like the familiar end page interview or regular last word in a print magazine, signal the end.[34] As at the beginning, the programme closes with the conversation still flowing, but names of presenters are overlaid on the screen and the invitation is displayed on-screen for the viewer to 'Drop in Again'; however, the discussion does not draw to a close, and no one wishes the viewer goodbye.

The intimacy and intensity achieved through the *Houseparty* style owe something to specific and skilful camera direction and varied and imaginative uses of the studio spaces. Changes in camera shot and angle provide accented variety in discussions and avoid a sense of potential stasis at the table: close-ups were not always of the speaker as the responses, verbal and non-verbal, were equally significant; individual and group shots emulate the rippling of a conversation and the important empty side of the table, the 'natural' space for the viewer, is a clear invitation for the woman at home to both occupy the eye of the camera and come and join in the conversation. Even the finishing 'round-table discussion', where presenters often have to pull up a chair to squeeze in, still leaves a space for the viewer. It became a mode familiar to viewers, and many viewers' letters demonstrate their engagement and desire to participate. The kitchen demonstrations were more structured and always viewed from the near side of the counter, but as much camera time was devoted to the conversation as the food, varying between mid-shots of presenter and worktop to close-ups of cook and participant. Similarly, craft demonstrations at the table limit close-ups of the item, enabling the viewer to feel like a participant, with the camera often emulating the human eye in moving to watch whoever is speaking. Most handicrafts are carried out or shown to other presenters (not to the camera) at the table, so that the viewer shares the sense of firstly joining the group and then peering into the hands of another woman to see what she was making, often including other presenters in the peripheral vision. Larger equipment, such as the spinning wheel demonstration, would be set up in the window seat/ third space. For some intricate, traditional craftwork, there was a system of placing one presenter, acting as audience,[35] behind the lead demonstrator, so that the camera could zoom in over the other shoulder, emulating that angle of observation. For this set-up, Jean commented that the demonstrator had to sit at the far right end of the table to enable the close-up camera to be set up in advance. Alternatively, other items such as the mini-fashion shows pulled back to a full-length shot when the open area beyond the table was used. If presenters were standing, this often included a glimpse of the table on the left, to locate the space. The positioning of cameras and presenters, although not without its limitations on the set, was absolutely crucial to the feel of the programme

Figure 3.4 Marian Shuttleworth demonstrates traditional crafts.
© *Wessex Film and Sound Archive.*

and to the inclusion of the viewer at home. It was, moreover, a visual language, which would roughly follow similar patterns for each type of item, knowing that in a print magazine this familiarity with the visual construction of sections is important for the audience.

For all the air of everydayness about *Houseparty* and the freedoms afforded the presenters, there were, nonetheless, a few golden rules instigated by Jack Hargreaves acknowledged as the expert in intimate televisual audience address. One of the most important directions was that the presenters must never look at the camera as this draws attention to the processes of the television. She was never to be gazed at, never to be addressed as a separate entity and never to be made to feel that she was an outsider, and this became normal procedure, as Jean said, because you never looked at the camera, 'you very quickly forgot there were cameras there'. Instead, the technique was to try and make the viewer feel as though she were in the *Houseparty* home, participating as a silent guest. One apologetic note from George Egan points out that they 'had to stop recording' because one of the ladies spoke about attending a function as a result of appearing on *Houseparty*, and 'I know that Mr Hargreaves has always insisted that we should never refer to their involvement in this way in the actual programme.'[36] This was absolutely crucial to the feel of the programme. But it was not something that went unnoticed by viewers. In making comparison to other programmes for women at the time, one view remarked that in *Houseparty*:

> There is no inadvertent glance at the camera to give the game away. The new programme 'About women' is completely spoilt by the 'looking at you, helping you out' approach. I hate being lectured at![37]

This intimacy, the pretence of ignoring the distance of camera and television screen, meant having no formal studio audience and even at one stage, banning contributors and friends from coming to watch as 'the girls are not their happiest with any kind of audience – however small'.[38]

The naturalness and intimacy of the presentation of *Houseparty*, frequently remarked upon by viewers in their letters, was a most deliberate intention.[39] At Hargreaves' instigation, *Houseparty* opens with presenters already talking so that the camera 'drops in' on their conversation. The programmes always open in the middle of a conversation between two or more women around the dining table, the viewer's arrival is not acknowledged and the conversation appears to be mid-flow, appearing to the viewer to have already been underway before the programme was transmitted on the screen. Jean recalled that the 'eavesdropping' technique had to be learnt: the action started with the director drawing an arm diagonally across, and conversation regarding the first item would start mid-way through, this opening item was never taken from the 'top' and for this reason, one of the more experienced presenters would always start the programme off. She might start with an explanation that seemed to respond to an unheard question, or a question that implied that the demonstration was half-way through, an actual positioning or introductory statement might be made through the course of conversation, but the show would never open that way, so that cookery demonstrations rarely came first as they must start at the beginning. This 'eavesdropping' style was a technique, brought back by Jack Hargreaves from America, and a signature pattern of talk on the programme, expected by the viewer and skilfully worked by the presenters. It was part of the house style and drew the viewer in to the conversation, it has its parallel in the way readers tune into the lexicon and sentence construction of particular print magazines.[40]

Magazine communication: The *Houseparty* 'ladies': 'I love them all'

The female presenters on *Houseparty* demonstrated how to conduct friendship, and this, I suggest, was the real exchange of meaning,[41] and a deep communication strategy of the magazine. In this context, the rule about never looking at the camera was significant in maintaining a sense of the viewer as 'insider' and 'sharing' the moment. For the same reason, the viewer was never to be mentioned in any context, so that presenters were never to say, 'Viewers at home' or 'Viewers might be interested in this.' This was to avoid bringing the reality of televisual communication to the fore[42] and was an alternative to the authoritative presence of other modes of television presenting. In *Houseparty*, the illusion and feeling of inclusiveness was worked at and maintained at all costs, hence the key notion of eavesdropping. If viewers had written in – and they did in their hundreds – they might be referred to quite obliquely in front of the camera as 'friends have told me...', as Jean said, 'You quickly became professional because you knew how everything worked and if something went wrong with a newcomer, you could pick it up, but at the same time you still had to be natural because if you started to be grand, the viewers saw through it and we saw through it.' One of the reasons the programme seems so 'natural', perhaps, is because the presenters tried to include rather than 'perform' for the viewer, and they managed this in a particular way, as Jean explained: 'The only way you thought about the woman at home, curiously enough, was them watching it and watching their group of friends. But they weren't really considered, not in that same way. You didn't say this would be good for the viewers.'

Friendship was constructed and demonstrated on-screen in various ways, and one of those was companionship. No matter what was being presented, there would never be a presenter on her own, she would always be displaying her handmade craft, demonstrating her recipe or showing off her dress, to someone else, as Jean observed, 'you always had to talk to someone'. This interested audience, physically close and paying careful attention, asking questions and making suggestions, even disagreeing or suggesting alternatives, means that a woman was never left on her own; being with someone is an important aspect of *Houseparty*; it is vital to the feel of the programme. There is no trace of housewifely drudgery even though many items centre on domestic skills, and most of the women were not 'just housewives', presumably just like their viewers. This is unspoken communication, implying that women have something interesting to say, and through this they assume status and gain companionship. The spaces of the set allow the performance of validated and valued female interests and female companionship.[43] The technique emulates the intimacy of the printed magazine, a mass media form intended for private consumption, where the magazine is projected as offering companionship, being the reader's friend.

Sociability was embodied in differently-textured ways on *Houseparty*: sometimes through sharing and showing of hobbies, at other times through confessional or heartfelt conversations, and also through enjoyment of each other's company. Jean remembered that Marshie and Cherry, long-term close friends and colleagues, 'were the funniest two together - at times they really were a comedy duo'. In one episode where Marshie makes her 'Mystery Cake' containing low-cholesterol fat and a can of tomato soup, the cake is outshone by the familiarity and friendship (Figure 3.5). Cherry, the haute couture model, is supposed to be helping, or at least performing the role of listener for the verbally-given recipe, but is barely able to conceal her distain at the ingredients, dumbstruck at the prospect of the can of soup, can only find the words: 'Ugh how funny.' Marshie, capable and determined to make a success of her cookery slot, carries on telling Cherry that her husband needs to have

Figure 3.5 Cherry Marshall and 'Marshie': Friends baking a cake.
© *Wessex Film and Sound Archive.*

low-cholesterol foods, and deliberately reminds Cherry that she has eaten this
cake plenty of times when she has visited Marshie's home. Following this, in
a particularly uncoordinated (and presumably unrehearsed) moment when
Marshie is sieving the flour and asks Cherry to pour in the soup, Cherry tips
the bright red contents of the can over the bottom of the sieve. This causes
Marshie to spill the flour onto the worktop. Marshie then, natural as ever,
lowers the bowl and sweeps the spilled flour back in, just as you might do
at home, but perhaps not as most cookery presenters would do in front of
millions of viewers. A few moments later, Cherry, still 'helping', tries to burst
the bag of walnuts by firstly stamping on the bag, then trying to tear it with
her teeth, an action curiously at odds with her glamorous demeanour and
high-class accent. Her failure to open the packet leads to a laboured search
for a pair of scissors. Still not embracing the idea of this mystery cake, Cherry
uninhibitedly goes on to remark on how much the already-cooked example
has sunk in the middle, and rather pointedly, the cake does not appear with
the end-of-programme tea.

There can be little doubt that the main event in this item is not the health-
oriented cake, but the friendship. The viewer cannot help but smile; these are
women so comfortable in each other's company, with a familiarity borne of
a long friendship that cannot be undone by culinary mishap, clumsiness or

even criticism. What the viewer witnesses, much more than the making of a peculiar cake, is women enjoying each other's company. They are not even really pretending to teach each other anything, there is an assumption they have seen it all before, they are just being together and playing their part in television cake making, but with knowingness and an enviably long-standing familiarity. Marshie uses her natural humour to jolly along an item that is in danger of becoming farcical, and presumably they enjoyed the unintended hilarity of their performance later. In this way, the cookery sections were immensely valuable, way beyond the home economics lessons: the viewer could learn much from women at ease with themselves, their abilities and each other. By allowing each other into that most private of female spaces, the home kitchen, by conversing, sharing skills, laughing, joking, teasing and playing to each other's strengths, a very positive and robust mode of behaving towards other women is performed. And yet, as Jean recalls, as the years went by this was hardly a performance. These women got to know each other very well during the *Houseparty* years, living locally, and forming close, supportive friendships outside the programme, explaining the informality and familiarity evident in the programme. This is a very appealing aspect of the programme and viewers frequently commented upon this in their letters: 'so real and natural'.[44] In a decade where women were uncertain of their role regarding family and work, and felt isolated because of social pressures, such overt demonstration of friendship was a powerful aspect of the communication of *Houseparty*.

Magazine communication with the viewer at home takes place in other ways too. To refer to the earlier example of Marshie modelling Ann Ladbury's dress, on one level all advice is given to the other presenters present, and of course by extension, to the viewer at home, but there is a deeper communication too. Regular viewers knew that Marshie was qualified to give advice about clothes and fashion from her career as a size 16 'matron' model, so that her authority lent itself to giving particular advice to women conscious of their size or shape. This level of familiarity with the histories of the presenters, and the assumption of this shared knowledge by the presenters themselves, enables an imagined friendship to seemingly flow back and forth between presenter and viewer despite obvious barriers of television presenting. Such familiarity and appreciation of the presenter's experiences and past lives revealed in conversation, to say nothing of a decade of watching these women talk about their lives is, just as in long-standing friendship, an essential part of the enjoyment of the programme.

Houseparty was a magazine that worked specifically to privilege companionship and familiarity over formality and these priorities also extended to the privileging of opinion and conversation over factual accuracy. Viewers' letters were a further important aspect of the cycle of communication between presenters and viewers, and George Egan replied to many of these himself, sometimes quite wittily, even acerbically, defending the presenters against sexism, racism and undue criticism. One example demonstrates his support for the conversational, rather than factual, mode of televisual delivery:

> It is really most kind of you to take the time and trouble to write to us, pointing out where you think we have gone astray. [...] One of the essential ingredients of the Series is to encourage the ladies who take part to be as natural as possible. This, of course, means that they do not always achieve perfection. However, if you remember the discussion was to try to provoke amongst the ladies present the awareness of the fact that it is all too easy to break the law through ignorance, misinterpretation, etc. And I think you must, in all fairness, agree that we achieved this.[45]

In this letter, Egan is defending the presenters' conversational exchanges against criticism from a police officer who wrote in to point out that the *Houseparty* ladies were mistaken in their understandings of the law, suggesting they 'needed to check facts' before the programme was aired.[46] This instance of discussion of the law of the land demonstrates *Houseparty*'s departure from any Reithian information/education axis of authoritative television, and prioritising of a more natural, everyday, human and therefore flawed, mode of communication. The presenters were not talking about the law, they were talking about their (mis)interpretation and (mis)understanding of it: they were having a casual, not an informed, conversation. Whilst this raises complex questions about authority, accuracy and trust in television journalism and transmission, in the context of the present discussion, Egan is very clear about what the programme is trying to achieve: uninhibited women's conversation. He makes this point even more clearly in a response to another viewer's letter who has queried why *Houseparty* does not give its recipes more clearly on the programme. Egan replies:

> One of the main reasons why we don't put recipes over on the screen is because we try to make these programmes as uninhibited by television techniques as possible. We hope that anyone who wanted details would do just as you have done and write in for them.[47]

Egan may not have been popular on the programme with the presenters, but he had worked closely with Jack Hargreaves for some years and he was fully aware of the challenges of such a programme. When responding to what he sees as 'healthy criticism' he says:

> the very challenging thing about this programme is that it is viewed by rich and poor alike; male and female; young and old. Now it is impossible to please everybody all the time but what we try to do is give viewers an insight into the lives of different people, and, as we all know, we all have different tastes, therefore some of the things we do will not suit some of the people.[48]

Furthermore, there is an appreciation of the qualities needed in the presenters in order to maintain the successful formula of *Houseparty*. In his reply to a job application from a successful female presenter from the programme *About Women*, with an interesting and fashionable specialism in palmistry and other astrology-related topics, he says:

> the essential qualitie [sic] for all of the women is that they should not be 'presenters' in any television sense. Seemingly ladies like this were tried in the early days of the series and they were just not successful in the form that we have developed.[49]

The spectacle of genuine friendship, that *Houseparty* worked hard to achieve, earned the programme a loyal viewer following across all age ranges.

> I am grateful too for the age range Houseparty covers, my Grandma who is 82 loves it, my cousin is 10 years, I'm 27yrs and my Mum is 59yrs and we all love it![50]

Most importantly of all, viewers wanted to be a part of the programme; so much of an impression did this kind of female companionship mean to viewers at home, that they wanted to participate: 'How I enjoy being one of the party,' said one viewer,[51] whilst another demonstrates huge dedication, following the cake-baking recipes from her sickbed, with the aid of a food processor and husband.[52] Lest there is any doubt about the affection in which the *Houseparty* presenters were held, this is a letter from one viewer that stands for many. This viewer has made handmade gifts for the presenters: aprons, tea cosies and a beach bag for Marshie, all made with the individual personality in mind. The viewer also suggests that Avril might pick up the gifts on her way to work as the viewer has discerned that she lives nearby:

I have done some crocheting for Ann as she said she can't crochet and I have had so much help with my needlework from her. [...] When the Queen was married I sent her a set of Tennereef mats, [sic] So, what is good enough for the Queen is good enough for you girls. [...] I am sorry I can't treat you all alike, my only wish is that I will meet you all one day.[53]

This viewer has watched and, in her mind, befriended the *Houseparty* ladies on television, she is grateful for the sewing techniques she has learnt from Ann Ladbury and noticing that Ann does not crochet, offers her own skilled work as a mark of that gratitude. The affection felt is palpable in the humorous raising of the presenters to the level of royalty, and in her longing to meet the 'girls'. Others wrote in to offer their services, suggesting items of interest that they could talk about, presenting themselves as contributing something new to the mix.

Viewers were far from naive and most of the *Houseparty* presenters project a certain class confidence, if not class allegiance; this was not lost on the viewers and some were very conscious of class differentials between themselves and the presenters. However, in one particularly telling letter, unsigned and handwritten in a halting style with interrupted prose, a reader expresses an acknowledgement of the distance between herself and the presenters:

Dear Friends,
    I have watched your programme in fact I look forward to it and take all in and often do I wish I was as intelligent as you all are and I sometimes think I under-estimate myself and I can do it if I want to enough, must tell you this though I have a daughter and a son [...]
    What I would like to know are you wealthy middle class and I am [sure?] not the working class, as every programme I have my favourites Marshy and Cherry great [...] may the programme continue,
    a mum in her fifties. [sic][54]

This viewer, who has discerned class differences between herself and the *Houseparty* ladies, nonetheless has chosen to learn from, and be inspired by, the programme and the presenters. Moreover, she indicates that she has not reached her own potential, she has brought up two successful children and now finds time for herself. For this reader at least, the *Houseparty* presenters represent some degree of social and personal aspiration. Thus through this programme some viewers might enjoy the benefits of broadening their social circle.[55]

***

The question remains about the contribution this exceptional programme made to women's lives in 1970s Britain. The presenters themselves were women of the 1970s with varying relationships to the world around them and to the feminism of the decade. Acting as their own researchers, they put forward topics for discussion that were current and, in this 'feminist' decade, pertinent to women and women's interests. Their choices were haphazard but largely unconstrained, ranging from lace-making and the construction of ribbon-covered espadrilles, to pregnancy termination and women in the workplace, to children's problems or hilarious stories of family life. The women on *Houseparty* were friends, giving and receiving handmade gifts, interested in their homes and their families, in making and crafting, in taking responsibility for their own happiness and in having a view on aspects of their wider worlds, *despite* their position of secondary power as women. Never overtly labelled as feminist, nonetheless, the programme worked for women in making women's lives and women's cultures significant and important,[56] with an underlying sense of female politics informing the presenters and the programme in this period of feminist consciousness.[57] Jean knew the relevance of the issues on the programme, and she had a strong sense of the issues that were mobilising women, but when she was asked if she was a feminist she answered no, rationalising and justifying her answer in terms of allegiance, 'because I thought "I don't belong to any group"'. As in feminism, contradictions in women's lives may not have been resolved, but they were openly aired on *Houseparty*. The presenters, as working women in their own right, away from the programme as well as within it, echoed, in this complex position, the actual situation of many women in the 1970s.

Just as a woman's domestic print magazine ensures regular appeal and familiarity through the continuity of its editor and regular section writers, so *Houseparty* in its regular production arrangements and values appealed to its viewers and by carefully and deliberately structuring the presence of the viewer, she was invited to join in, to be part of this circle of friends. Jean knew that people made fun of the programme, often suggesting it was little more than 'A lot of women sitting around chatting.' But she also had evidence that there were many male viewers too, writing in under the guise of their wife's opinion. Looking back at the programme across the decades she concluded that, 'My instinct is it is all so slow. There is room to breathe. It is cut, cut, cut nowadays. No depth.'

Ultimately the programme served a need to raise the importance of women's quotidian reality. Like the soap opera televisual genre, it acknowledged the everyday within the context of real female lives.[58] The whole point of the programme was to make the viewer feel a part of the gathering. And it worked, there were many letters from viewers writing in to say 'how *Houseparty* had helped their loneliness'. *Houseparty* promised consistent and reliable female companionship to a lonely generation of women, achieving an exceptional televisual magazine intimacy. It took the magazine format and made it a real-life experience enacted through female presenters who, through conversation, demonstration and presentation provided companionship.

'Improving the Public Image of the Lesbian' in *Arena Three*

Arena Three (1964–1971) was, if not the very first lesbian magazine in Britain, certainly the first to openly announce itself as such and because of this has a weighty significance in British gay and lesbian history as a 'first attempt to speak as a lesbian community'.[1] It is an example of a magazine that helped to bring about social recognition and acceptance of an unacknowledged group of women and its position as a magazine is surrounded by complex and contradictory factors: if in many ways it was a first, it also was part of a tradition and longer history; it sought to reach an isolated readership, but the organising group had already established a number of connections; it was to be the mouthpiece for research into lesbianism, but also needed to function as a nexus of community for a timid readership; it presented itself as brand new, but also apart from the existing lesbian social scene. Consequently, as a magazine it needed to function in disparate ways, finding a mode of expression that addressed broader concerns and organisations whilst also empowering insecure individuals at an intimate level. Above all else it tried to build confidence about lesbianism in its readership groups, and to bring lesbianism to the attention of the wider public. It tried to base itself in serious enquiry, but to also adopt a light, confident tone, inspiring a collective self-belief which could laugh at the silliness of the ill-informed prejudice of some commentators. At that time, lesbianism occupied a marginalised position in British society and *Arena Three* sought both recognition and acceptance of lesbianism by bringing lesbianism into the mainstream.

This periodical was set up as part of another organisation that had a broader remit regarding lesbianism in Britain, called the Minorities Research Group (MRG). The founding member of MRG was Esmé Langley and she was also editor of the magazine. Langley (1919–1992) was no stranger to controversy or prejudice in her private or public life, and her autobiography *Why Should I Be*

Dismayed? written under the pseudonym of Ann Bruce charts a period of her life as a young woman surviving independently with her baby son.[2] However, her achievement was highly respected, 'Esmé Langley shouldered the sole legal and financial responsibility for breaching the public wall of silence and bringing lesbianism into the arena of public debate.'[3] Her interest in minority groups had caused her to set up the MRG, having previously started a magazine for the homeless, *Mainland*, before embarking on *Arena Three* in 1964. Langley as the driving force behind the MRG and its magazine, was the embodiment of an enterprising spirit and along with three other women, can be identified as the founding member.

The MRG committee was made up of four professional, middle-class women: Esmé Langley, the initial driving force; Diana Chapman (shortly to become Esmé's partner); Cynthia Reid and Julie Switsur.[4] Reid and her partner Switsur had already considered the possibility of a lesbian social club, and Antony Grey, Secretary of the Homosexual Law Reform Society (HLRS), introduced them to Langley and suggested combining the magazine and the club. Initially it was productive to join forces under the umbrella of a common minority group, and at the outset the magazine attempted to cover these divergent requirements; however, later on the understandably different aims of a research group and of a social club caused problems. The obscuring title of the MRG was chosen as an ambiguous, unspecific compromise, a tactic learnt from other similar groups across Europe.[5]

In targeting a specific group, *Arena Three* may be viewed as a magazine approaching its audience with an objective far removed from that of the more mainstream magazine offerings in the previous chapters, even though some of the functions of the magazine may be the same. This chapter examines the potential of a magazine to galvanise a social movement. Although, as I will discuss, *Arena Three* formed part of a longer history and a wider, international landscape of campaigning around gay and lesbian rights at the time, it nonetheless played a very distinctive role in the British context: it operated as a social movement organisation (SMO) in its own right. John McCarthy and Mayer Zald argue that social movement theorists have traditionally made strong assumptions about the significance of shared grievances in the emergence of social movements. However, they also point out that recent research has disputed this link between a shared grievance and outbreaks of social movements, and go on to emphasise the importance of resource aggregation and mobilisation.[6] This is a helpful model in understanding the broader context for *Arena Three*, and for making sense of its very varied content. It helps to explain how this magazine set about achieving its disparate aims of both bringing lesbianism to public attention, of dealing with writings, 'research' and literature, and reassuring a disparate group of women frequently isolated by their sexual identity and a desire to remain private about their outlook.

Resource mobilisation relies on the effective organisation of power and resources from both inside and outside the movement, and resource mobilisation enquiry, therefore, is interested in the ways that movement organisers use the resources available to them in positive ways to mobilise and further their cause.[7] Such resources might include: people, both organisers and members, able to give of their time and energies and expertise; resources such as technology and funds; agencies such as the media and governmental groups; and links to other related social networks and societal support. Edwards and McCarthy have argued that there are five ways of categorising resources: material, moral, social-organisational, human and cultural, and that these include a range of physical and intellectual resources which can be utilised and brought to bear on the project of furthering the cause.[8] The positive desire to mobilise a range of resources towards a purpose is seen as a more important motivating factor than grievance and deprivation in social movement behaviour. To this end then, an SMO, it is suggested, will have clearly defined objectives, 'a set of *target goals*, a set of preferred changes toward which it claims to be working,'[9] and an entrepreneurial spirit working towards an issue of public interest is one way of seeing the energising force of such movements.[10] As a social movement, the MRG members played a critical part in resource mobilisation: their personal resources of support, expertise, intellectual and cultural capital firstly established the social movement and then increased its numbers.

This chapter reflects upon how *Arena Three* approached these differing calls in order to play a central role in galvanising a social movement. *Arena Three* as a 'pressure group periodical' was significant as a form of 'movement media', demonstrating the 'potential of print as an organisational and mobilising tool' to encourage and educate both its own members and the general public and other agencies at large.[11] The function and reach of *Arena Three* extended through and beyond its pages to serve as a nexus for women's social movement at a time when lesbianism developed from a position of invisibility and marginal legality to a group with a public profile striving for social acceptance. It has been suggested that lesbian feminist mobilisation might be understood according to three factors in the construction of collective identity: boundaries, consciousness and negotiation, where 'boundaries' refers to the establishment of difference between the minority and dominant groups, 'consciousness' to the interpretive frameworks of definition and 'negotiation' to the everyday actions groups use in their resistance.[12] *Arena Three* can be understood to be dealing with a series of tensions within and outside the magazine, operating against external stereotypes to establish those boundaries, as well as working to offer different frameworks with which lesbian women could identify in order to develop consciousness, whilst also negotiating with the media.

Lesbian culture in Britain, of course, does not start with *Arena Three*, and amongst others, Rebecca Jennings has written *A Lesbian History of Britain* that starts in the early modern period; Emily Hamer's *Britannia's Glory* has provided a history of lesbians in the twentieth century and Laura Doan has argued for the basis of a quite visible English lesbian cultural style in the 1920s.[13] Studies of other cultures have also sought to recover long-standing histories of gay and lesbian culture. For instance, Lillian Faderman in *Surpassing the Love of Men* discusses lesbianism from the Renaissance onwards, and the collection *Hidden from History* contains numerous essays on same-sex love and relationships in different cultures from as early as the medieval period.[14] Some of this work of historical recovery argues for lesbianism as an important but often ignored part of history, whilst other work is more critical and reflexive. The present chapter does not give a full history of *Arena Three* magazine (1964–1971), and its contribution to the lesbian cause over that six-year period,[15] but rather considers how the magazine and the movement established itself. It examines the efforts of its editor and founding members, the SMO's 'elite group', to establish a social movement through addressing sometimes conflicting needs.

The motivations of the MRG and the resources needed and mobilised, the time and energies and intellectual resources given and acquired, the links to other societies in foreign countries and the engagement of the media to work on the group's behalf, all mark the MRG out as an SMO. In line with McCarthy and Zald's sense of positive mobilisation rather than grievance motivation within social movements, I suggest that although the MRG was irritated by the portrayal of lesbianism in British culture, rather than simply decry those ignorant images, it mobilised its resources towards the more positive project of creating a different set of images and ideas about lesbianism. Announcing itself as, 'an association of people who are at present concerned about the problems of female homosexuality', it declared it was open to anyone:

Membership is open to anyone who has a bona fide motive for applying to join the Group, whether this is directly personal, or sociological, or from disinterested good will. This point must be stressed, because one of the objects of the Group is to free homosexuality from the prurience, sensationalism and vulgar voyeurism with which it is associated in some minds.

This is a statement of an open policy, and indeed some supportive men, quite a few married women, as well as social service, medical or academic professionals joined, alongside single lesbian women. From the very start, the MRG was aware of the titillating, voyeuristic way in which lesbianism was represented and consumed by some, and naturally the group wanted to keep out that portion. Below this, the group set out its five aims:

1. To provide a centre wherein homosexual women can meet others for discussion of their differing views, problems and interests. It is now becoming generally recognised that isolation is a potent factor in inducing neurosis.
2. To provide material for medico-social research workers and writers who wish to investigate the condition.
3. To seek ways of improving the public image of the lesbian by familiarising this fairly common condition, and of removing from it the aura of social stigma.
4. To publish and circulate monthly to its members the magazine *Arena Three*, in which items of particular concern to homosexual women can be discussed, but which will also publish material of more general interest.
5. To arrange meetings, debates, lectures and conferences and to promote intelligent and properly informed press and radio comment in relation to this minority group.[16]

Like other SMOs, this group had clear objectives which can be summarised as follows: offering a meeting point, providing research material, improving the public image, publishing a magazine, arranging meetings and lectures and achieving press coverage. The 'preferred change' in society underlying these extensive plans for resource mobilisation, including people, their skills and their intellectual capital, publication of a periodical and intervention regarding the press, is to improve the public image of the lesbian.

One of the ways the MRG set out to achieve their 'preferred change' was to strengthen links with other lesbian and gay networks with similar objectives in Britain and elsewhere. The HLRS was formed in 1958 to lobby for legal reform and it established the Albany Trust, a charity to deal with social and psychological issues associated with homosexuality. Lesbians also naturally gravitated to these organisations, and it was from the HLRS and Antony Grey, its secretary, that Esmé Langley sought advice about setting up a magazine for lesbians.[17] In this way, *Arena Three* did not operate to a single agenda of intimate communication with its reader; it needed to pay attention to the wider issues of the movement, including the workings of the MRG. In this it operated, especially in the early issues, to give voice to a new social movement and the resource mobilisation of its elite group, as well as attempting to educate and establish links between a membership in its very early stages. Whilst Langley and her team were indeed trying to promote a new or rather, alternative, kind of lesbianism, it should be remembered that lesbianism in Britain has a long association with print media.

Setting boundaries: *Arena Three* and its print media context

As Taylor and Whittier have argued, one of the ways of understanding lesbian feminist mobilisation is through the 'Boundaries' that mark the social territories of a group: 'Boundary markers are, therefore, central to the formation of collective identity because they promote a heightened awareness of a group's commonalities and frame interaction between members of the in-group and the out-group.'[18] Within the context of the available lesbian print media, its history and contemporaneous publications, this section brings to the fore some of the social territories already established, and others that were available for Esmé Langley to draw upon. *Arena Three* is often claimed as the first lesbian magazine in Britain, probably because it was the first to label itself as such; however, nearly five decades earlier there was a periodical called *Urania* (1916–1940), circulated privately to interested individuals and sent to women's university colleges. Eva Gore-Booth is believed to be the inspiration behind *Urania*, and she along with a few others including her partner Esther Roper were members of the Aëthnic Union, a small group which campaigned to 'overcome all distinctions based on sex'.[19] The magazine was started in 1916 and printed in India for T. Baty, Paper Buildings, Temple, London. Thomas Baty (1869–1954) was also a member of the Aëthnic Union and the magazine's editor, writing copy as his alternative persona, the feminist Irene Clyde.[20] *Urania* calls for support by urging 'those who respond to the ideal of freedom advocated by this little paper to do us the favour of intimating their concurrence with us'. It seeks 'spiritual progress which far transcends all political matters. It is in favour of the abolition of the "manly" and the "womanly"'.[21] However, the periodical seems mostly about women, particularly those women who adopt what would have been considered men's roles socially, culturally and professionally. There are impressive feats of womanhood reported with a general air of proving that women are as good as men. In some contexts of 1920s Britain, this depiction would have been seen as the mannish woman; however, *Urania* idealises an androgynous, futuristic version of womanhood. There is an international flavour to the magazine, with a particularly strong Japanese interest, presumably reflecting Baty's time working in Tokyo. And in issues from the 1920s there are articles, many copied directly from other newspaper sources, about women in men's clothes, women with the strength of men and women marrying women.

Culturally the 1920s was an important time in lesbian history; there were suffragettes and flappers, both arguing for different kinds of female and sexual freedoms, and lesbian literature became more overt. In discussing Radclyffe Hall's fiction and the 'Mannish Lesbian', Esther Newton has noted a shift between first-generation New Women of the *fin de siècle*, trapped by familial constraints, and second-generation lesbians of the early twentieth century, constrained by their bodies and their sex.[22] This shift to an individualised responsibility for subjectivity and sexual consciousness, in terms of appearance, functionality of the body and psychological awareness, was explored and developed in these early twentieth-century texts such as *Urania* and lesbian novels.

The seriousness of the pursuit and portrayal of alternative models of womanhood in *Urania* and the responsibility for subjectivity and sexual consciousness are helpful frameworks for understanding the project of *Arena Three*. The MRG and *Arena Three* present research in a manner of enquiry, proceeding from a point of individual subjectivity and self-knowledge, and project any findings outwards with the intention of developing a wider consciousness in the broader society.

In promoting *Arena Three*, Esmé Langley, of course, made links with contemporary organisations to form a sense of an 'in-group'. Perhaps the strongest link, the greatest influence on Esmé Langley, and certainly her editorship of *Arena Three*, was the American magazine called *The Ladder* (1956–1970). This was published by the group called the Daughters of Bilitis (DOB) and was well established when Langley set up what was called her 'companion' paper in London. The DOB (named after an erotic poem) was set up in San Francisco in 1955 initially with the intention of providing a lesbian social life away from the gay bar scene already in existence. *The Ladder* soon expanded into more public-minded objectives and joined forces with Mattachine, a left-wing men's homosexual group, and *ONE* (1953), a magazine for men and women, into the 'homophile' movement. The wording of the objectives of DOB, including educating the public and integrating the 'variant' into society, owes much to the communist-initiated language of the Mattachine society. *The Ladder* was published monthly by DOB and intended to provide personal support and experience to isolated lesbians, whilst political engagement was mostly left to members of the wider organisation.[23] *The Ladder* continued until 1970 when its role was effectively undermined by the gathering strength of the US women's liberation movement. Its stated intentions and objectives were printed on the inside cover of each issue and its purpose was to promote 'the integration of the homosexual into society', and the aims were fourfold: 'Education of the variant'; 'Education of the public at large'; 'Participation in research projects' and 'Investigation of the penal code as it pertains to the homosexual'. By January 1964, the start date of *Arena Three*, *The Ladder* was into its eighth volume and had an established feel, and Barbara Gittings (a prominent gay rights activist) was editor while Jane Bell was president and Matty Elliot was vice-president of the DOB. It was produced in approximately A5 size, with a coloured light card cover, often with drawing or illustrated image on the front. By mid-1964 there were many photographic covers, also with a back photograph often featuring two women, and from 1964 it carried the subtitle 'A Lesbian Review'. Its monthly content consisted of articles, reviews, short stories, a letters section and a section called 'Cross-currents' that contained snippets of news about homosexuality in the wider world. It started to keep a close eye on the British press and followed significant discussions across the Atlantic, such as Tony Geraghty's article about homosexual fear of employment dismissal in *The Guardian*; and in May 1965 reprinted an article by Monica Furlong on the MRG from her column in the *Daily Mail*.[24]

The Ladder offered *Arena Three* support, gave it publicity and access to its subscription list and, consequently, most of the initial subscribers to *Arena*

Three were American. In the January 1964 issue, *The Ladder* describes female homosexuality in Britain simultaneously giving *Arena Three* a puff, claiming it as a 'sister magazine' and announcing the editor, Esmé Langley, as secretary to the MRG.[25] Later that year, *The Ladder* gave advice on subscribing to *Arena Three* 'our British counterpart', indicating a new more realistic subscription rate and advising American subscribers not to send a cheque, but a bank draft or international postal money order.[26] Close ties and close communication were implied between these two magazines at *Arena Three*'s start-up, indicating at least one established interface for the new British magazine. As an established and supportive associated group, this was a highly important resource for the new lesbian group in London.

Given that there were no other groups in London, Langley, in addition to the DOB in the United States, also found connections and support from more established mainland European groups; after all, the first lesbian magazine had appeared in Germany in the 1920s.[27] As well as the DOB, two other groups are mentioned in Esmé Langley's opening editorial: Arcadie and C.O.C.[28] In Paris, André Baudry had created *Arcadie: Revue Littéraire et Scientifique* magazine in 1954.[29] *Arcadie* was an offshoot of *Der Kreis-Le Cercle-The Circle*, a Swiss 'homophile' movement and magazine, with French and English pages. *Der Kreis* itself had also started out in 1932 as a lesbian magazine called *Freundschaftsbanner*.[30] 'Marc Daniel', pseudonym for Michel Duchein, a major contributor to *Arcadie* and an English-speaking historian,[31] was thanked in particular for 'very friendly help, advice and practical encouragement' in this first editorial by Esmé Langley. In the Netherlands the C.O.C., also a 'homophile' club (Centre for Culture and Recreation), had been set up in 1946 to provide personal support, opportunities to meet others and political lobbying on behalf of homosexual men and women. The Dutch C.O.C. was also based on a magazine called *Levensrecht*.[32] Many of these post-war groups had links to the pre-Nazi German gay and lesbian scenes, and often used oblique titles to avoid attention from authorities or to remain unattractive to those only interested in the gay bar social scene. These groups aimed for an intellectual, political and even genteel approach to homosexuality, hence their preferential use of the term 'homophile' and not homosexual, signalling support for the cause, rather than an exclusive focus on sex and sexuality.

Part of the function of the MRG was to maintain contact and dialogue with other homosexual societies, and Langley followed the established pattern of these other groups in setting up an overarching organisation that sought to spread its message outwards through a variety of channels, using whatever resources it had at its disposal. In a similar way to these other societies, the role of the MRG was manifold and extended into different arenas, all of which demanded a high level of input from the committee and very often from Langley herself. The range of activities undertaken by the small committee group included keeping up with publications, producing the magazine for members, facilitating social events and meetings, offering a lending library and utilising the media to spread the new message. In addition to all this, extra resources were used to provide a drop in counselling service for members which became overwhelmingly popular and in the results of a questionnaire, sent out at the end of their first year, counselling was given top priority by the respondents.[33]

Negotiating with the mainstream: Mobilising the media

Langley understood the power of the media and the importance of getting a positive reception for this new social movement within the wider press. From the outset, the MRG had a mission to 'promote intelligent and properly informed press and radio comment' in relation to lesbianism, with its fifth aim being very specifically to achieve appropriate media coverage. Utilising the media, part of the 'negotiation' process, is understood to be a very important aspect of establishing a new social movement, often crucial to its success. The magazine itself was a foray into the world of print media representation, and in its production Langley was able to draw on her own resources, both intellectual and financial. Her previous experience in magazines and her own financial backing provided the impetus required to bring this publication to its audience. Langley had also worked for BBC at Caversham in her early career and had produced a magazine before and so had some knowledge of the media world; so that industry know-how alongside her own talents in writing and typing[34] were a key resource for *Arena Three* and in helping to build this social movement (Figure 4.1). Besides being a new venture in print, a persistent theme running through the magazine is the presentation of lesbianism in the press. After all, Esmé Langley was inspired to start the magazine as retaliation to Dilys Rowe's article, 'A Quick Look at Lesbians' in *Twentieth Century*.[35] From the very beginning of this social movement, the debate about lesbianism was carried out, positively and negatively, within the print media. As discussed

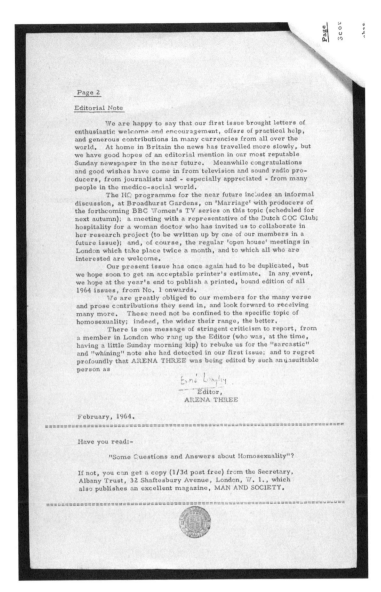

Figure 4.1 Esmé Langley's editorial, *Arena Three*, February 1964, p. 2.
© *Estate of Esmé Langley.*

earlier, Langley's very first editorial thanks to other European and American homophile magazines established the position of *Arena Three* in a print media context of periodicals.

The intention was to mobilise the media twofold: to advance their cause, educate the public and respond to media representations of lesbianism; but also to reach people who felt isolated by their sexuality. By November, this is articulated quite clearly in the magazine:

> M.R.G. has this month embarked on a nation-wide advertising campaign. This is in accordance with Object 5 of our aim and objects as set out in our 1964 application form: 'to promote intelligent and properly informed press and radio comment'.
>
> Quite apart from the obvious value of press publicity in dispelling the assorted myths and fantasies still current about female homosexuality, it is of tremendous importance in reaching the many isolated, lonely and often desperately unhappy people who would otherwise never hear of our existence. We want to emphasise this point, as from time to time people ask us why we want to 'make a fuss' about lesbianism. We don't. It is society that makes a fuss about it, and we aim to persuade them that fuss is unnecessary, that it is high time, after all these millennia, that homosexuality in men and in women was accepted and taken in the social stride.[36]

Small ads were regularly sent to various established newspapers, magazines and professional journals advertising the work of the MRG and informing people how to get in touch with the organisation; some of these were rejected at first, but Langley persisted.[37] At first, television and newspapers were hesitant to engage with lesbianism.[38] However, there were some successes as early articles appeared in the *Observer* and the *Sunday Times*, both in March 1964. Esmé Langley was also interviewed in April 1964 for television's *In the News* programme in her role as MRG co-founder and *Arena Three* editor about lesbianism,[39] and other invitations for radio interviews and other television appearances followed, though some of these broadcast media programmes took time to be transmitted. It seems that there was more reticence in broadcast than print media forms as newspaper articles about the magazine and group started to appear more regularly. An article in the *News of the World* by Ron Mount opens with a sense of intrigue and titillation in his discovery of 'the headquarters of one of the strangest organisations in Britain'. He nonetheless goes on to give a very fair account of the MRG group and gives Langley generous quotation space to describe the work of the group and get across her account of lesbianism (Figure 4.2).[40] There is little doubt that Langley took every available opportunity to mobilise media resources and advance the MRG and the new public image of lesbianism, through interview, press release or by placing small ads.

Figure 4.2 Esmé Langley and the MRG in the *News of the World*: 'Women Only' by Ron Mount, *News of the World*, 13 December, 1964.
© *News of the World/News Syndication.*

Raising consciousness in *Arena Three*

The overall tone of *Arena Three* projects an authoritative, lively and multi-faceted investigation into a new lesbian identity. The first issues appear assembled with professional intent, but without professional printing and production techniques, with foolscap pages stapled together in the top

left-hand corner and a standard Courier typeface. Indeed, *Arena Three* opens
with an apology: 'First, we must apologise to all our members, at home and
overseas, for the inordinate delay in getting out our first issue.' This was due
to delivery problems, and an implied unhelpfulness, from 'the gentlemen
of the printing world'. The *Arena Three* committee decided to produce the
first issue themselves on a Roneo duplicating machine, which meant no
'artist's illustrations', but was nonetheless an 'all-female effort'. Mobilisation
of alternative resources in this instance shows a clear determination that
resistance or hindrance from the male-dominated printing industry would
not deter publication (Figure 4.3).

Aspects of the magazine overlap with more conventional magazine
structures, for example: news from the editor, letters from other readers,
reviews of books, suggested reading and so on, all centred around its central
theme of lesbianism, providing frameworks for consciousness. However, the
magazine focused on negotiations or actions too: it advertised its counselling
service, set up face-to-face social meetings and offered the prospect of making

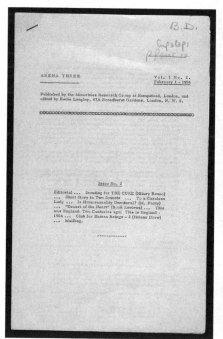
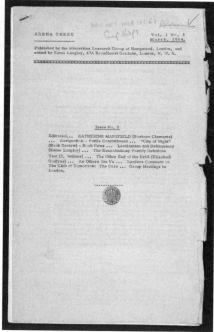

Figure 4.3 Early 'roneoed' first issues of *Arena Three*, *Arena Three*, February 1964 and
March 1964, front covers.
© *Estate of Esmé Langley.*

connections through a classified ads column. The actual size of the readership is unclear, the circulation of the magazine was over 400 in mid-1965, the print run was 1,000, but 2,000 copies were produced in 1971 for subscribers and newsagents sales. However, Esmé Langley suggested that the readership might be 10,000 or more, with the informal distribution of the magazine amongst friends.[41] Whilst there is humour in the writing, particularly in the printing of some of the more outlandish letters to the editor, this is not a light-hearted magazine intended to entertain or distract a casual reader. This is a movement periodical with every intention of involving itself, along with its research branch, in the current debates, functioning to inform its readership of literature concerning lesbianism as well as responding to those ideas. This important function within the context of the SMO is to offer, bolster and encourage a new collective consciousness. Within *Arena Three* there is an overwhelming desire to move its readers from the margins to the centre of British society. It sought to offer lesbians, anticipated by the magazine to be isolated and unconfident in their sexuality, a new way of thinking about themselves and one that permitted women to publicly acknowledge their sexual orientation whilst participating fully in mainstream society, something, it was further assumed, that many readers felt unable to do at the time.

The following three sections look at three ways in which *Arena Three* sought to raise consciousness within its readership. Firstly, the magazine had been set up at the inaugural committee meeting of the MRG, with the intention of using it as a periodical to report on its 'Research' element, so that *Arena Three* served the group by acting as a mouthpiece for the activities of the initiating research group. Secondly, there had always been a social imperative behind two of the founding members, Reid and Switsur, and forming a club and facilitating meetings and social events became an important function of the magazine. Thirdly, consciousness was raised by the firm establishment of a fiction reading practice within the membership.

Conducting and collaborating in 'research'

Esmé Langley describes the MRG in terms of its activities, which are:

> to conduct and to collaborate in research into the homosexual condition, especially as it concerns women; and to disseminate information and items of interest to universities, institutes, social and educational workers, writers, poets,

editors, employers and, in short, all those genuinely in quest of enlightenment about what has been called the 'misty, unmapped world of feminine homosexuality[']'.[42]

This is a high-minded approach to an opening editorial, setting out the privileging of research and the wider dissemination of that information into the public domain. Marianne Cutler has discussed how the American lesbian magazine, *The Ladder*, by publishing the research of the DOB, was compelled to enter into a public dialogue which firstly asserted the magazine as 'possessors of important information regarding homosexuality' and secondly that lesbians were 'legitimate participants in the discussion of this "problem"'.[43] The element of the MRG called 'research' was a multi-faceted mode of enquiry and similarly required and facilitated different modes of discourse: as a generic term, 'research' stands rather obliquely in *Arena Three* for any form of serious engagement with the subject of lesbianism. However, through the publications within *Arena Three*, it can be seen that there are quite specific interpretations of the term research.

One interpretation was the engagement with current discussions about lesbianism, be they scientific or personal opinion, dedicated, specific publications or more casual remarks as part of another project. These were reported to the readership through articles and snippets of commentary, disseminating the information in easily assimilated ways. Some articles came laced with heavy irony such as 'Scouting for ... The Public Image' by Hilary Benno (one of Esmé Langley's pseudonyms) which, in a sweeping conversational tone, lightly makes reference to extreme and offensive images of lesbianism presented across different public domains. There is no shortage of inaccurate images according to Benno/Langley, starting with Rowe's already existing discussion in *Twentieth Century* magazine of, 'classic English partnerships of elderly well brought-up women'; followed by the BBC, with its 'High-level shush-shush policy', and reluctance to engage with lesbianism; and then the law, where a judge declared, 'that "a Lesbian" was a creature of the "grossest unchastity", on a par, indeed, with the common prostitute'; and the 'headshrinkers' who are full of contradictions about lesbianism with comments about 'Arrested Development' with lots of 'mental blocks to be removed'. However, the article ends with two quotations from Iris Murdoch's letter of support: 'Anything to do with "special relations with the police", or "treating these people kindly as persons in need of treatment" must be got away from.' And then, 'What needs to be recognised is that homosexuals are perfectly ordinary people, and vary as much as heterosexuals.' Murdoch's words are employed to summarily dismiss any ideas of a special pathology, distinctive look or particular public image.[44]

This is research derived from the generalised opinions of others, opinion that has reached the public domain, and so is offered up, together with editorial interpretation for consideration by the reader. Articles such as these set up a framework for readers to understand the different quarters from which commentary on lesbianism is derived and the different interpretations available. The second issue, 'Scouting for … the cure' by Benno/Langley continues its light-hearted dismissal of any notion of a cure (Figure 4.4).[45] Her first stop is 'at a doctor's house' where it was considered that:

> Girls who came striding into the consulting-room shooting their cuffs and twitching at their bow-ties, in the butch-heroic manner would, in due course, go tittupping out again on stiletto heels with a bag full of mascara and lipstick, demanding to be led to the altar by the next presentable and eligible male citizen.

Taken together, these two articles of 'public image' and 'cure' offer an easily-understood retaliation against two of the most common misconceptions of the time about lesbianism. Written in an ironically-resiliant way, these articles provide personal assistance in an intimate way to the individual reader, they prepare lesbian readers for the criticisms and comments they might receive, they offer support and by example they give readers answers to have to hand if faced with these commonly-held prejudices. Whilst misconceptions are dismissed, for the less informed reader these articles nonetheless serve as warnings about those misconceptions too.

Some 'research' discussions based on public opinion have a more specific focus such as one by Michael Forty who wants to ask 'what can it mean to say that homosexuality is "unnatural"' and he takes ideas of nature to task, concluding that any sense of 'purposive' nature is flawed, especially concerning population increase.[46] Two conflicting approaches to lesbianism are explored in 'Bent or Straight Mates'. Here, the idea of homosexuality as an 'acquired neurosis' is challenged, mentioning that both Beran Wolfe and Simone de Beauvoir, 'regarded homosexuality in women as a flight from, or reaction against, the inferior position allocated to women in our culture'. The other psychological notion is that of a failed relationship, perhaps with the father, which 'engenders

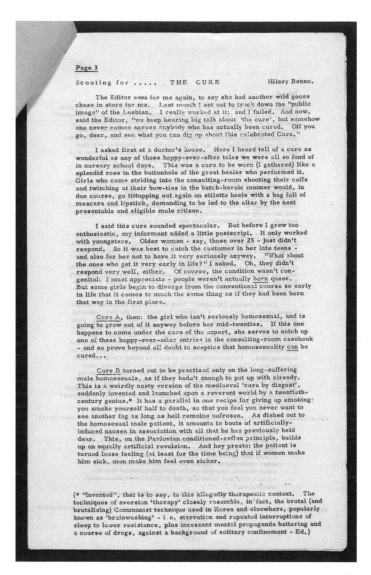

Figure 4.4 'Scouting for … THE CURE' by Hilary Benno, *Arena Three*, February 1964, p. 3.
© *Estate of Esmé Langley.*

in the female child a fear of men'. Although it is noted that over-identification with the father is suggested as the 'cause' in Radclyffe Hall's *The Well of Loneliness*, despite the fact that Radclyffe Hall barely knew her own father. These theories are dismissed for their lack of statistical evidence.[47]

Arena Three presented views, hearsay and information on lesbianism in its pages; in addition, it gave readers ways of thinking about objections, criticisms and commonly held beliefs, ranging across questions of appearance, cures, nature and psychology. It also, to some extent, kept abreast of new publications about homosexuality: Daniel Cappon's *Toward an Understanding of Homosexuality* (1965), for example, was dismissed by Barbara Gittings, editor of *The Ladder*, as 'an epitome of all the most grotesque clichés about homosexuality'; with the spare copy she proposes to start a 'Black Museum of homosexualia'.[48] In this way, expressions of defiant opinion were interleaved with reviews and notifications of publications or commentary about lesbianism and homosexuality. Not only, then, did this kind of research and reading help to keep the membership informed of current debates and publications, but, as with the general opinion articles, it offered a way of thinking about them too. In January 1965, one year after the magazine started, a Literary Circle was suggested 'for talks, discussions, readings, etc.' as an 'extension of the sociological roots of the M.R.G.' and so offering another mode of group research.

These aspects of MRG research drew attention to views about lesbianism, whether published opinion, attempts at scientific discovery, proposed 'cures' or just public hearsay and gossip and this covered respected commentary as well as outlandish, sometimes ridiculous, statement. Responses were articulated to all manner of things, building a collective consciousness of the group, and sometimes the explication and the response happened at the same time. Nevertheless, for the magazine subscriber these operated differently: one made the reader aware of prevailing discourses about lesbianism; the other expressed modes of reaction, perhaps speaking for those without the perspective brought by wide reading, or the political stamina to speak up for themselves. The committee and writers for *Arena Three* can be seen to be fighting back in their pages, speaking sometimes for those portions of the membership who wanted to remain silent and invisible.

The most direct mode of research, however, and perhaps the most controversial, was involvement with, and endorsement of, research projects into lesbianism. In the first issue, Juliet Switsur, one of *Arena Three*'s founding group of four, discusses 'The Bene-Anthony Family Relations Test'. This was a process of assessing a child's sense of his/her relationship to the rest of the family, now being applied to adults to see if there is a difference between homosexual and heterosexual familial relationships. Switsur calls for volunteers who might be interested in helping with this research.[49] *Arena Three* then, was of use to various research projects in different ways: its readership network formed a pool of potential test subjects for various psychological or sociological studies of lesbianism, and there were volunteers from this source; it also supplied an audience interested in the results, even if results were viewed with scepticism.[50]

However, *Arena Three* was not a research journal in the academic sense. The articles are often written in a light or ironic tone, and sometimes offer limited depth in analysis, at times, all that is being discussed is hearsay. That is not to say though that these issues were of little importance to the readership: readers, through their letters, expressed gratitude for the frankness and openness of this 'research', whilst at the same time reflecting back the editorial tone: ' "The Cure" was well done! I enjoy articles like this that are factual – but also poke a bit of fun at those facts'; 'Reading the magazine has sparked off a thousand points for comment'; and 'I am glad to see the inclusion of a few humorous, not too desperately serious items. I think this is necessary to counteract the possibility of a note of maudlin self-pity creeping in.'[51] Furthermore, the very term 'research' may, in some degree, have been employed in the title of MRG as an obfuscating tactic, a misdirective even, to obscure the purpose of the group, in much the same way that the Dutch C.O.C.'s title hides its interests. Nonetheless, the idea of research does provide a useful way of understanding different processes at work within this social movement: Esmé Langley and others used their cultural capital, their reading, political engagement and understanding, and their confidence in their sexuality as an intellectual resource to disseminate information, publications and opinion to what they perceived as a less confident magazine readership. Many letters were printed in the Mailbag section of the magazine, some offering congratulations on the publication of *Arena Three* and others wishing it well, some telling the story of their own journey to lesbianism and the confidence and companionship that the MRG and *Arena Three* have offered on this journey. One long letter, perhaps printed in full because it seems to speak for many, ends by expressing the desire for this movement to reach others and acknowledging the growth of the movement:

> Finally, there is one niggling anxiety. How can we reach those who have either not yet heard of use or who – through fear or ignorance – dare not yet make contact? They are the lonely and the desperate ones. Those of us who read A3 and/or write to you are at last no longer alone.[52]

One way in which this magazine tried to service the social movement was as a dependable and supportive conduit for opinion, writing and even research test projects into lesbianism. In this it supported its less informed readers through education and through bolstering confidence in its dismissal of exaggerated or ill-founded commentaries on lesbianism. However, a social movement needs more than written responses to blossom; it needs people, meetings and argument and 'negotiation'.

Building community: 'A Club for Human Beings'

Georgina Turner has discussed lesbian publishing of magazines as a means of building communities and bringing like-minded people together,[53] and another very important way in which *Arena Three* served this social movement in its early stages was in opening up a number of channels of communication between women (Figure 4.5). Already discussed is the access the magazine gave its readers to the world of commentary on lesbianism, if they were not already aware of both bigoted opinion and the diversity of writings on the subject. It informed of lectures or meetings of interest in gay and lesbian circles, and it kept the individual reader informed of the broader engagement of the work of the MRG. In addition to this, despite an air of privacy and anonymity afforded by a private subscription, *Arena Three* ventured to suggest face-to-face meetings between members. From the outset, it was seen as very important that members of the MRG group and subscribers to *Arena Three* should have the opportunity to meet each other, if they so desired. Some members of the MRG would have already known each other as it had been founded a year earlier than the magazine, and meetings had been held. Furthermore, connections with other similarly focused groups abroad had also already been made. However, this was only a starting point in forming a substantial group in Britain. Both MRG and *Arena Three* offered a number of ways for ordinary members, reluctant perhaps to announce their sexual orientation, to become more involved, to participate in the cause, to give of their labour and energies and to meet socially, in short to network in ways which would establish meaningful connections and require a commitment, even a personal declaration.

Alberto Melucci has discussed how submerged networks operate as a source of new collective identities, and how specific individuals negotiate a sense of group membership. He suggests it is in 'face-to-face interaction where collective identities are developed in submerged networks' and this takes place 'through a process of social negotiation'. He points to the idea of 'opening skirmishes' between members of the submerged networks and between the dominant cultural code as a way of defining that identity,[54] and Carol Mueller

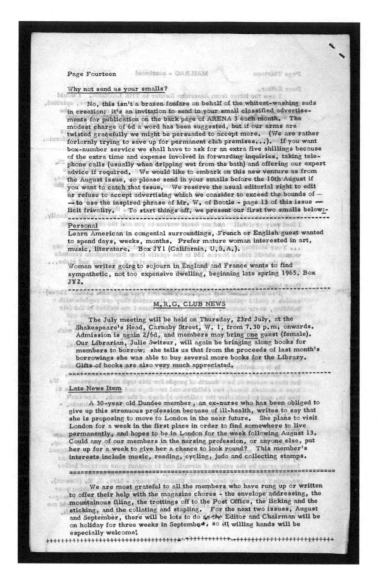

Figure 4.5 Running the magazine and opening up channels of communication, *Arena Three*, July 1964.
© *Estate of Esmé Langley.*

has applied these ideas specifically to the development of women's liberation.[55] For the MRG, a 'submerged network', these social gatherings brought out hotly contested issues for women, and dealings with the press, as discussed in the magazine, were slippery and fraught. The recording of the gatherings and the participant responses in *Arena Three* are highly significant in terms of the work of the magazine. They record the foray of the group into wider society, and 'opening skirmishes' that define collective identity, as well as the way individuals negotiate their way to the group. The meetings themselves, much anticipated and variously regarded, were very well attended and certainly raised issues of identity formation for this group.

Thus, in the very first issue of *Arena Three*, Helena Drew's article entitled 'A Club for Human Beings' suggests face-to-face meetings. Drew starts her call for meetings with an underlined quotation, a call to action and a cry for support:

> '*We must meet*' says this contributor, '*because we need support and friendship. We must meet in decent surroundings, because most of us are decent people*'.

Drew continues:

> There are two needs, and the club would serve two purposes. First it would offer a place where Lesbians could meet one another. A decent, open and above-board place – no different, in fact, from hundreds of social clubs in England, except for the people it existed to serve. Second, it would provide a venue for talks, to which men could be invited without falling foul of the existing laws.
>
> It would be pleasant to think that it might serve a third important purpose as well: to show the general public that Lesbians and male homosexuals are just ordinary people who like ordinary things, who can behave in an ordinary fashion; who are no better and no worse than anybody else; who are, in fact, human beings who happen to be attracted to members of their own sex rather than the opposite, but who are ostracised and penalised for this as if they were guilty of some dreadful crime.

She calls for a kind of social club, 'a decent, open and above-board place' for women to meet each other and to hold talks. However, the most poignant purpose is to demonstrate that they are 'ordinary people who like ordinary things' and through this demonstration of ordinariness, they might even have an impact on the legal position by influencing 'the public's image of the homosexual sufficiently to make it react favourably to any improvement in the existing law'. What is hoped for through the idea of this face-to-face club is a public display of unremarkable social behaviour. The club, the place and the act of gathering, is envisaged as an opportunity for group members to be understood, as people rather than objects of study or derision.[56] Readers wrote in mostly in support of the establishment of a 'Club of Tomorrow'. One reader saw it as an improvement on the 'kind of meeting-places which are familiar in Paris, Brussels, etc., where, simply to meet their need for companionship ... Lesbians ... only want to dance, chat, smoke'. Another saw it as destined to fail, 'It won't work. You'll be swamped with the luckless neurotics, and the others will keep WELL away.'[57]

By the third issue in March, there is a note on group meetings which have proved to be 'so popular and enthusiastically well attended' that they can no longer be held in members' homes and need a larger premises, perhaps a small public hall.[58] The Shakespeare's Head public house in Great Marlborough Street, Soho, London, was suggested, and this was engaged. However, other readers remained uncertain about this 'Club for Human Beings', and one reader was unclear who, exactly, would be allowed to join:

> People join clubs to meet others of similar tastes. What possible reason could any heterosexual have for joining a homophil club? You'd attract the voyeur, the husband and wife team anxious to make up a threesome, the bored married woman seeking idle diversion, the people ready to try anything new for 'kicks'. And what about the people for whom the club would be founded – the homophils? If you are going to serve only light refreshments, this will at least deter some of those lesbians who prop up the bars of the dismal 'clubs' already in existence watching out for an easy pick-up. But who else would the club attract? A woman obliged to live discreetly (whether alone or with a partner) because of her job, relatives, etc., would be very cagey of joining any club with such a non-selective membership. [...] Who wants to be left with a bunch of inquisitive heterosexuals gaping at exhibitionistic lesbians? Not for me, thanks.[59]

This letter raises many important issues of the moment: for lesbians in general in Britain at this time it voices the need, still strongly felt by some, for discretion and modest behaviour. It points with disdain to the mostly working-class lesbian scene already in existence, as well as acknowledging the potential for voyeurism and titillation to be associated with lesbianism. The reply from Helena Drew states that the men to be invited to talks were homosexual men, and that she hoped for inclusivity of lesbians of different 'class, income, behaviour, and the hundred and one other ways in which Lesbians differ'. It seems there were misunderstandings about the club even before it started, and members had written in asking about other clubs, and an editor's note at the bottom of the page promises a 'brief tour' of some of these in the next issue. In the May issue, two clubs are described, one a gay bar full of men, the other is described as 'dingy and uninspired' in decor, with a range of lesbian styles of different nationalities and classes, but 'most of them come into the "lower income bracket"'. There are 'occasional fights, quarrels, black eyes', and it is a place where 'Change of partner appears to be frequent.' The jukebox and fruit machine and the noise at closing time indicate a completely different type of social club than the one envisaged by the MRG,[60] and it points to class conflict between the MRG membership and the working-class lesbian club scene.[61] As the magazine records these different 'skirmishes' and 'negotiations', so opportunities for identity definition are offered to all readers, not just those who could attend.

The first large meeting was held on 14 May 1964 and over forty members turned out to make a 'notable stride towards this "club of tomorrow"'.[62] The mailbag section of July's issue was full of letters about the meetings, some full of praise and some raising questions about definitions and perceptions of 'butch' dress, and this seems to hinge around the discussion of wearing trousers or slacks, seen as exhibitionism by others. One reader raises the issue of transvestism, 'I assume because I have attended meetings held by the MRG wearing trousers and tie that I am to be classed as one of the so-called "exhibitionists" mentioned in this months issue of *Arena Three*,'[sic] and she calls for the '"natural" carefree atmosphere' to be maintained. The response from the editor reminds her and other readers that one of the objectives of the MRG is to 'improve the public image of the Lesbian'. Langley also points out that the room is booked for a 'business and professional women's club' and that one member was stopped by the pub manager, 'saying, "I'm sorry, sir, you can't go up there; it's a women's club meeting"'.[63] Evidently from this editorial response, the room was booked under slightly false pretences and the appearance of women in masculine clothing was not only remarkable, but could possibly have revealed the true nature of the club and damaged the image the MRG was trying so hard to project. In 1964 the mere wearing of trousers by women was surely unlikely to cause outrage, but as another reader, D.M.C., put it in her letter printed below the editor's response, 'All we are griping about is extremely "butch" dress' and she goes on to call for a more private room, so that 'everyone could come dressed as they like'.

Identity expressed through clothing took on a particular inflection for the women of the MRG meetings. There were members who wanted to express their sexuality through masculine dress as an invocation of the freedoms afforded by the 'Club for Human Beings' and there were those who thought prudence and discretion would benefit the collective aim of the group to become more normalised within society. Esmé Langley in her editorial in August 1964 acknowledges the 'heated discussion about "drag"', but also makes light of it too, ironically noting a new fashion trend for women's suits, which may be new to haute couture but less so in lesbian history.[64] The tone for this discussion had, perhaps, already been set up in issue 6 with the Fashion Note: 'I haven't a thing to wear' by K. H. who, rather conservatively, advises that for lesbians it is better to 'look female than funny'.[65] The debate about appropriate clothing for lesbians rumbles on in the mailbag section of the magazine, with some seeing 'full drag' as an expression of their sexuality and others seeing it as exhibitionism that does not help the aim of improving the public image of lesbianism. Dress codes apart, judging from the letters, the meetings themselves were a great success. The role of the magazine was to assist the social arm of the MRG in getting these meetings off the ground and it did so by opening up debate, printing opinion and then informing readers about place and time. Yet this magazine was more than just a vehicle for information, it also provided a place for readers to express their emotional responses. Some were overjoyed to meet other lesbians, others expressed disdain at butch dress and those early tentative reflection of the community of this movement had a home: the magazine. It was the receptacle for the extended pleasures and conversations written in the aftermath of the meeting.

As the membership grew, regional groups were formed and regional meetings held more locally for those outside London, such as in The Old Vine, Winchester. In addition to group meetings, the MRG went a step further and offered the possibility of more individual introductions through the facility of a personal small ads feature. However, from February 1965 onwards, small ads as well as news of London meetings and regional activities were to be circulated as insert sheets to MRG members only. This decision marks something of a division, creating a distinction between the magazine readership and those who also belong to the MRG, supporting its work through additional subscription. If it can be assumed that the personal ads were much sought after, this was a way of securing extra revenue; it is also a way of being discrete about disclosing names and addresses in a magazine, suspected by Langley of being read by many, many more than actually bought it.

Arena Three is a complex publication and in playing its part to garner and raise support for a social movement, it had to speak to its readership in a number of different ways. As part of the SMO it tried to bring all its readers to an educated awareness of 'research' undertaken about them. Additionally, it managed the necessity of social interaction, broaching the topic of face-to-face meetings, conducting open discussions and providing space for post-meeting analysis, it also offered a personal ads column. In all these ways, the magazine helped to establish ways in which members could demonstrate their support for this new social movement. But *Arena Three* was a personal, intimate magazine too, not only a newsletter or a mouthpiece for the more politically engaged sector of the MRG, and this is evident through the very strong reading sections provided by Claire Barringer, whose articles indicate some measure of literary discernment and in this, her cultural capital is deployed for the good of the movement.[66]

Encouraging reading: 'Drawing the line at "sludge"'

Recent critics have been interested in the function of literature for lesbian women. Kate Flint suggests that lesbian literature can be dated back to the nineteenth century, and that as early as the 1890s some novels 'had begun to exploit the fact that not every woman's primary sexual orientation is a heterosexual one'.[67] Sally Munt argues further that: 'Books have functioned as rites of passage, and signs of kinship for lesbians. Our literary tradition is a history of the linguistic traces of a common identity'.[68] It was intuitively assumed within *Arena Three* that lesbian literature was an important source of identity formation, a point of contact and common reference. The editor and writers for *Arena Three* understood that they were dealing with a multifarious lesbian readership: it was not expected that all lesbian readers would be single women, confident in their sexuality and necessarily interested in medico-scientific enquiry into their 'condition'. Many readers and members were married and some were mothers, and one interesting anomaly is that to avoid duplicity the application form had to be signed by husbands of the married women who wanted to join. The book sections tend to assume a middle-class, educated readership.

From the very first issue, the *Arena Three* editorial team assumed a literate readership and used literary references to make their case. Names such as Iris Murdoch, Katherine Mansfield, Simone de Beauvoir and Radclyffe Hall, employed in different ways, lend an authority to the first few issues, and a literary section of the magazine is established from early on. A well-stocked library is seen as an important aim achieved in the progress report produced at the end of their first year.[69] The common experience of reading, both sociological and fictitious literature about lesbianism and lesbian subjectivities, was seen as one way of alleviating loneliness. *Arena Three* intended to broaden this solitary experience of reading by forming a lending library and reading groups. The first novel to be reviewed, *The Desert of the Heart* by Jane Rule, was given conflicting reviews, firstly two quite scathing accounts followed by a more sympathetic one from a reader who objected to those earlier reviews.[70] Other books were reviewed such as *City of Night* by John Rechy and *The Dark Side of Venus* by Shirley Verel, who also wrote a retrospective about her novel for the magazine.[71] Recommendations, suggestions, guidance and book lists were all offered to *Arena Three* readers.

In the fourth issue, the editorial note announces that 'Our Literary Editor, Claire Barringer, is now drawing up a booklist for publication in later issues of ARENA THREE. She will be most grateful to any members who have recommendations to make for her list.' For these recommendations, she offers the following guidance notes:

> I draw the line at including 'sludge'; I am also excluding titles where the passing reference is too slight to be eligible for this list. Also I have kept it to the female angle, since that seems to be within the terms of reference. I will also include some revised editions, reissues and paperbacks, for interest's sake.[72]

This then is to be a particular kind of lesbian literature, in line with the tone of the magazine and attracting a particular personality type to this new social movement. Novels must be of some literary merit ('not sludge'), openly committed to the lesbian theme and with women's interests at their heart.

In the very next issue, number 5, a book list duly appears, and Barringer's first recommendation is a survey of lesbian literature by Jeanette Foster, *Sex Variant Women in Literature*: 'This fascinating goldmine was published in Britain by Frederick Muller in 1958, and should be begged, borrowed or – better sill – bought by anyone wishing to build her library on a solid foundation.' Following a plea not to be 'too readily lured by the paperback editions' for the classics such as 'Colette, Proust, Rosamond Lehmann, Elizabeth Bowen', there is a suggestion that 'presentable' paperbacks can be bought of some of the 'lasting favourites' including *Nightwood* by Djuna Barnes, *Orlando* by Virginia Woolf and *The Rainbow* by D. H. Lawrence. However, the seminal lesbian text, *Well of Loneliness*, is dismissed as that 'diehard … got up in a flashy jacket by Perma Books, looks more than ever like yesterday's mutton dressed as lamb'. This then is to be a list that keeps abreast of new publications not just of fiction, but biography and social science too. Barringer goes on to recommend four 'recent titles which reflect a welcome sense of humour' rather than viewing the subject as a 'sacred cow', and these include *The Group* by Mary McCarthy and *Honey for the Bears* by Antony Burgess. The tone of this book list is familiar, entertaining, at times sardonic and written with a certain literary knowledge and authority, demonstrating a pride in the body of literature itself; it is written with care and for women who care about literature. The recommendation of 'The Clique', Foyle's second-hand book searching service and a note that this book list has begun, 'auspiciously' thirty-seven years after Rosamund Lehmann's 'incomparable' *Dusty Answer* was published, and thirty-seven years before Renee Vivien's unpublished poems will 'see light of day', all indicate an uncommon and very detailed engagement with the literary world.[73]

Clare Barringer continued to reflect on the importance of reading: in 'The Fringe Benefits of marginal reading' she weighs up those who would 'rather plough through an otherwise deadly novel in search of an isolated lesbian episode, or read about one entirely unsympathetic homosexual character, than tackle any kind of "straight" book at all'. She reflects on some borderline books which lean towards the subject rather than meet it head-on, in 'literary limbo-land' where women are written about in all guises including loving friendship. Authors such as Woolf, Lehmann, and Antonia White are recommended in this article as a way of broadening the group's sense of helpful and interesting reading in the 'BOOK LIST'.[74]

The literary section was a regular feature in *Arena Three* and the book list was extended, reviews continued and a lending library was established, with Julie Switsur, the MRG Librarian, also offering a postal service. By the September issue, it was announced that the library held over a hundred books, a selection of which was brought to each meeting. Interest had also been shown in collecting details of plays with lesbian themes and assembling a tape library of sound recordings, and forming a Literary Circle for the MRG as an 'extension of the sociological roots'.[75] All this kind of activity gives a sense of gathering information and sources together, of amassing evidence, of finding ways of understanding lesbian subjectivity and of discerning individual ways to reconcile inner and outer worlds: it was a way of educating a movement.

Literature, fiction and non-fiction publications of significance or relevance to the individual and the movement continued to have a strong presence in the magazine. It was a binding force, an already assumed and continuing interest, a point of commonality already undertaken and experienced by most and a way of educating members. It was also a means of offering a collective identity, with history and subjectivity, of raising consciousness and keeping the membership informed and up to date with the progress and history of the movement. The power of literature was understood to bind the group together, and that literature could also help to explore and even explain what might be, for those women readers within this 'submerged network', a tumultuous and little-understood inner life. That literature was significant to this group as a source of collective identity is undeniable: women over a considerable period of time had taken refuge and sought solace in literary texts that encompassed or permitted alternative sexual or friendship preferences. The magazine spoke intimately to its readership about a literary canon and in so doing offered the hand of friendship, helping to assuage the isolation of some lesbians, by recommending and critiquing the body of lesbian literature.

***

By early in the second year of publication, and after much publicity, the establishment of a social scene, the lobbying of the government and the production of a magazine which both recorded the larger scene and spoke intimately to each reader, Esmé Langley was able to report that 'The tidal waves of correspondence, telephoning and unheralded visits that followed our bouts of publicity in December and January have begun slightly to abate.'[76] As a periodical for a social movement, a lot had been asked of *Arena Three*: what started as a very focused group, with its magazine clearly directed, became more disparate. Regional groups splintered off, and some wanted more social or recreational groups. One particular development a couple of years later in 1966 was the formation of a breakaway group, Kenric (the Kensington and Richmond Branch). This group, formed by Cynthia Reid amongst others, had a more sociable remit: and a long time in advance of gay marriage, they produced a small number of Kenric rings, to be given as wedding rings.[77] However, disputes crept in over the running of the MRG and its finances; Langley disappeared abroad with the proceeds and *Arena Three* and the MRG seemed to come to an end in 1971. Some members established the more feminist and political *Sappho* magazine, led by Jackie Forster.

There was also a diminution of the research element of *Arena Three*. The lesbian enquiry of *Arena Three* had a complex relationship to the Gay Liberation Front and to second-wave feminism. For some lesbians, this shift from medical and sociological interrogation of lesbianism to 'feminist assumptions about lesbianism' has caused something valuable to be lost: Elizabeth Wilson has lamented what she sees as the reductiveness of lesbianism into a major theme of feminism, and how, 'for some women lesbian sexuality came to be seen as an immediate source of liberation'.[78] For, by the time the *Arena Three* magazine was reinvented as *Sappho*, the political climate had changed for women: lesbianism itself had become a political stance.

The MRG and *Arena Three* can helpfully be seen as major components of a lesbian social movement that tried to pursue goals of serious investigation into, and improving the public image of, the lesbian, but ultimately had to accept that different members of the group had different objectives. Such fracturing forms a developmental stage of the SMO. However, the resource mobilisation evident through the pages of *Arena Three* indicates that this periodical played a crucial role in helping lesbianism as a social movement to develop from a clandestine group to mainstream visibility.

'Our Culture in a Racist Society': *Mukti*

Mukti (1983–1987) was the magazine publication of the Mukti collective which, in the face of increasing white racism in Britain in the 1980s, sought to offer different spaces for women of particular ethnicities to express themselves. Although this was another magazine response to prejudice against a group of women, it was in many ways quite different to the organisation of *Arena Three* and the Minorities Research Group discussed in the Chapter 4. For one thing, *Mukti* was not battling for recognition from a position of underground status, but was supported with public money and sponsored by a local council that provided offices and funding. For another, *Mukti* was not so much trying to rally and galvanise women into a social movement, as working to educate and politicise its readers. *Mukti* made their attempt to do this in two distinct ways: firstly, the Mukti collective used the magazine to disseminate factual information to readers, about their legal status as female immigrants, their rights as citizens, wives and women in Britain; and secondly, it presented itself as a forum for readers' self-expression through personal writing. In encouraging women to talk about their lives and experiences, the magazine's objective was to empower readers frequently stereotyped as 'Asian' who were suffering various and multiple forms of oppression.

However, despite good intentions to provide a positive space to discuss and express women's identity, *Mukti* was not a great success as a magazine. The collective produced only seven issues over four years, and these reveal a number of calls for contributions and help with the production of the magazine. One obvious reason for the magazine's curtailment was the cut in funding. Another less obvious reason was the complex range of communication strategies within the magazine itself: at times communication was unclearly focused, functioning in disparate ways, and even contradictory. The following discussion considers the project of *Mukti* against a backdrop of contemporary discourses of race and feminism, reflects on *Mukti*'s overall ambitions to address identity as a minority community group and then analyses in detail some of the ways the magazine communicated with its readers. This was a magazine that tried to write its opening editorial and its leading, positioning article by committee, or rather, by collective, and this last factor raises important questions about levels of political engagement, editorial power and disparate audiences.

Recent feminist reflection on the ways in which South Asian women in Britain have been viewed by the mainstream has expressed great concern about the way British policy has shifted 'from multiculturalism to multi-faithism', and Sukhwant Dhaliwal and Pragna Patel have considered the impact this has had:

> A new settlement is taking place between 'faith groups' and the state in which 'faith groups' use the terrain of multiculturalism to further an authoritarian and patriarchal agenda. These groups use the language of equality and human rights while at the same times eschewing these very ideals. The result is that secular spaces and secular voices within minority communities are being squeezed out, which in turn means that fewer alternatives will be available to minority women and others given restrictions on their fundamental freedoms.[1]

Concern is expressed that, 'since mid-2000, there has been a proliferation of faith-based projects which seek to undermine the feminist projects' that groups such as the Southall Black Sisters have struggled to establish. Feminist approaches to social problems, they suggest, have been delegitimised by this process, while debates about violence against women have been 'circumscribed within a religious framework'.[2] This has meant that minority women have been 'corralled within their religious identity whether or not they wish it' even though, according to work carried out by Southall Black Sisters, women interviewed did not see religion as the basis of a social identity.[3] This has led to a complex position for women, subjected to 'religious-based local orders premised on new communitarian philosophies', but trying to promote the emancipatory and alternative aspects of feminism: trying to 'retain our secular spaces, our secular voices'.[4]

Mukti as a magazine defined its target readership not by faith, but by gender and minority group. Just as South Asian feminists today may argue that women feel oppressed by the all-consuming 'faith-based' agencies at large, Asian women in the 1980s were oppressed by an increasingly restrictive immigration legislation, alongside more general racist hostility. By aiming at a diverse collection of women of six different languages from the subcontinent, both the

Mukti group and the *Mukti* magazine tried to help this marginalised group of women establish a positive sense of social identity on their own terms, supporting their fight against the racism of the time and the prevalent stereotypes of Asian women: 'We must start to write our own stories, create our own pictures, share our struggles and our triumphs.'[5] Stereotyping, as Stuart Hall has pointed out, maintains the social order by creating divisions between what is seen as 'normal' and 'other' and occurs 'when there are gross inequalities of power'; inevitably, it sets up a hierarchy.[6] This chapter examines how this particular magazine, with its very specific sense of audience, tried to help women achieve a sense of their rights and to interpret themselves. The project of the Mukti collective, in its feminist imperative, trying both to raise consciousness and to educate its readers, should be viewed against the backdrop of black feminism and its uneasy relationship to mainstream white feminism of the second wave. *Mukti* tried to position itself as part of the black feminist movement, although ultimately this proved to be a troubled relationship.

As early as 1974, nearly a decade before *Mukti*, the Combahee River Collective had been meeting in America, as a consciousness-raising and study group, then moving into education and activism. They wrote a statement and explained their problematic relationship with mainstream feminism:

> A black feminist presence has evolved most obviously in connection with the second wave of the American women's movement beginning in the late 1960s. Black, other Third World, and working women have been involved in the feminist movement from its start, but both outside reactionary forces and racism and elitism within the movement itself have served to obscure our participation.[7]

The statement goes on to express a troubled relationship with the Black Liberation Movement too, 'We struggle together with black men against racism, while we also struggle with black men about sexism.'[8] This was a group intent upon understanding their cultural and experiential oppression, 'No one before has ever examined the multi-layered texture of black women's lives,'[9] but they understood the difficulty of this task: 'There is a very low value placed upon black women's psyches in this society.'[10] Their work, both practical and educational, had taken them to workplaces and colleges, seen them protesting about inadequate health care and setting up rape crisis centres.

This very early set of problems about the specificity of black woman's feminism was famously described by bell hooks in *Ain't I a Woman*, where she reflects on white American feminists who were still regarding women unlike themselves as 'others': 'Consequently the Sisterhood they talked about has not become a reality, and the women's movement they envisioned would have a transformative effect on American culture has not emerged.'[11] The problem may be discerned in regarding racism too generally and not specifically enough, as 'a general evil' rather than confronting the 'reality' of racism in women's lives. But hooks also points to a greater polarisation between the two groups of feminists: 'Rather than black women attacking the white female attempt to present them as an Other, an unknown, unfathomable element, they acted as if they were an Other.'[12] This led to animosity between black and white women's liberationists in the United States on two counts: disagreement over racism in the women's movement; and an environment of jealousy, envy, competition and anger.[13]

Similarly, women of colour in Britain in the 1980s faced a problematic relationship with the Women's Liberation Movement (WLM) where feminism, from at least the early 1980s onwards, was accused of having adopted an assumed whiteness and middle-class identity as a given social position in an imperial white feminist discourse.[14] It was thought that the WLM in Britain did not take adequate account of the groups it excluded such as working-class women or women across a range of ethnicities, and so alternative organisations were formed. The Organisation of Women of African and Asian Descent (OWAAD) started in 1978 and called for Afro-Asian unity to challenge the official racial discourses. It had its own newsletter, *FOWAAD*, and was the first national network of its kind for all women of ethnic origins and offered an opportunity for its members to articulate demands as an organised body, with many members rejecting feminism as a secondary concern to racism. However, major ruptures were caused by naming all of its members as 'black', and this inadvertently turned what might have been a united force for good into an inward one of individualised identities.

There were other issues with white feminist politics too, some of which, whilst they seemed to support women's liberation in general terms, actually worked against minority groups. One area where feminist and anti-racist objectives came into conflict was immigration, where some white feminists expressed opposition to immigration laws because of the implied enforcement of the nuclear family and heterosexual norms, and yet for many immigrant women who were separated from their families, this was, understandably, not viewed as supportive.[15] In addition, some white feminists have argued that 'the black family is a qualitatively different proposition' from the families of white women, claiming differences in dependence on men and family oppression.[16] Such sweeping, generalising views from white feminists were widely unpopular, but so was the generalising use of the term 'black'. Politically, copied from the American Black Power movement, for some the label became a term of pride and resistance against racism; however, for others it was too restrictive as a term that 'denies Asian cultural identity'.[17]

Immigrant women in Britain had long been marginalised and disempowered from various quarters and whilst post-colonial migration from the 1940s is far from the beginning of this history, it does mark a point at which many women came to Britain, of their own accord or accompanying the men of their families, and started to experience discrimination.[18] Rosina Visram describes the racism that women faced in the decade that *Mukti* started:

> In the early 1980s black women organised not only to protect their rights in the workplace, but to engage with the sustained fascist and racist onslaughts of white British politicians, their vanguards, the police and their lackeys, the white street mobs which inhabited (and still do) the heightened sensitised place that is the national racialized terrain of late twentieth-century Britain.[19]

Britain in the 1980s had an increased atmosphere of open racism and racial discrimination. There were riots in the capital city as a result of heavy-handed policing strategies, alongside personal attacks on individuals and other crimes motivated by race. Since the Race Relations Act of 1965, public discrimination has been illegal, but nonetheless racism was rife in Britain in this decade.

This complex scenario of long-standing oppression, of increasing public racism alongside increasingly restrictive legislation as well as feelings of exclusion from the white feminist movement and a racially fractured black feminism, was the hostile and differentiated environment into which *Mukti* emerged. However, despite this range of political oppressions and sometimes oppositional viewpoints, many of which were still in the early stages of debate, in its five years of operation, *Mukti* made a number of contacts with other women's groups around the world, as well as links with other groups in Britain, and it made an impressive contribution to the exploration of individuality for British Asian women at a time of troubled race relations in Britain. *Mukti* appeared alongside other groups working and producing magazines for specific readerships, based on racial identity, within the British population. In printing its pre-publication letters of support from, amongst others, *Eve's*

Weekly, in Bombay (Mumbai), Outwrite Collective, Women in Print, Asian women's advice centres, Sheba Feminist publishers, *Spare Rib* magazine, Grass Roots Books and Southall Black Sisters, the collective of *Mukti* editors firmly locate the magazine within a publication field of feminist organisations and protest media.

Mukti's voice: I have a mind but I can't express

Some feminists have called for greater voice for theoretical discussions in women's history, seeing 'race as an unstable and "decentred" complex of social meanings constantly being transformed by political struggle'.[20] Furthermore, the language of race has been seen by Bakhtin as a double voice, at once serving the voice of black oppression and the voice of black liberation.[21] In 1978, Amrit Wilson, activist and writer who immigrated to Britain from northern India in 1961, entitled her book, *Finding a Voice: Asian Women in Britain*, in which Asian women describe their experiences of immigration and life in British society. Wilson covers various aspects of women's lives regarding family, work and marriage. The life of Rezia, who lives with her husband and son in one room, is described:

> Rezia spends almost all her time in this room. She rarely goes out and has never been beyond the street she lives in on her own. She speaks no English and knows hardly anyone. In her first year in Britain no one visited her. Her husband is a restaurant worker. He is out all day from 11 am. to midnight. Where does he work, I ask.
> 'I don't know the place. [...] He never really talks about his work. There isn't the time.'
> The isolation and emptiness of Rezia's life is typical of what many Asian women in Britain face.[22]

Throughout this series of interviews, issues of terrible isolation, racial prejudice as well as violent racist attacks, and huge problems regarding language barriers and unfamiliar social customs, become clear. The lack of communication, especially the silence of women, is particularly poignant.

Whilst new forms of feminist interventions, mobilisations and understandings for Asian women of many counties are seen as changing and developing alongside the diversity and expansive possibilities of third-

and even fourth-wave feminism,[23] the question of voice, authenticity and diversity still remains central. One recent study by Sariya Contractor sets out to 'challenge the accumulated "mystery" around Muslim women'.[24] This recent work tries to reinstate the Muslim woman as 'a storyteller who tells her own story', rather than seeing her as feminists have done in the past where 'the proto-feminist pitied her and wanted to rescue her from her "inferior" culture' or as a woman, 'locked up in her cage waiting to be rescued by whoever was narrating the story'. In this book, Contractor has offered a space for women to write about themselves from a multiplicity of standpoints. The relationship to feminism is again understood as complex and insensitive, with the sexual liberation of second-wave feminism perceived as problematic for Muslim women, and later feminist discourses 'dominated by anti-veil and anti-Islam ontologies'.[25] Muslim women, previously seen as 'mis-voiced or un-voiced' in almost all the discourses surrounding them are, in this project, given a space in which to speak and to explore the effects of being heard.[26]

It was such a voice that *Mukti* hoped to give members of its own collective, and the very first item inside the magazine is a quotation, suggestive of a typical reader's opinion and outlook, telling of her frustration, her oppression and her desire to write about women's lives:

> I have a mind but I can't express because no-one taught me how to express. I want to write on paper but I can't, I feel that something is stopping me. Maybe I feel that I'm not good enough to write, because what I want to write I can't write – I wish I could. I've got many things in my mind, it's full of thought but I can't express it. Our society doesn't want our brains to be developed in case we ask for human rights. Soon as we grow up we are locked up inside and get trained as housewives, they think that's what we need, after marriage they want us to learn patience so we can cope with everyone better … So I would like to write about women's life. [Sic]
>
> Rifat Jabeen[27]

The opening address of the first editorial letter exclaims 'SISTERS!' and uses Rifat's quotation to guide the direction of the magazine:

> Many of us feel like Rifat and it was with the conviction that we must start to write about our lives and the changes that we can make that last year a group of us started to meet to talk about bringing out a magazine. We wanted to write about the many aspects of our lives, the good and the bad. We wanted to read about our sisters [sic] struggles against oppressions we face as women,

black people and workers. Our experiences are almost absent from the media, controlled by white men. If stories about our lives do appear they concentrate on us as victims of our culture. Also the black press rarely gives us space on its pages. We feel that the white feminist press has until recently ignored us and often only print articles that again make our culture a problem without understanding the need to hold on to our culture in a racist society. We must start to write our own stories, create our own pictures, share our struggles and our triumphs.[28]

This opening paragraph not only indicates the implied reader of the magazine but also tries to give substance to a sense of oppression felt, but perhaps as yet not expressed by that reader. It highlights the importance of the life story as a political experience. A troubled relationship to second-wave feminism is indicated from the start: whilst it follows the importance of the personal testimony in the movement as a means of consciousness-raising, it is critical of the lack of detailed cultural investigation and understanding in the feminist press. Furthermore, the editors call for a collective creation of presence and identity through written expression, and see this as their activism.

Such politics of feminist consciousness, and self-definitions of identity and self-representation through writing are to be found within the magazine, and they express both positive and negative 'voices'. One long abstract poem in the first issue, entitled 'my peoples mould that I will not accept' by Josna, rails against her society:

Do you know that 'respect' and 'honour' according to your books are tools that crush us women?
Do you know that these tools were needed for uor [our] feudal society to function in the way it did?
Our society needed us women to be child bearers and home minders.
No more, no less.
Our society needed us women not to be Fully human.
It treated us as less than human beings, its demands upon us were less than human.

This poem goes on to express defiant choice, a path perhaps of solitude and isolation, but one of growth and self-knowledge.[29] Poetry, short stories, cartoons and testimonials were all part of a new creative mode of self-expression of the feminist movement in Britain in the 1970s and a decade later, *Mukti* opened up this same opportunity for a group of women marginalised by that same organisation.

Mukti: From our perspective

A leaflet marketing advertising space in *Mukti* states: 'MUKTI is a feminist journal focusing on racism, sexism and imperialism from "our perspective." ' It goes on to state the intention of the magazine to report regularly on 'women's struggles and achievements worldwide, in fighting male violence; racism; struggle for equal pay; struggles for control over our bodies and sexuality, fiction and poetry'.[30] It was targeted at an audience that was hard to reach, including women who did not yet speak English, and in order to facilitate as wide a readership as possible it was published in six different languages: Hindi, Gujerati, English, Bengali, Urdu and Punjabi. The actual issues of *Mukti* were non-commercial productions, of twenty-four pages each, A4 size and printed in black and white, most with coloured paper covers. The contents were a fair mix of items in the usual way of a magazine of this kind at this time, with longer discursive articles and shorter snippets. Photographs and drawn illustrations break up the text, as do different fonts and sizes of print. A strong international feel is developed through an 'International Focus' section relaying women's experience in countries such as India, South Africa and Sri Lanka. There is also a 'Local Focus' page on London boroughs. Other regular sections include items on law, women's health and women's campaigns and individual oppressions, and there are regular profiles, items of poetry and notices of support groups. Care has been taken to make this journal visually appealing and varied and given that it is without colour, gloss or capitalist backing, it has been produced with skill and attention. The front cover of the first issue, June–August 1983, tells us much about the intended magazine to come: a large image of an angular, graphic and heavily shadowed Asian female face, with a bindi applied to the forehead, dominates the yellow front cover, complemented by a line drawing of an Asian woman in a simple sari and T-shirt choli, with her left arm, complete with bangles, raised with a clenched fist in a militant pose (Figure 5.1). Such signs of protest locate the magazine politically and the powerful illustration of the dominant and serious face with its direct gaze and the militant pose of the smaller image, disrupt any racist associations or stereotypes of submissiveness associated with the sari. *Mukti* itself meaning freedom, liberation or release, proclaims this further.

The Mukti collective, providing a service to a minority group, earned grant sponsorship[31] from Camden Council and was given an office on its premises at 213 Eversholt Street, London NW1.[32] As such, the magazine

Figure 5.1 *Mukti*'s defiant first cover, printed in six languages, *Mukti*, July-August 1983. © *Mukti collective.*

alludes to the responsibility the collective felt towards their target audience and the ways they viewed their remit within the Asian women's community:

> *Mukti* is not only about being a magazine – it is about our participation in the community. Our work also encompasses holding workshops to pass on skills, developing and contributing to various forms of representing Asian women's experiences, working with Asian girls in schools and youth clubs. Our members have been involved in various groups which meet on our premises which are wheel-chair accessible; Incest Survivors Group, Black Women Photographers Group, Asian Women Youth Workers Group, Aurat Shakti exhibition group, Black Women and Representation Group.[33]

This strong sense of community participation, alongside a semi-official position, helps to explain the diverse modes of address within the magazine.

The meetings of the Mukti collective were sometimes related in the opening editorial of *Mukti* magazine, and as I discuss later, these had a significant, and sometimes detrimental impact on the magazine itself. After the first issue was published, a community meeting was held to 'discuss, comment on and criticise the magazine'. The first issue sets the feminist tone of resistance to the status quo of Asian women's oppression and marginalisation in Britain and it does this in diverse and complex ways. At the first post-production meeting to discuss what was wanted in future issues, those women present decided that they wanted a different format and that each issue should be 'devoted to a specific theme as well as containing the regular features such as health, legal rights, education etc.'. Community and reader feedback therefore had a significant impact on the remaining six issues, setting the topics as family, sexuality, work, education, racism and prejudice, and housing. These were seen as fundamental aspects of women's lives and understood as vital components of identity formation. In addition, the collective calls for articles and contributions: 'We would also welcome ideas for covers for MUKTI, cartoons, graphics, illustrations and photographs.'[34]

In this structure, which comprises at least three groups of women: the editorial committee, the broader collective and an even wider group of readers, we might start to discern different, or at least layered, objectives for this magazine. This might help to explain the varied forms of address and political engagement within the magazine. At the outset, *Mukti* was produced against a backdrop of other politically informed magazines for women, with mentions given to *Spare Rib* and *Manushi*, an Indian feminist magazine. However, with time, different approaches to feminism become apparent, ranging from overtly feminist address to a milder, but nonetheless female-centred tone. Moreover, as the editorial collective had pointed out, *Mukti* was always more than a magazine, and whilst this may have led to valuable workshops and education programmes, the differing objectives and outlooks of the collective caused problems for the magazine itself. This was most apparent, not so much in the opening editorial, but in the lengthy positioning article that performed a number of sometimes conflicting functions. On the one hand, these main articles set out debates, outlining racial or gender injustices, and on the other, they interpreted those debates for their readers. The articles were supposedly jointly written by the collective, and yet there were often statements of dissent, and to add to this complication, sometimes those dissenting voices were printed alongside the main article. Sometimes, these articles tried to both give a sense of the overall thematic problem that determined the focus of each *Mukti* issue, whilst also reflecting the face-to-face discussions held by the wider group. This raises all sorts of questions about the production of content for a magazine: it draws attention to the efficacy of multiple authorship of politicised magazine content; it queries whether a magazine can represent the outpourings of a community meeting and, perhaps most of all, the role of the editor(s) is brought into sharp focus.

Whilst all the community faced racism and oppression, there seem to be different levels of discourse and engagement with political agency evident within the magazine. At times there is a well-informed collective directing a less well-informed and less politically engaged readership. Indeed, whilst it is impossible to know the readership of *Mukti*, some women might, implied by the range of languages necessary, have recently immigrated from third-world conditions, and quite possibly be fully occupied with the more basic aspects of day-to-day survival in a hostile country, like those described by Amrit Wilson. In this there may well have been a distance between the politically informed opinions of the committee and a timid, house-bound readership, frightened of being attacked on the streets of London. Consequently, there are tensions discernible here between groups within the collective, perhaps brought about by differing levels of political and feminist engagement, perhaps caused by different levels of 'Westernisation' or acculturalisation regarding language and society or perhaps, more fundamentally and simply, caused by women having different views on the matters in hand.

Mukti magazine attempted to do a number of difficult things simultaneously: it tried to inform a readership of women from the Indian subcontinent of varied nationality and language, of their legal positions and basic rights; it tried to educate its readers in discourses of race in order that they might analyse and so resist the racism they regularly experienced; it tried to raise feminist consciousness and encourage activism and engagement; and it tried to offer up creative spaces where women could assert and take control of a more positive projection of their personal identity. This stretched the capabilities of a single magazine not least in terms of its focus. Even though naming each issue after a particular concern, 'work', 'family', 'sexuality', etc., might have offered a certain cohesion to subsequent issues, the disparate aims of the Mukti collective, and perhaps overambitious expectations of the work that *Mukti* magazine could do for their community, meant that although diverse voices were to be encouraged, no single position which an oppressed reader might occupy, ever emerges with clarity.

Having discussed the environment into which *Mukti* introduced itself, the next few sections investigate the different ways that *Mukti* staged approaches to understanding identity and the ways that a range of individual women responded to the magazine in terms of two presiding frameworks: self-identification and a relationship to feminism.

'Becoming racialised'

Heidi Safia Mirza has suggested that, 'being "black" in Britain is about a state of "becoming" (racialised); a process of consciousness, where colour becomes the defining factor about who you are.'[35] Mirza summarises that, 'Located through your "otherness" a "conscious coalition" emerges: a self-consciously constructed space where identity is not inscribed by a natural identification but a political kinship.'[36] No matter the editorial intentions towards feminism, colour certainly became the 'defining factor' of *Mukti* and 'political kinship' as a route to identity is prominent throughout the magazine. *Mukti* tried both to address and to argue with the contentious issue of colour being the most important aspect of their readers' lives, but at times this feels as though it pulls the magazine in opposing directions. One contributor, photographer Mumtaz Karimjee,[37] reflected upon the imposition of ethnic categorisation of her work, and the way this led to associated problems in defining herself:

> The word Asian has, I feel, been misused and come to mean something that it isn't. Yes, just as I am Black, I am also Asian, but so too are the Chinese, Malaysians, Japanese and all the other peoples of Asia. How can I claim the term Asian for myself only when I come from only a very small part of Asia?[38]

This contributor underwent a process of 'becoming racialised' under pressure from external factors, even though these were never truly distinctive: 'The Black community in Britain is no [so] monolithic, and while I consider myself part of the Black community, there are clearly occasions when the word Black does not include me.'[39] In contrast, an interview with a young drama student, Venu Dhupa, reveals an internalised, self-reflexive mode of 'becoming racialised'. Her experiences of being cast in roles of servants, maids and prostitutes demonstrate ways that being a woman of colour was manipulated: 'I was a novelty, "a middle class white with a brown face," ' being employed by directors to make a 'social comment' in their productions. However, her own relationship to culture was complex, and being middle class, she only learnt about the hardships of many working-class immigrants through the work of theatre groups like Tara Arts[40]:

> For example, one production I saw explored the exploitation of male and female workers coming to this country and being shoved into factories at low wages. In particular it helped to highlight the problems faced by families

who did not speak english [sic] which meant that they were immediately ostracised and harassed socially.

These experiences left her sufficiently motivated to 'learn my own language' and to start Hindi classes,[41] evidently a strong conviction as Dhupa has had a long career in arts and culture.[42]

Crucially, *Mukti* offered an arena where being 'Asian', a very broad range of nationalities and ethnic groups, is identified as the norm. In this way, the magazine challenged British stereotypes of 'Asian identity' by making its reader the total and absolute focus of the magazine, the intended subject of the content, that is, both the target reader and the contributor. It does this in part by presenting Asian women in all guises: as 'racialised' certainly, but also occasionally as the victor against such categorisation, as a marginalised group, but also as central to family and community. The magazine in its breadth and reach tried to expose the contradictory and disconnected aspects of its readers' lives, regarding women as anything but one-dimensional and stereotyped. One area where notions of 'political kinship' seem to be apparent amongst this group of women is in the oppression that many subcontinental women felt was imposed upon them by their families.

Family life

Views expressed about the family foreground the sense of a double oppression felt by the readership, combining external factors of law, politics and society with internal pressures from family, culture and even other women. The Mukti collective introductory article covers a number of important aspects of Asian women's family life, and although there is mention of the 'togetherness of Asian and Black families', the article mostly concentrates on the oppression of women within the Asian family, suggesting that sexual segregation and dress taboos are used as means of control, and whilst an education for girls may be granted, it may also be used as leverage and 'conditional on acceptance of marriage'. In particular, for the Asian woman who is becoming Westernised, it is suggested that there are further layers of confusions and conflicting pressures:

> It is true that our relationships with particular Asian communities are often made difficult by assumptions the community makes about us as women. However even as 'free and independent' women we strongly identify ourselves

with the larger Asian/Black community. We don't find it easy to break away from or ignore our families. If and when we escape the constraints of our families we don't necessarily see ourselves as 'free and independent' Western women, because we live in a racist white society which often denies us normal family life through its laws and which views normality as us conforming to Western habits of food, dress, social behaviour etc. In short it expects us deny our Asianess. Those of us who are forced to deny our Asianess completely *do experience* a deep loss, conflict and alienation.[43]

The conflicted sense of self is explored, where denying 'Asianess' and trying to belong to both the community of family and Western community leads to alienation.[44]

Asian family culture is particularly criticised over the controversial concept of the dowry. 'Dowry…the cost of marriage' is an article compiled from information in other magazines, *How* and *Manushi*, and explores the custom of transferring goods and money between families when a young man and woman get married. Both dowry and bride price (compensating the bride's family for the loss of an asset) are seen as ways in which 'women are being exploited by men for their own gain'. The economics of this practice, it is argued, cause great hardship to the bride's family as well as bolstering middle-class accumulation of wealth and private property, even leading to the horrific outcome of 'dowry deaths' or 'bride burning'. The 1961 Dowry Prohibition Act is seen as ineffectual, and readers are urged to take direct action.[45] One reader's response makes the point about dowries in much stronger feminist terms:

> it is at best, a system whereby, an older male pays a younger male to get rid of the older male's rubbish viz a female child…and Dowry at worst is a Contract taken out by men to kill women with impunity. Why this is so should be linked to the 'Theory' of Patriarchy.[46]

However, a different mode of response is offered by a cartoon emphasising the ridiculousness of dowry exchange and finding humour in conflicting interpretations of this traditional process (Figure 5.2). This range of responses encompassing feminist, cultural and humorous, demonstrates how a politicised magazine such as *Mukti* simultaneously houses multiple opinions on one issue.

Mukti attempted to play a part in dispelling myths of 'Asian' female stereotypes and disrupting the sense of locked-in prejudices in its multi-dimensional objectives and presentation. Susheila Nasta, discussing British

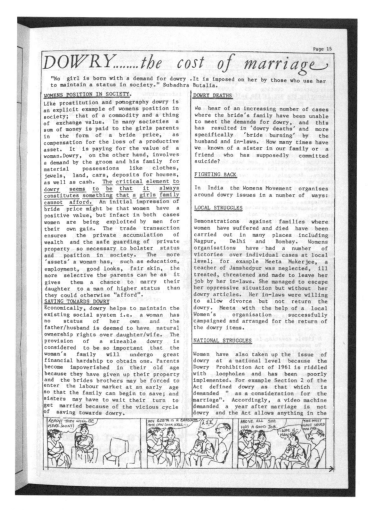

Figure 5.2 Varied approaches to the subject of the dowry, *Mukti*, Spring 1984, p. 15.
© *Mukti collective.*

Asian fiction and writers of the 1980s, has argued for 'the need to unlock the static notion of a monolithic vision of citizenship and ethnicity'.[47] This comment is both a criticism of a previous obsession with citizenship for ethnic groups and the projection of a hope for a multi-dimensional, subtle exploration of ethnic identity. Whilst *Mukti*'s project is focused, even founded, upon women's rights, interpreted sometimes as legal citizenship, this basic, practical concern was not the only objective of the magazine. Citizenship was an overwhelming concern of readers in 1980s Britain, but *Mukti* tried to set its sights higher, to move away from the 'monolithic vision' trying to establish a broader sense of identity and trying to embrace the diversity of Asian women, by bringing debate, discussion and disagreement to the fore, and by allowing women to air their opinions, their experiences and their differences.

Mukti tried to open up a space for its community of women, a private space, away from the gaze of men and other women, by restricting the magazine to concerns of women of Indian subcontinental origin and making it a publication where South Asian women's 'otherness' would not be so keenly felt. There is encouragement to participate in and partake of the world, and, in this identification of this specific readership group as underconfident personally, and under-represented politically, this magazine, through exclusivity, tried to dispense with stereotypes and concentrate on building consciousness and courage through its pages. One important political impetus for *Mukti* was feminism, and in the hugely varied responses to the feminist politics of the time in this magazine, a glimpse of the diverse readership and differing levels of political engagement may be discerned.

Life as a feminist

For *Mukti* readers then, the relationship to women's liberation, perhaps especially radical feminism, was complicated by family ties, cultural bonds and tradition. Many felt that the WLM did not address their particular situations or demonstrate sufficient understanding of the additional restrictions placed by families from the Indian subcontinent on young women, where the weight of expectation regarding marriage was especially heavy. Some of this may be seen in the opening article of the issue focused upon 'Sexuality'. This discussion, 'Self-Fulfilment', starts with the disclaimer that '*This article provoked much discussion and dissent. It does not represent the unanimous feelings of the Mukti collective.*' Further explanation reveals that a tradition of inhibited discussion about female sexuality in the *Mukti* readership means that so many aspects of women's development and sexual experiences are kept hidden, even from women by women. The world, the article continues, closes in on young Asian women, where domestic duties, family Izzat and arranged marriages prevent them from 'fulfilment of desire to sexual pleasure and self-determination', and even if Asian women do seem liberated, 'We are constantly battling to discover who we are and what it is exactly that WE want.' The Mukti collective, rather than attempting to develop a solution to these deep-seated problems, sees its project as, 'trying to create a non-judgemental space where we can safely acknowledge the fact that we have experienced sexual intercourse, willingly or otherwise, and that we are actually experimenting sexually as we recognise and accept our sexuality'. In opening up the subject of women's sexuality in this way, those members of Mukti who chose to be identified are following many of the WLM's discussions about female sexuality. Such sexual freedom is wanted for Asian women too, where there are options for women and choice of sexual partner, Asian or non-Asian, male or female, without prescription or oppression, and this is envisaged as a goal worthy of all women:

> None of us feels that we by any means have the perfect answer. What we do know is that each of us in her own way is striving for non-oppressive, loving, sharing and joyful friendships both sexual and otherwise and that we will be involved in this process for the rest of our lives.[48]

This is an introduction to a complex field of discussion, of importance to all women, but a difficult and sometimes taboo subject within the community addressed by *Mukti*. This leading article covers a range of topics, but leaves more personal and radical discussions to others. One individual voice of a woman coming out as an Asian lesbian explores her own history: both rejected by her mother and finding racism at the heart of the white lesbian subculture where she felt 'tokenised' and objectified, she has found solace in black feminist writing. Finding little compassion in the discussions available, her intention in being so open about her sexuality, is to bring comfort to others.[49] In contrast, another anonymous contribution takes a more cynical view of the 'right-on' lesbians who announce their sexuality. This reader does not want to be 'an object for scrutiny' and whilst she is aware of the pressure that the feminist movement puts on women to explore their sexuality, and that lesbianism is a viable alternative, her experiences have made her cautious: 'When one has lived for most of one's personal life in secrecy, one is not going to trust people easily'. Her remarks indicate the difficulties of women's liberation for Asian women:

> 'Hiding – from one's own parents, one's friends' parents especially if they are Asian is a far worse problem than for white women. Something a lot of white radical feminists do not seem to realise. Your family is your culture. It is hard for me however, not to be bitter at some feminists who walk round with planks in their eyes. Please don't criticise me before taking a close look at yourself first.[50]

The contradictions and subtle implications of being influenced by two different cultures are painfully obvious in another contributor's estimation that an obligation of care for elderly parents is only really possible from within marriage. She explains that, 'In a society conditioning us in favour of Western ways and preaching "freedom and love", we're *not* free. We don't have the same privileges and options as the white people, so in essence it's harder for us to be independent.' Marriage provides no answers being, 'A cage full of, if not financial dependence, at least psychological dependence.' This reader understands the conflict between her needs and her parents' needs, but is powerless to find a resolution.[51]

Whilst women's liberation and sexual freedoms may have been a prominent concern for some of the *Mukti* editorial group and those who wrote for the magazine, others took a more moderate view. An interview with someone already well known in the British Asian community, Jayaben Desai (1933–2010), famous for leading a two-year strike of Asian workers at the Grunwick film processing plant in London, gives some insight into the complex relationship with feminism for some Asian women. Despite her defiance of her employers, her determination and her personal resolve on the picket line, in her interview she presents a very moderate, even conservative feminism:

> I believe in women's progress, but not extremist feminist ideas. I don't like extremes – it brings disaster. In your home, you can talk and co-operate. My husband and I discuss things, sometimes I guide, other times I am willing to be guided by him. I don't feel I am lowering myself by doing that.

The philosophy she advocates for young women today, based in mental strength and the step-by-step system of Hinduism, gave her resolve at Grunwick. She emphasises this for women:

> Women carry 'sickness' in the self. You have to understand with a healthy mind. I couldn't have fought at Grunwick submissively. Understanding between people is not submission – sharing can carry us forward. Extremes don't work. We need to get self-satisfaction from doing something – so you don't put yourself to depression. The effort we put in does not bring the equivalent amount of outcome. Nothing changes overnight.

It is clear for Desai, that struggle must be faced:

> Life is about struggle, you come up against things and you fight. The girl has to create herself, she can help herself; she can be guided, but at the end of the day she has to decide for herself. The decision has to be implemented. I don't run

away from life and its struggles. Circumstances of struggle will always be there. I have taught my sons to find ways of responding to that. You have to learn ways of solving problems.[52]

Struggles and problems were key themes in much of the writing in *Mukti*, and this articulation of a personal relationship to feminism speaks for a particular approach to the layers of oppression experienced by this particular group of women. Whilst the impact of a single magazine interview on its target readership may not be known, it might be expected that this would appeal to the more moderately minded members, those who were not in agreement with the collective's main article, perhaps. However, it is clear that Desai had to show great strength of personality in the face of unreasonable employers: 'Mrs Desai', said the factory owner, 'You can't win in a sari, I want to see you in a Mini.'; 'Mrs Desai, I'll tell the whole Patel community that you are a loose woman.'[53] Desai interprets this behaviour: 'You see he knows about Indian society [...] He knows that Indian women are often easily shamed.'[54] This notion of shame, easily felt by a particular community of women, may go some way to explaining the disparate levels of attachment to women's liberation and tensions between the Mukti collective and the readership over women's sexuality, the collective clearly tried to follow a second-wave feminist line in offering space for women to openly discuss their sexualities; the readership may not have been in the same liberated frame of mind.

Mukti tried to foster a different kind of kinship, political yes, but not one of single identity, more a community of discussion, expression and sharing of the, largely oppressed, experience of being an 'Asian' woman in 1980s Britain. Despite the intention to broaden the scope of the magazine to include the voices of its members in the feminist mode of consciousness-raising, *Mukti*, like other feminist magazines, also had to include in its pages an element of political education. However, unlike other feminist magazines targeted, certainly in the early days of the second-wave movement, at an assumed white female readership, *Mukti* carried the burden of exploring and explaining discourses of race, evidence of racism and examples of racial prejudice, and the editors assume a responsibility to educate their readers. They discerned an urgent need to offer advice to Asian women about their fundamental rights in Britain, and this was clearly important and crucial work.

The following two sections examine the way *Mukti* presented two most urgent discussions on 'Immigration' in issue 1 and 'Racism and Prejudice' in issue 6. The editorial collective sought, through the editor's letter 'Sisters!' and the introductory articles, to share their knowledge, their understanding and experiences of oppression and their interpretation of the Asian woman's position in Britain of the 1980s, and much of the following discussion focuses on these two sections of the magazine. Whilst *Mukti* may be seen as important documentation of some aspects of the social history of the British Asian women's community in the 1980s, exposing the double oppressions of racism and patriarchy, nonetheless, its communication and perspective is not always clear, and layered communication opens up a distance between editors and their readership as well as between the editors themselves. This can be seen in the close analysis of the ways in which debates are framed and responses are managed in two most crucial issues for this particular group of women: 'immigration' and 'racial prejudice'. From these we may discern in the first section on immigration, the varied levels of communication strategies from the committee to the readership, and in the second section on 'racial prejudice', the wide range of readership response.

Life as an immigrant

Mukti made efforts through its content to offer its readers the personal, individual qualities of magazine participation, but the magazine contents were often dominated by the well-informed editorial essays, as well as the dissemination of legal or official information sometimes more typical of a governmental or formal set of documents. A number of the collective's editorials give very serious, pertinent and important information for the Asian women's community they address, and these magazines can be seen as manuals for coping with life in Britain as an immigrant Asian woman. In many ways each issue operates as an information pack on its subject matter: on aspects of the law, the social services and rights to citizenship, with some consciousness-raising material, intended to build and bolster individual and collective identity. The *Mukti* magazines suggest ways of adapting to the demands of British culture, systems and agencies whilst still retaining an Asian identity. This is a complex magazine address to a readership of already diverse cultural backgrounds, added to which there is a problematic overlaying of official and legal rights with attempts to draw out personal accounts of Asian female identity. This is a difficult outlook for a magazine and there were a number of calls for material for future subject/issues in the opening editorial letters, indicating that heavy encouragement was needed for this group of women to come forward and discuss their lives, to use this space to make their own voice heard.

Mukti's first issue sought to expose the blatant racial discrimination in Britain's Immigration and Nationality laws: 'Our Right to be Here Challenged' is politically assertive and points out how 'Black women are treated as appendages of their husbands rather than as individuals in their own right,' detailing changes in the law and the consequent implications for women's citizenship.[55] 'Asian women', it is explained, not only encounter difficulties with the state, but are also 'forced into ignorance' by the men of their families (Figure 5.3). This article explains that the Immigration Laws are 'complicated' and the editorial suggests it will 'try to outline just some of the ways in which they affect women'. There is little doubt that the editorial was trying to offer useful information, but there also can be little doubt that there was a hierarchy of knowledge.

The following piece, 'What we should know', urges women to be proactive and self-reliant regarding their status as citizens, and not to remain dependent upon men. Application for citizenship is advised in order to secure the rights

Figure 5.3 Fighting immigration laws: 'Our Right to be Here Challenged', *Mukti*, June-August 1983, pp. 4–5.
© *Mukti collective.*

of female readers and their children; all the information that women will need when making an application is clearly listed and addresses for resource centres are also given. Urgency, due to unease and uncertainty over changes in the law, is emphasised: 'The new Nationality Act has made many of us very uncertain about our future in this country.'[56] This theme of uncertain citizenship and a fragile legal status continues with a report on the 'Bangladeshi Divided Families Campaign', which aims to reunite families kept apart by immigration control, and highlights three individual cases of women fighting for the right to stay in Britain.[57] These rejected applications are clearly situated in a wider political context when it is remarked that:

> The right for a man settled here to have his family with him exists under the present immigration laws. But now that black workers are no longer economically useful they face redundancy, increasingly blatant racism on the streets, in the workplace, in the provisions of the welfare state and the National Health Service, and above all in the exercise of immigration control.[58]

This is a woman's magazine, then, that opens with issues of citizenship and immigration, communicating, in practical and accessible ways, in six different languages, matters of fundamental importance to a vulnerable target audience. There are imports from *Eve's Weekly* (India) giving a sense of feminist activism in India, whilst individual accounts of deportation give the magazine a pressing and immediate feel. In such serious articles, and there are many, it is evident that different levels of communication are in progress: there is a desire to inform the reader of her rights and this sits alongside news reports on immigration situations in Britain and elsewhere, making *Mukti* a place of convergence, a practical source, for information on this subject, in the mode of an advice bureau.

However, in terms of *Mukti's* communication with its readers, this starts to reveal a substantial inequality in political engagement and understanding between editors and readers: those who are writing these informative articles are doing so for the benefit of other women who, the editors assume, are not yet as politically aware of their situations, do not yet understand the complexities of the legal and immigration systems and are not yet politically engaged. Whilst it seems evident that the collective was genuinely and sincerely striving for equalities of all kinds, there is still a tone of benign authority in the editorial of this magazine; unfortunately this seems to set up one group of women with a voice, and another without.

As further issues of the magazine came out, the *Mukti* editorial collective made their own voice stronger, where the political viewpoint of the editorial became even more prominent and the magazine itself was moved to the centre of the debate:

> As Britain becomes increasingly right wing, women are being pushed back into the home even further as more and more oppressive laws are daily being introduced. In such a political climate, it is crucially important that we have a magazine which accurately reflects issues of concern to us.[59]

It is stressed that all women of colour are being increasingly policed, and that fighting back is becoming crucial.[60] Illustrations of prejudice and intimidation in different guises such as road blocks, body searches, arrests and being denied access to children are all depicted in a reproduction of a poster by 'The Brent Campaign against the police bill' (Figure 5.4).[61]

This is not to imply that *Mukti* became nothing but a didactic rallying cry. As in other magazines the form embraces an eclectic mixture of items, and other topics include a discussion about the absence and stereotyping of Asian women on television;[62] opinion expressing the oppressiveness of the 'persisting Imperialistic attitude' of the British education system resisting teaching Asian children their own languages;[63] health concern over 'rickets' caused by vitamin D deficiency; and a film review of a documentary drama, *Courtesans of Bombay* (1883), an enclosed community of women entertainers.[64] The international dimension occupies the central four centre pages, crediting articles to *Outwrite* and *Eve's Weekly*, *Manushi* and *Maitreyi*, with a montage called 'Issues Indian Women Fought in '82' that highlights activism and campaigns in India concerning domestic violence, trafficking and exploitative employment. Activism is, by implication, promoted as a way of bringing oppressors to justice and of changing the weight of discrimination against women. However, lighter elements also make up the mix, with snippets and cartoons and some single-authored pieces regarding matters concerning the self and the inner woman. This eclectic mix places this magazine at the centre of Asian women's politics, and it remains dominated by racial identity, and in accordance with a central tenet of second-wave feminism, *Mukti* tries to be both political and personal, whilst still maintaining a practical approach to helping its readership.

The political voice becomes stronger and is evident in issue 4, Autumn 1985, on paid and unpaid work, where there is both explanation of Asian women's position, legally and socially and engagement with feminist arguments in the

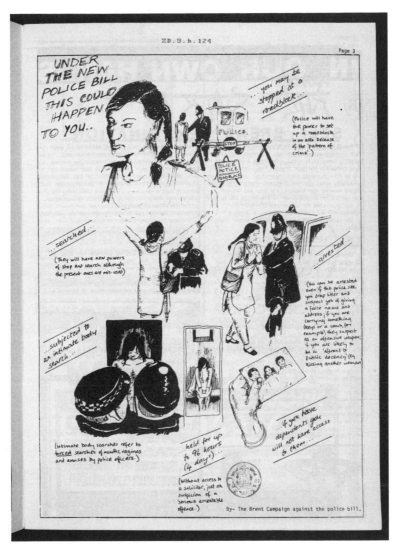

Figure 5.4 Supporting the Brent Campaign against the police bill, *Mukti*, Spring 1984, p. 3.
© *Mukti collective.*

illumination of the particular needs, and lowly status of Asian women. The urgency of this matter is brought to attention when readers are informed that the Wages Councils, which provided minimum pay protection for 'poorly paid un-unionised industries', have been abolished. The disastrousness of this situation is interpreted for the reader: it means that, 'hundreds of thousands of low-paid Black workers will be left without even minimum legal protection.'[65]

The introductory article, again written jointly by the collective, and therefore covering disparate aspects of the discussion, gives a good deal of background information, ranging widely in its approach to the subject of the 'Asian worker'. It opens by touching on a discussion of European Imperialist determination of the Indian subcontinent, and then moves on to emigration to Britain:

> There was an active policy of recruiting cheap labour from our countries of origin. Many promises were made, assurances given, but when we arrived here we found that we had been brought here under false pretences. The work available to us was basically that which the whites refused to do. Menial, dirty, degrading, hard and thankless.

This raises issues of class and caste, which combined with race, leave the woman immigrant worker exploited by global capitalism and in fear of being punished or even 'murdered for existing in this country'. Related to this lowly status is the relationship between work that women perform in the service sector, and the work they perform within their homes: 'This type of work has no social status, nor is it well paid.' A call to action is the conclusion:

> For the Black community and black women in particular, the contradictions inherent in work are central not only to our struggle against oppression but also how we are oppressed. Because of the way in which white society controls and defines the structures in which we work, Black women have to struggle for space and survival or risk co-option. In order to continue to survive we have to reclaim power on our terms and use it by whatever means possible to sabotage the system.[66]

Taking a lead from a more radical feminism here, there is a call for direct action to sabotage the system. There are other political approaches rising to the surface in the magazine too, such as a Marxist feminist account of the sexual division of labour: 'Our subordination as women is firmly rooted in this sexual division of labour, a division which has no logical basis.' An essentialist argument is also invoked regarding women's 'natural' caring roles, work which is de-valued and seen as inferior, and the argument is turned to become particularly relevant to Asian women:

> The government cuts and close-downs of various health care sectors has serious effects on us as Asian women in Britain. Government policy hits us far harder and much sooner than our white sisters, and will continue to do so.

This, the article implies, is because Asian women's work in the caring or service industries is often related to and viewed in terms of their domestic roles.[67] This argument attempts to conflate both Marxist feminist arguments about housework with an argument about the low status of Asian women in the workplace related to the work they do in the home. Moreover, Trade Union exclusion of Asian women is noted, with the betrayal and neglect of Asian women workers at Grunwick's film processing laboratories and Imperial Typewriters given as examples. It is concluded that, 'The struggle of Asian women and men to resist exploitation is complicated by racism,' and that, 'Racism and sexism have a deeply-rooted connection to work, and until the Trade Union Movement seriously begins to challenge these issues it cannot have any credibility as a Worker's Movement.'[68] As well as varied political approaches, there is a sociological investigation into the reasons why some women accept the poor pay and vulnerability of homeworking, that is, performing piece work at home. A small survey suggested that some women sought to work from home to avoid racist and sexist harassment, but for others it was a necessity as work in the 'formal' economy has contracted, forcing work in the 'informal' economy. Conclusions are drawn that homeworking 'does little to improve the position of Asian women in Britain.'[69]

These articles are written by educated Asian women from a range of political perspectives; they address areas assumed to be of particular concern to other Asian women and they talk of false pretences, work of low status, governmental and Trade Union neglect, of low-paid homeworking, racism in the workplace and ultimately call upon their readers to take both feminist and anti-racist action. With limited response from the readership group, it may not be known how this was received on a wider basis, but certainly for some this was an opportunity to have their voice heard.

The strong editorial element of *Mukti* magazine seemed intent upon making readers better informed and therefore better able to make judgements about events and conditions surrounding them. At times, *Mukti* has an educative feel as it delivers straightforward information, evidencing the strong guiding hand of the editorial group and many articles, by laying out facts of law or process of agencies, by examining the relationship between state and immigrant and by reporting on world events, inform women in a number of ways. However, the editorial group also wanted this same readership to take up the feminist cause, to be politicised and politically active. So that the readership was sometimes seen as women without certain citizenship, without rights, status or security in the workplace, and yet at other times there was an expectation that these vulnerable women, oppressed in society, in the workplace and possibly at home too, would be willing to take further risks in becoming politically active. *Mukti* as a magazine was, it seems, addressing numerous audiences at once, and even within the Mukti collective, there were complexities of identity too great to permit a single unified political position. These fractures show when *Mukti* tried to address perhaps the most contentious subject of all in issue 6 called 'Racism and Prejudice'.

Living with racism

The difficulties experienced by the editorial team of achieving clarity in defining terms of reference for race and racism and then differentiating between white and black racism become evident in issue 6. Presenting a united front against the British government's increasingly racist policies, against the double oppression of racism and sexism and against racism targeted at women in the workplace might have been obvious ways in which the Mukti community could come together, even from different perspectives. However, finding modes of expression and acceptable ways of exposing and bringing intra-minority group racism to general consciousness caused enormous problems and these are reflected in the editorial sections of the magazine. This exposes rupture and fracturing of the Mukti project, but it nonetheless represents the difficulties faced by the community at the time. In this issue there was a structuring of the debate mostly around the educational collective articles.

It was with good reason, perhaps, that the editorial collective had waited to devote a whole issue to the topic of 'Racism and Prejudice', and although it was clear that they thought race was the central focus of all, it was evident that there had been a degree of controversy and argument about the content of this issue. Hesitantly, then, the main article expresses a desire to open up 'an active discussion', with a determination to approach racial oppression from within as well as from without, and the question of prejudice from within the community is reflected upon:

> In all previous issues of Mukti racial oppression has provided a major focus in our analysis of the issues and themes covered. But in the past we have not actively or consciously considered the effect of prejudice within our own communities

and families. We feel that had we taken on the issue of prejudice the slant of the articles in all previous issues might have been different. Prejudice, linked with social and economic conditions, is destroying us physically and mentally in the Indian Sub-continent, for example through communal violence all over India, and in this country. Our selection of articles highlights the experience of being racially oppressed as well as having the power to oppress on religious, economic, racial and cultural grounds.

The editorial reveals that the open pre-publication discussion had brought forward a wide range of remarks and definitions regarding racism and prejudice with individual responses, and these were printed uncensored, for example:

> Globally racism has to be seen in terms of white domination.
> We need to include not only our resistance but also our collusion with racism.
> Racism as expressed today is tied up with the capitalist system and multinationals.
> There is such a thing as black racism. Racism from black people can be more devastating.
> We must accept that perceptions of racism are different for different people.

By reprinting these, some contentious positions are made plain. Out of these responses, the editorial group guided the formulation of further questions, one was concerning absorption of the dominant culture, and concerns are expressed about young people and whether they were born in Britain, or have come to Britain having grown up elsewhere:

> Young people who come to the UK from the Indian Sub-Continent know what and who they are and feel secure amongst their own community. Whereas often their peers who have been brought up here may try to become what others want them to become because they have never been encouraged by the dominant culture to feel positive about their identity.

This potentially sets up further hierarchies of cultural loyalties, where young people born in Britain are likely to deny and refuse Asian habits, customs and language, raising the very complex question of racial identity across different cultural experiences. Another perceived problem is those who deny racism's very existence and claim they have never experienced racism or racist violence; they, it was suggested, shield themselves with a 'form of psychological protection against the hatred that prompts these attacks'. Related to this is the matter of identity and a particularly divisive problem is in defining and discerning the very meaning of the term 'black':

> Since Mukti first formed as a group its aims and objectives were based on its identity as a Black women's group. This has had to be openly and clearly stated in all issues of Mukti, particularly because of our awareness that many Asians still continue to interpret the word 'Black' as only applying to people of African or Afro-Caribbean origin. On the other hand, some Africans and Afro-Caribbeans assert that the term 'Black' is the prerogative of people of African descent. Some Asians consider themselves as being superior to 'Africans', as more intelligent and more cultured and therefore find it demeaning to be put in the same category.

In an attempt to be inclusive, and perhaps to appropriate broader political momentum, the editorial team adopted 'black' as an umbrella term for a variety of ethnic groups, including women of the subcontinent; however, this evidently sat uncomfortably with some who unfortunately felt entitled to further distinction and, in their opinion, hierarchy. Furthermore, prejudice from within the community of women from the subcontinent is brought to attention and raises yet more difficult questions:

> When loved relatives say 'you're too dark to be married off', it's as though they are stating a matter of fact – dark is not lovely, and the relatives of another say 'don't go out in the sun – you'll lose your Kashmiri complexion', they are proclaiming that paleness is to be protected and admired. The skin colour of the woman or girls being spoken to is all important in the eyes of the outside world – be it in the Indian Sub-Continent or in the Asian community here.
>
> Both comments were said by loving and affectionate females, which made it all the more hurtful and bewildering [...] A woman's intelligence, personality, and in some cases humanity are subsumed by the lustrous dark tones of the skin. The predominant 'ideal' of physical perfection and beauty in South Asian societies is of the fair skinned, aquiline nosed, straight haired woman or man, the 'Aryans' in fact who inhabit the Northern part of the sub-continent.

The Mukti collective took it upon themselves to expose the racism and prejudice, that they had discerned, on both the outside and the inside of the 'Asian community', arguing, in a spirit of self-examination, that to acknowledge racism is an 'important first step in challenging it'. Introspection, they argue, is required, and they expressed this in self-critical terms as follows:

> We have to recognise the way we, as Asians, are perceived by others. At one and the same time, we have to ask ourselves what the term Asian means to us, just

because we are seen as Asians (or South East Asians) does not mean we have a unified identity or common aims with other 'Asians'. The differences between Muslims/Hindus, Sylhetis, Bengalis, East and West Bengalis, Gujaratis and Marathis etc are brought with us from the Indian subcontinent and develop in the hot-house of prejudice which our communities often condemn themselves to. We have to overcome our prejudices through accepting our differences and drawing strength from them.

This densely packed and wide-ranging article lays out a certain kind of introspective debate about racism and prejudice for the *Mukti* reader, acknowledging difficult and differentiated attitudes to racism and, quite pointedly and uncomfortably, criticising the Asian community for its own part in permitting prejudice and failing to work together to counter racism in Britain.[70]

The discussion of racism extended to other articles in this issue, as did the exposé of prejudice, causing a fair degree of disagreement, argument and criticism. One particularly controversial article, 'Maids and Madams in the Natal Indian Community', was discussed at the pre-production meeting and elicited some heated responses. The article describes wealthy Indian women employing and abusing Zulu African women as domestic servants and criticises the 'inhuman treatment' in a particular example of one wealthy family who adopted the illegitimate child of one of their maids, 'very likely sired by one of the landlady's teenage sons', whilst retaining the mother as servant to the family. This case is considered an 'indictment of the divisions brought by racism and compounded by artificial class structures that the natural mother was never deemed fit to share in the upbringing of her child, and was, to all intents and purposes, regarded as racially inferior'.[71] This article had in fact been voted out of an earlier issue and for one member, Najma Kazi, that decision undermined the credibility of the collective and called into question the sincerity of the collective's intention to publicly challenge inter- as well as intra-community racism. In her response, Kazi says, 'For me the worst thing about that Sunday Afternoon was that we sounded like a bunch of liberal white people as we uncomfortably laboured out our cliches [sic] against publishing this article.' This reader-member clearly felt that it was necessary to publish:

> Let us not live under any illusions when 'Maids and Madams' is published in *Mukti* it will only be the beginning of us confronting openly and acknowledging the part we Asians have played and continue to play in

perpetuating white dominated racism against African Black people and ultimately against ourselves.

It is understood that 'white people' will use the article to cause division, but this is not new to *Mukti*, 'Haven't we always acknowledged that everything we publish on *Mukti* can be used against us as a community?' None of this, however, according to Kazi, provides any reason to expose sexism or inter-group racism.[72] This strongly voiced response exposes divisions within the Mukti collective and warns against using the tactic of blaming ruling classes rather than racism wherever it occurs.

This same article, 'Maids and Madams', elicited a number of objections: to the data, to the age of the survey, but also to the confused use of terminology in that it 'lacked a clear political analysis of racism'. The responsibility expected of the magazine collective to its readers is made clear:

> In conclusion I feel that if this article was written to ensure a serious discussion on the issues facing Black women domestic workers in Southern Africa and to elicit support for them then the article has failed. I feel that Mukti has a responsibility towards its readers to provide clear political discussions rather than emotional responses in a vacuum. Mukti should not have allowed itself to be blackmailed into including something in case they are 'accused'.[73]

For this reader, it was not enough to print the article and its responses; it was expected that *Mukti* would provide interpretation, clarity, leadership and even censorship. The Mukti collective had a difficult role to fulfil, they had hesitated to publish this article, had held an open debate, decided to publish in a later issue, been criticised for not being radical enough, 'a bunch of liberal white people' and, lastly, for not giving a responsible clarity in the political discussions. For this reader-member at least, the collective's group editorial role became confused with its already partially adopted pedagogic role, merged also into a politically instructive authority. This raises many questions about the role of an editorial collective for a woman's magazine as opposed to a caucus. For these editors, producing a magazine as well as running a community group, the questions of consensus, censorship and intellectual leadership were all raised over this article.

This issue of *Mukti* must have been produced with mixed feelings: on the one hand, it was an important objective of the committee to represent the views and voices of the whole collective community, and yet the prejudice and racism expressed and reprinted are plain to see. The pre-publication meeting exposed experiences of racism, but much more problematically, also racist views from within the community. It also evidently produced discontent and dissent, with some members appalled at the views of others, some members unhappy with the committee and some members wanting censorship. Publishing some of these views presented enormous difficulties; it was after all, the voice of the readership that the collective had wanted to promote. The collective discussion had made some feel uncomfortable and the content of the magazine was mostly structured around that uncomfortable debate. It seemed that neither the collective editorial group nor the wider readership community were happy with what was produced. The questions of whose needs this magazine was serving, and whose views it represented, must be asked. If the magazine had become little more than a collection of responses to, and a continuation of, a face-to-face debate held at a different time and conducted in a different discursive space, then this stretched the capacity of a magazine to serve its readers to the limit.

***

It is clear that running the collective Mukti and producing *Mukti* the magazine were projects of a difficult and demanding nature. In the penultimate issue it is explained that original support for the group came from 'subscribers, individuals and organisations, who wrote to members on the Council on our behalf. Owing to this we secured a three-month lease. In December '86 we secured a grant enabling us to employ a worker'.[74] Ultimately though, the dependence on the council grant had significant implications for the magazine: the collective was eventually evicted by the council, which claimed the offices had been abandoned, and so cut their grant. Efforts to find alternative funding and premises failed and so *Mukti* came to a close. However, in the last issue readers are asked to check Mukti's address when sending in contributions, as the position has become insecure and if they were not at those premises then readers were advised to use the address of *Outwrite* magazine or *Spare Rib*. *Spare Rib* had already carried an article two years earlier about 'black women's groups' around the country in crisis over funding,[75] and a reader letter in the same year that *Mukti* closed, discussed the cuts in Camden council's support for minority groups, sardonically remarking that cuts and redundancies would be 'handed out in an Equal Opportunities manner'.[76]

By *Mukti*'s editorial letter in 1987, the fight to look for renewed funding from authorities was conceded; it had proved too difficult to produce a magazine in six different languages, with no collective member able to translate into all languages and with insufficient funds to properly pay translators the going rate. Ultimately, it seems there was not enough practical help:

> Women have repeatedly supported our continued existence but have not found it within themselves to come forward and give commitment and practical support in the production of the magazine. The hardest thing to come to terms with has been the lack of encouragement from Asian feminists, particularly those who were unwilling to write in the form provided by *Mukti*.

The magazine grew, according to its editors, from 'the idea of being a small circulation, duplicated magazine. We have come a long way to now being circulated internationally' and this expansion had exhausted the committee, who were forced by funding authorities to change roles from volunteers to 'reluctant managers', and run Mukti as a business.[77] *Mukti* then, in trying to serve a barely visible community of women, fell between a lack of official funding and the absence of Asian feminists' support. In trying to provide a forum for women of a range of languages, ethnic origins, education, political engagement, caste and class it was a publication of diverse views and disagreement, trying to serve a fractured population, some of whom were beset by taboos and some entrenched within prejudice.

Mukti was of the WLM in its project to provide a forum for oppressed women to speak up and have their voices heard, and in that it endeavoured to operate against racism in Britain by educating its readers and presenting debates. Throughout the magazine the double oppressions of racism and patriarchy are made clear, and experiences of family, working life and individual consciousness are proffered. This was a magazine that tried to serve a community which was particularly difficult to access and to persuade that community to a political position. Ultimately though, the community of women did not come forward in sufficient numbers or strength to sustain the collective. Furthermore, in assuming an exclusively Asian identity, *Mukti* felt unsupported by the feminist movement. Indeed, the pages of *Spare Rib* in 1987 demonstrate not only an extensive appeal to a broader range of minority group women, but also the readers' letters reveal an inclusive readership too, suggesting that this more mainstream second-wave feminist magazine had expanded its scope sufficiently to include women of all ethnicities and sexualities.

Mukti was a brave attempt to provide a minority and gender-specific group with a voice, and an attempt to politically educate and engage its readers. It tried to bring together women divided by feminist consciousness and political awareness. If elsewhere, 'Asian' women were marginalised, faced increasingly harsh immigration laws and poor working and home conditions, had in the early stages been paid no attention by the WLM, whilst also tolerating an inferior status in their own families and communities, then *Mukti* went out of its way to provide a safe forum. By keeping race and racism at the top of the agenda, but by diversifying into other areas of tension too, the magazine worked towards disseminating a more diverse understanding of immigrant life in Britain. Consciousness-raising about race was the starting point, but the aim was towards an appreciation of a broader range of feminist issues. Appreciating racialisation as disempowering, *Mukti* tried to empower its readers through expression of their diverse subjectivities, encouraging readers to think of themselves as individuals with particular familial circumstances, cultures, desires and dreams of their own, offering women who were not often heard, an opportunity to tell their own stories. The question remains whether such focus on minority group identity was embraced as an integral part of the wider women's movement.

Mukti was a publication beset by oppositional views and diverse outlooks from within the editorial collective, the wider discussion group and other reader-contributors, and whilst the materiality of the magazine could encompass such breadth and scope in its formal structure, *Mukti* seems eventually to have lost the support of its readership and its political partners. Diversity of magazine form was not enough, and in this case may even have worked against the project.

A Magazine of Letters, CCC

The Cooperative Correspondence Club (CCC) (1935–1990) crafted a magazine unlike any other under discussion in the present volume. Their magazine was a single issue hand-collated assemblage of letters, produced once a fortnight for decades and then towards the end, every two months. It consisted of correspondence from the CCC members, written under pseudonyms and sent to the editor in advance of the production of the magazine. The editor organised the mostly handwritten letters within a cover, and then sent this 'magazine' on its way through the post to the first name on the roster. Each member had just twenty-four hours to read her way through everyone's letters, and was then obliged to send the magazine to the next name on the list. This circulation of letters amongst a self-selecting group of correspondents continued, with only a few changes of participants, for over fifty years. Only women were allowed to join, and only women who were mothers; married status was not a requirement. The membership of the club comprised housewives and mothers at home as well as a number of working and professional women, a good number of whom were university educated. All, regardless of circumstances or formal education, were interested in extending their life experiences beyond the confines of 1930s British hearth and home.

This was far from the only correspondence club in Britain in the twentieth century, but it was one of the earliest. A large body of material related to the CCC has been collected and preserved under the auspices of the Mass Observation Archive at Sussex University,[1] and it has come to recent attention through the detailed and important recovery work of Jenna Bailey.[2] Bailey's oral history research into the lives of the CCC members, sometimes through their families, through her collaboration with a surviving member, Rose Hacker, and her use of the letters, has enabled this private organisation to be brought to light and to life in numerous ways.[3] Ten years before Bailey's work on some of the *CCC* contributors, Rose Hacker (1906–2008), a long-time member of the group, foresaw the potential importance, in historical terms, of the CCC's letters and undertook the enormous project of collation, information gathering, summarising and describing the club, resulting in her unpublished manuscript, 'Sisters Under the Skin', also held at the Mass Observation Archive.[4] The club meant a great deal to Hacker, who had a lifelong interest in people and their social circumstances and relationships. She was a socialist, a member of the Labour Party and the Fabian Society, and an interview on *Woman's Hour* (BBC R4) revealed a lifelong commitment to campaigning for social justice; and crossing social divisions was an important aspect of her life.[5] She wrote books on sex education such as *Telling the Teenagers* (1957), and worked in marriage guidance counselling. Aged 100 she was invited to write a column for a North London newspaper, the *Camden New Journal*, which she did until she died.[6] Hacker's detailed contextualising account of a correspondence of over a thousand letters, Bailey's history and the fortuitous preservation and donation of many original letters, have made it possible to develop the discussion of this unusual magazine in new ways.

Whilst Bailey's book focuses on individual lives, and Hacker's unpublished manuscript recounts and collates the story of the CCC, the present discussion is most interested in reflecting on how this fortnightly collection of letters functioned as a personalised, even tailor-made magazine for women. This chapter is particularly interested in how the magazine functioned, was organised and received, how it related to regular magazines and the letter-based communication styles that facilitated such a strong bond between writers and readers. I argue that this private circulation of letters sustained its readers in multiple and substantial ways giving the kind of support, friendship and personal attention to which commercial magazines may only aspire. Paradoxically, its unusual format offered a greater engagement with what might be considered the essence of women's magazines: the intimate communication and companionship as hoped for through each magazine purchase, and as aimed for by each editor; and it did so with a far greater intensity than any commercially produced women's magazine could conceivably achieve. Brita Ytre-Arne has discussed how a regular woman's magazine offers three significant textual aspects: the repetitive and recurring nature of columns, headings and section titles, offering a reliability in its structure; multiple entries and exits to the text, meaning it need not be read in any particular order; and metatexts that invited the reader to look forward to the next article or issue.[7] The CCC, whilst it had none of these formal printed properties, apart from a list of contents written by the editor, nonetheless, gave its members the reward and private relaxation that Ytre-Arne discusses. The CCC was intimately relevant to members' lives, it was 'down to earth' and it represented 'the way things are', on top of which it also offered insights into varied lifestyles for women, all things claimed of the commercial magazine. CCC, I suggest, could be understood as a personalised distillation of a woman's magazine, achieved as a result of constructed connections, but executed through a lifetime's communication though letters.

The *CCC* magazine, however, without gloss or professional editorial control or any financial backing, disrupts the usual divisions in print media processes between public production and private consumption by crossing territories of all manner of writing forms: autobiography, magazine correspondence, diary writing, magazine feature articles, personal testimony and confessionals, reportage, instruction, fiction, self-help therapeutic writing, even questionnaires and more, and yet its content, in comparison to general commercial magazines for women, relies upon one dimension of magazine writing: readers' letters.

Strong and weak ties

Mark Granovetter has discussed the idea of strong and weak ties where strong ties exist within a collection of close friends or family, most of whom are in touch with one another, 'a densely knit clump of social structure'. And weak ties can be understood as 'a collection of acquaintances, few of whom know each other'. Each acquaintance will have their own group of close ties.[8] This way of viewing networks can shed light on the friendship group of the CCC. At the outset, the group of prospective letter writers had little or no actual connection to each other; they had things in common but under normal circumstances would probably never have met. The club was formed mostly out of women who responded to advertisements in *Nursery World*, and they were selected from their replies. The club came about as a result of a letter to a magazine for mothers, nannies and nursery nurses, *The Nursery World* (1925–ongoing).[9] Jenna Bailey describes the story of one reader who wrote in July 1935 to the letters section, 'Over the Teacups', expressing her feelings of loneliness, isolation and depression.[10] This reader explained that, 'I live a very lonely life as I have no near neighbours. I cannot afford to buy a wireless. I adore reading, but with no library am very limited with books. [...] I get so down and depressed after the children are in bed and I am alone in the house. [...] Can any reader suggest an occupation that will intrigue me and exclude "thinking" and cost nothing! A hard problem I admit.'[11] This reader was from Ballingate (County Wicklow, Southern Ireland) and she signed herself 'Ubique'; a nom de plume was quite usual in such letters' pages.[12] She had responses from other anonymous readers, many of whom felt the same way; some suggested letter writing as a way to combat loneliness. In her original letter, Ubique had already said that she 'adored reading' and wrote 'stories galore', and so had already established her love of writing. When she wrote back to the magazine in September to thank all those who had responded to her cry for help, she suggested a correspondence magazine.[13] In this way, the *CCC*, intended as a private correspondence magazine, was initiated from within the world of commercial print women's magazines,[14] already understood as a source of companionship. At the outset of the magazine, with seven women in 1936,[15] the women were not even acquaintances,[16] each with their own distinct world of family, household and other strong ties.

Granovetter's work is particularly significant in considering the rationale behind the CCC's formation. Granovetter suggests, from his 1973 paper, that 'individuals with few weak ties will be deprived of information from distant parts of the social system'. It was precisely the feelings of isolation and lack of involvement with life beyond the domestic that prompted 'Ubique' to seek other connections and start the magazine. It was the desire for 'weak ties' to other women with other social settings, beyond their own social circles, geographical locales and habitus, that motivated the group to assemble. Granovetter's focus is the employment market, but for the women of the CCC, their focus was on expanding their horizons beyond the confines of the domestic. Their need for 'bridging', to use Granovetter's term, was not to a new job opportunity, but access to a range of different female lifestyles, geographical locations and social and political outlooks. Differences of social background and class within this friendship group were sought out and considered significant and for many members, the potential contributions from women of different walks of life were an important aspect of the magazine, for instance, a sheep-farmer's wife in Scotland, or a woman brought up in the Jewish faith, are backgrounds that other members would never normally have encountered. The intended focus of CCC magazine was for women with limited access to other parts of the social system, to make connections with or 'bridge' to different circumstance, in order to enhance their own lives. Such diversity enabled the kind of insight and understanding of different social circumstances that class-ridden Britain of the first half of the twentieth century rarely afforded: it gave access to 'distant parts'. The women of the CCC were, I suggest, progressive in thinking that this would broaden everyone's understanding of life, and they were keen to learn from the frankness of each other's letters.

The diversity of social backgrounds was particularly significant to Rose Hacker (or 'Elektra') who, in her very helpful preliminary narrative of the club wrote, 'Ubique gathered together twenty-four women from a wide variety of class, income and religious persuasion.' Hacker reflected on the social significance of the group: 'Looking back, we see typical women of their time – putting family, husband and home in the forefront of their lives.'[17] The group was formed of women whose lives spanned the mid-twentieth century, who had lived through world wars and 'nearly a century of rapid changes', whilst dutifully looking after husbands, children, grandchildren and parents. However, Hacker emphasised that carrying the burdens of caring and domestic duties did not mean the end of views on the world or on life: many of these women 'held strong political opinions' and 'had searched for meaning' 'throughout their lives'. Explaining that, 'Ideas about the exploitation of women and their liberation and consciousness raising were powerful only in the subsequent generations,' Hacker nonetheless regarded the *CCC* as a support group for women: 'It seems that the frank discussion of troubles and problems was a source of information and sustenance when others in their turn had to face similar trials.' Hacker remembered that while help and support were offered through the letters, there were disagreements too, but 'familiarity and closeness' enabled argument over issues without sacrificing friendship.

In this way, Hacker's account recalls, not the letter writing itself, but a space in which women shared ideas and experiences, but also discussed their troubles over a period of great social change for women. She focuses on heterosexual marriage as a determining factor of those lives, and is obliquely critical of the oppressiveness and restrictions placed on women by the expectations of the institution of (middle-class) marriage. Hacker imagines that feminist consciousness came only for a later generation of women of the 1970s, but indicates a proto-feminist consciousness in the 'strong political opinions' and 'search for meaning' she describes. For Hacker, the CCC seems to have filled a gap, offering a space for expression and discussion of issues not catered for elsewhere in women's lives: it offered opportunities for intimacy not offered elsewhere.

Producing the magazine

As the CCC magazine was a private concern, it needed some structuring ideas in the initial organisation. The basic principles were laid down at the start but it took a while for correspondents to get into the routine:

> As editor for so many years I find it very interesting to see that it took us a full two years to get into regular habits of roster-making, sending out on the 1st and 15th, sending on in 24 hours and contributing regularly (well … of knowing it's a rule that we *should* anyway). There are arguments about expenses and subs and accounts, and suggestions by the dozen, even one that the editor should send p.c.s to each member to tell her when each mag should reach her! [18]

The magazine always had an editor whose role was also that of coordinator, however, editors were not expected to censor the letters, and one wrote that 'I am against censorship and feel that grown-up people should be able to argue and take hard blows without getting tearful, sentimental or spiteful.' As for the magazine's organisation, the editor's main responsibility was to collate the letters, organise the rota and keep track of the progress of the magazine. This last was complicated by a system at one time of two groups, A and B, with different sets of letters being circulated to each. Ubique had kept the magazine going until censorship between Eire and England made this difficult, and then the role moved through some other members. In one canvassing statement, 'A Priori' hints at what may have been areas of difficulty over this role:

> I do not believe that CCC can survive if the Editor is *nothing* but an accommodation address. There are ways in which she can stimulate interest and smooth out difficulties and also encourage new members, where suitable and approved by the club as a whole. A Priori also thinks that a small subscription is necessary, she is against censorship, and wants those members who have joined Rusticana's Club to promise not less support to CCC than they have given in the past. [19]

Just before the war, 'Ad Astra' took over as editor and she wrote editorials for each magazine. She also kept a tally of quantity as well as quality of contributions, and whilst the minimum was one letter a month, those who wrote more and were therefore in nearly every magazine were acknowledged at the end of the year with special mention. Ad Astra was seen to be very well suited to editorship and remained in the role until the 1980s; and whilst she did not edit or alter the letters she did compile and arrange the material, perhaps facilitating discussion about a more controversial submission.[20] She ran the magazine by gathering in the articles and collating them together in their covers, and in the early stages kept 'meticulous accounts' but 'Thank God we know one another well now and no one wants me to say how the shilling is spent. In fact, whatever you all may think, I am quite unmethodical about it today. I know it costs all the subs to buy covers, silks and stamps for tracing delays and keeping us all in touch, and probably a little bit more.'[21] Aside from the housekeeping duties, including buying the covers in bulk, Ad Astra understood the complexities of her role and the fine balance she sometimes had to strike, and this became clear when she had to acknowledge the magazine's demise. Towards the end of *CCC*, when the letters were written into notebooks, Ad Astra's frustration with a lack of contributions is evident writing: 'Xmas Number and last for me. Goodbye CCC. Its best to acknowledge that the old CCC is dead and you don't care enough to write for it.' The rota order follows, with dates received entered by the list of eight other names and further comments at the bottom. The last on the list is 'End – home and done for.' Later on in this issue she writes:

> From AA – last time. I have read through my messages in this book and I cannot see why they are called 'bitter' (after 50 years as 'co-ordinator') If anyone takes over the job and goes into it gaily assuming that she can say what she likes and remain friends with all members without any consideration of a's position, b's politics, c's family's interests, I warn her from experience she has a surprise in store – you'd think we were all so adult in thought as in appearance! I thought CCC was different but it seems it is not.[22]

The editor's role in CCC was more than an administrative task, even amongst this closed group, and although she did not alter the letters, she did manage their presentation, and, in later years managed the friendships of the group, smoothing difficulties, adding the personal touch that has no equivalent in commercial magazine communication exchanges. When Ad Astra was editor, she would deal with a member's controversial contribution by positioning it as a debate.[23] The editor's role was not predetermined, but was adapted according to different personalities who occupied the position, needing to be negotiated and renegotiated within the group. Whilst she did not occupy the role of a professional editor, this was nonetheless a pivotal position in ensuring the efficient running of the club and was adapted to the context of the CCC's requirements. In some ways she had less power than a professional editor, but in other ways her role was a centrally prominent one within the group.

When Ad Astra became editor she compiled the magazine by hand sewing the letters into embroidered canvass covers; later on, she bought card covers (Figure 6.1). The physical material appearance of the *CCC* magazine in its linen covers must largely be derived from clues available from the archive. Most of the letters from those hand-collated magazines have been unbound and the contents separated out and filed under the pseudonym of each contributor. Some letters were returned, as requested, to the writers, some were requested by families at a later stage. However, one card-bound magazine has survived intact (Figure 6.2), complete with cross-stitching along the spine to keep the papers in place. The opening page, titled 'CCC Christmas Number' also gives a date of 1 December 1987. The editor gives Christmas greetings and then, with clear instructions to 'Please get a pencil and your address book NOW' readers are given a new address to which they must send their contributions, but the roster for receiving and sending on the magazine contains only nine names,

Figure 6.1 A selection of embroidered and card covers for the *CCC* magazine.

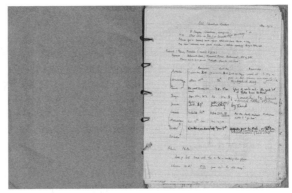

Figure 6.2 The construction and editorship of the *CCC* magazine.
© *Trustees of the Mass Observation Archive, University of Sussex.*

as this is late on in the life of the magazine and therefore in the lives of its members. Whilst members have taken it upon themselves to change the order of progression of the magazine, each recipient has carefully recorded when it was received, when it was sent on and added a comment: 'Splendid magazine' commented Waveney, and 'Lovely to hear news like old times' signed Freya. On the next page there is a handwritten index, with name, short description and page number for each of the contributions. Whilst this magazine of letters did not contain many items expected of a regular commercial magazine, there were enough aspects, cover, index, distribution list and even some editorials, to make it feel like a familiar artefact each time, and behind this compilation lies the editor's hand.

At some point the paper size must have been agreed upon: exercise paper with five holes punched, and the letters are assembled and sewn into the covers with black silk thread (Figure 6.2). A number of the original covers remain intact and they take a number of forms: the hand-embroidered canvass covers, designed for re-use, each incorporate CCC stitched into the design; the buff plain card covers often carry a picture postcard of a bird, taped to the front (Figure 6.1). Some covers had seasonal designs: an embroidered sprig of holly or a winter skating scene glued to the front. One of the most remarkable is the embroidered map of the British Isles, with dots depicting the location of members. The care and attention given to these embroidered covers, as well as the choice of picture on later covers, gave much pleasure to the members: they often remarked upon the choices made, all indicating the personal touch of the magazine.

Intimacy

Cynthia White has discussed how the inter-war period in the women's press reinforced the trend back to 'dear housewifeliness' and how, 'Almost without exception, the new periodicals dedicated themselves to upholding the traditional spheres of feminine interests and were united in recommending a purely domestic role for women.' With reference to the 'cloying, patronising journalism' of *Lady's Companion*, White states that:

> Throughout the fiction, the chat, and the answers to correspondents in this and other magazines, there was a sustained effort to curb restlessness on the part of wives and to popularise the career of housewife and mother.[24]

In the face of this, it is unsurprising that the women of the CCC wanted a magazine with a broader interest base.

Ubique replied to letters to *The Nursery World* that had interested her and suggested that they start a private correspondence club enabling more intimate and confidential writing than was possible in a public magazine.[25] The magazines were kept secret from husbands and children, and the adopting of a pseudonym maintained a level of hidden authorship, should the magazine fall into the wrong hands. But of course the women knew, or at least had access to, one another's real names, not least because of the distribution list, but also because over the years they would have been intimately familiar with the life stories of their fellow correspondents, as well as with their handwriting. Further, Hacker recalled that 'There were rules about confidentiality and unspoken rules about privacy. Although a great deal was written and discussed about sex and birth control … there was a general reticence in describing husbands' behaviour in bed.' The key point about the secrecy was that because 'everything was utterly confidential' it meant that a broad range of topics could be discussed.[26] As Bailey explains, 'Despite some hesitancy amongst the members, the confidentiality offered by the CCC gave the women the opportunity to write articles that went beyond what would have been socially acceptable in the public realm at that time.'[27] Consequently, sexual experiences, discontentment with roles of housewife and mother and unhappiness at home could be expressed, on the whole a female experience contrary to the one of contented housewife and mother promoted in many commercial magazines of the time, although it has been noted that there were magazine expressions of women's discontentment in American magazines after the Second World War.[28] The members of the magazine club were writing to a known audience, where privacy was guaranteed, and so could choose to express themselves in a manner and on subject matters that might not be acceptable in general society.

Lauren Berlant, in defining intimacy considers that it: 'involves an aspiration for a narrative about something shared, a story about both oneself and others that will turn out in a particular way. Usually, this story is set within zones of familiarity and comfort: friendship, the couple, and the family form'.[29] The idea of a narrative is a central premise of the CCC in both the expression of the individual's narrative of herself and the expectations of similar, yet unfamiliar, narratives from others. Further, Berlant suggests that 'intimacy builds worlds; it creates spaces' and even reproduces 'a fantasy that private life is the real'.[30] The process of gathering together the private narratives into a magazine of letters can be seen as the creation of an intimate space, and as the years progressed, this private world became deeply significant to its contributors, 'real' in the face-to-face meetings, but also real in the sense of the genuine attachments formed.

Whilst the appearance and the content of *CCC* were very different to commercial offerings, having no ideological or advertising-driven imperative in keeping women confined to the domestic sphere, it nonetheless offered an equally strong, if not stronger, sense of intimacy and personal contact through its letters. It did this in a number of ways, and one of the most important was in the creating of the private space for expression, and related to this is the sharing of confidences amongst the CCC group. They not only brought controversial topics to the fore such as childrearing, birth control, politics and war, some also shared very personal aspects of their lives. They created this intimate space, with the intention of sharing personal material, and it was created to the exclusion of others; some women were discussed as potential members and then rejected, others left of their own accord. Writers often started their letters with 'Dear CCC', addressing the group as a collective body. One member, describing the CCC as 'running like a living vein between us', did not want to include any 'new members (or should I say any blood transfusion?) for we are all so comfortable as we are'.[31] Cynthia White has discussed how, from very early days of magazines, writing to a woman's magazine might offer the opportunity to express opinion that could not be expressed elsewhere; if Georgian women 'felt unable to speak their minds' to irritating relatives, they could write 'to women's periodicals for the purpose of "conveying, under the assumed fiction of a story of exactly resembling circumstances, some precept or admonition which could not have been communicated or would not have been attended to in any direct manner".[32] Magazines have acted as private discursive spaces for women for centuries, offering an intimate zone of confidentiality and friendship. Indeed, one of the ways in which magazines of the 1930s encouraged the housewifely mode in women readers was through the device of more companionate and intimate aspects of magazine writing.[33]

Letters in magazines

The idea of 'correspondence' is central to various media forms, including print and periodical cultures and in particular, journalists with a special brief have long used this notion to describe their output and the role they occupy. Journalism through the letter form is nothing new for professionals, and letters from readers have always been crucial to women's magazines understood, as White explains, as a 'channel of communication through which women could exchange the fascinating trivia of everyday life [...] The "letter page" has since become one of the most popular features in women's magazines; the average reader turns to it first, and then to the "problem page".[34] They also provide a 'valuable editorial guide' and were introduced to forge closer links with readers.[35] The letter as magazine communication from editors permits the reader to feel addressed personally; and letters from readers let editors know they are on track and allows the reader to relate to aspects and offerings of the magazine as they wish, such as advice from Agony Aunts.[36] In the case of CCC, the magazine consists only of letters, and even more specifically, these are not letters of enquiry, but correspondence of a narrative nature. The letters of the CCC, and Hacker referred to them as letter-articles, take many forms and fulfil many functions: some letters give diarised overviews of events, whilst others look back to different periods of life, some are amusing anecdotes or descriptions of places or events. Some writers address a general audience, but many address a group of confidantes and discuss private matters. There is self-consciousness evident in writing that relates boring or depressing aspects of women's lives, but there is skilled writing too, showing flair, proficiency and education. The work these letters performed in fulfilling both the ambitions of the club, and the role of magazine content, is the subject of the discussion below.

One of the reasons both for the delighted surprise and occasional strong disagreement between contributors seems likely to have been their very different circumstances and belief systems. For many members, including Rose

Hacker, an insight into others' lives was an important aspect of the group's correspondences. There was intentional diversity across members with regard to location, lifestyle, religion, political affiliation and personality, and this was appreciated by all. Hacker commented that the members became close friends in spite of an enormous difference in class, politics, religion and education across the group, and her careful record tells of teachers, musicians, writers, farmer's wives, an army wife, a hotelier, housewives with particular knowledge sets, such as gardening, a miner's daughter (who went on to be a well-known writer for television) and others who had lived in interesting places or had unusual experiences of life.[37] There was a clear intention to encourage a spread of interests, livelihoods, social position, geographical location and religion. However, not only was this sense of difference sought, it had also to be facilitated within the content of the magazine. Some of the members continued to represent what they saw as their unique contribution to the group, or originality within their writing. This was seen as making a valuable contribution to the magazine, and to the wider project of diversity of experience too.

Letters as fragmented autobiographies

Many of the letters to the CCC might be seen as partial stories of a life; in one sense this was the agreed mode of contribution; however, the different interpretations and implementations of this idea are interesting and raise questions about the work that the letters might have performed for their writers as well as for the group. Whilst some letters tell of a single event, others are structured as ongoing life narratives. Some letters were recalled by individuals because they recorded important aspects of those lives, and others were recalled by families for the sake of keeping information private, but of the many letters that remain one of the lengthiest series is by 'Accidia', who tells of her emigration and her husband's work in Canada. The commitment to letter writing for the CCC group is evident in the length and regularity of her letters, although how the postage of the magazine worked to Canada is not clear, and there are also hints that she writes for another more local group too. However, the important point here is the way she narrates her life: the human contact projected through letter writing was perhaps especially important for those who lived, or had moved to remote locations. Surely no one could miss the loneliness, clear in the minute detail and circuitous telling of her long, long letters from Toronto:

> John left for Winnipeg on Saturday, travelling by our crack, stainless steel train, the 'Canadian'. He goes to Vancouver, via Saskatoon and Calgary, at the end of the week, but beyond a brief note written in the peace of the train, I have heard nothing. He is not unfortunately Ursula, a good letter writer (talking is his form of expression) so I shall not hear much of the trip until he gets back. He has a heavy schedule, including radio and TV dates, and looks like getting back flat out, though first class travel and hotel facilities should help. I just hope he doesn't tell me too much about the meals as we are on the basic at home and butter beans taste sour if you know that the best beloved is surfeited with Winnipeg Goldeye fish or Victoria Salmon [...]

And so Accidia continues for six or eight sides, relaying the minute details of her husband's life, living vicariously even though she was a Cambridge English Literature graduate herself. For this writer, filling the pages with her detailed, conversational style may have helped assuage her sense of isolation. The intimate and confidential tone of the letters invokes an atmosphere of one woman speaking to a group of trusted women friends, as indeed they became. For some, this group appeared to be a lifeline and, for this writer, the opportunity to relate the detail of her life to interested parties fulfilled her commitment to the group, but also gave her an audience. Writing in this case fulfils a need for companionship, which is something that regular magazines offer. However, whereas in mainstream magazines, emotional revelation is there to be understood and related to, in the case of CCC there was the possibility of actual participation.

The magazine did not, unlike commercial magazines, have a house style and so women contributed in the mode that suited them best, or that accommodated their needs at the time. Roberta, for instance, wrote movingly about her painful divorce from her husband in Switzerland. She chose to construct her retrospective narrative in a particular way. She tried to bring a wryness to her closing episode, 'Finale a la Noel Coward' bringing a touch of irony to her own dramatic scenario. And yet the detail of her account reads like a love story, heavily influenced by the romantic fiction genre:

> and we had our last words together.. he thanked me for everything and asked me to be brave etc. etc.. we made our last money arrangements for the next few months.. and then he was off after putting his arm round me and kissing me and stroking my hair.. what ever he felt inside him I shall never know.. nor does he know my real feelings.. or may be we both do.. any how off he went.[38]

This typed letter is written almost as a stream-of-consciousness narrative, in the style of immediate thoughts and impressions, with its drifting double full stops and ellipses. The mixed emotions of Roberta's last few meetings with her husband are carefully expressed, tender and controlled in tone, but moving too, even to the point of near-reconciliation at the divorce lawyers where they both admit that they could still 'make a go of it'. The most painful parts are where he sees the children again, and Roberta's relief that these meetings do not overly upset the children is palpable. It has evidently taken much courage to think about this episode in her life and to write it out as a personal account for the group.

For Roberta had a purpose: 'I must try and clarify my thoughts and not give any false impression.. hard to do will try my best.' Later, towards the end of her tale, she even made her husband welcome in their flat with dinner and flowers, 'pride pride.. knowing SHE does nothing in house', still competing for her husband's affections and approval. Writing the story of her divorce afforded Roberta a sense of self-control. It helped her to feel satisfied with her own conduct: 'I feel most strongly that to feel as I do, that is to say certain love, pity and charity is so MUCH better for my well being than if I felt anger, hatred, bitterness towards Walter […] it is better to feel a kind of tender love and pity without remorse, than be het up and wild in side.'[sic] Whether it was the anticipation of writing this account that helped Roberta to behave with dignity or whether this retrospective account has solidified a version of events may not be known. Either way, Roberta wanted to account for herself well, and the very process of writing this series of letters has performed cathartic and therapeutic work for this contributor in dealing with a tumultuous and potentially destructive episode in her life, giving closure and distance.

To narrate an entire life in letters is an impossible task, but many of the letters of the CCC contain carefully chosen episodes of life, selected to illustrate a wider social context perhaps, such as the first day at school for working-class children, or to be representative of family life, or personal achievements. Some letters record important days, others retrospectively tell a story once the events have settled or emotions permit. This raises the question of honesty, and whilst accuracy is hard to prove and some members were thought to exaggerate, on the whole, the letters have a ring of truthfulness and honesty about them.

The *CCC* accommodated different kinds of temperaments, there was no control over tone or content and women responded as they pleased. The group was compassionate, giving sympathy and concern freely, and sometimes this was supported by telephone calls and visits.

Letters as reportage

A number of members of the CCC interpreted the function of their letters slightly differently: for some the sense of their unique offering was strong, and consequently their 'letters' were not necessarily less personal but they emphasised the particular distinction or skill set they offered. Producing letter-articles, with headings underlined, this type of contribution is deliberately informative, providing running interest in matters of history, literature or botany for example. These writers were deeply interested in their particular subject, and this might have been why they were chosen. The tone of such contributions varies enormously. For example, the detailed research work of Robina, about Bacon's authorship of Shakespeare's plays, pursues a very specific point, and its subject matter is far removed from many of the more regular accounts of women's daily lives:

> It has been very difficult to condense such a mountain of evidence and I have not dealt with such corroboration as is contained in the codes, cryptograms and numerous F.B. signatures and masonic numbers throughout the works, not the recent interesting discovery of the Morgan Coleman mss at St Albans – as also Henry Seymour's confirmation of Mrs Gallup's life work deciphering the Bi-lateral cyphers which he tested in Bacon's prose work 'Henry VII' (the only King without a play!)[39]

However, Robina, whose father edited the *Baconiana* journal, elicited many interested responses to her articles, judging by the detailed comments squeezed on to these pages in different handwriting and different ink. This occurred to such an extent that she had to make a request: 'May I ask if, in this instance, comments or queries (which I value!) be added at the end or on a separate sheet in order to give all members a chance of reading right through legibly.'[40] Robina's writing adopts the tone of a harassed researcher, without enough hours in the day to do justice to the evidence before her, using the jargon of the work of the literary decipherer.

If Robina brought discussions about Bacon and Shakespeare to the magazine, then 'Cotton Goods' was certainly the magazine's correspondent for the working classes. This was conscious self-presentation as the one working-class member of the group, taking her name in relation to her father who worked in Woodstock spinning mill, Lancashire, and all her father's family who 'had good positions in cotton'. Although with a middle-class father and a good education,

Cotton Goods was proud of her working-class status,[41] even though she herself was a teacher. She wrote to the magazine carefully bringing class differences to the fore, her contribution to the group being to represent the working classes. Interestingly, according to the files, her handwriting seems to have two styles: one is simple, clear and printed, perhaps her teacher's writing; the other is a more cursive mature style, perhaps her adult hand.

When Cotton Goods wrote about taking the children to see Gracie Fields in the film *Sing As We Go* (1934), she broadened her narrative to describe the working-class context to her middle-class fellow CCC members:

> I don't suppose any of you have even attended a children's matinee such as we have. It used to be 2d (it's 4d now) for children who in their hundreds crowd into the hall. Lots of the children are clean and respectable, but there is a percentage of neglected, dirty little gamins who have got 2d each by hook or by crook. The hall fills up long before the pictures are due to begin, a pianist plays popular tunes on a tinny piano, and the children sing at the top of their voices, while attendants have their hands full in keeping order among the rough element.

Further letters arise out of her experiences, written retrospectively as anecdotal sketches, and are highly accomplished at bringing aspects of the working class to life. One such letter recounts the tale of the help she received from pupils when she moved her belongings two miles away to a friend's house in order to keep her company for the duration of the war. There were no local buses and she describes the amusing sight of 'a dozen little lads' helping her by carting all her possessions in their home-made wheelbarrows. Each boy had one, she notes, just as boys have tricycles or bicycles nowadays. To maintain order, the procession kept to the 'backs' of the houses in the busy part of town, the passageway, she explains, that ran between the backs of terraced town houses. She herself, to keep a sense of dignity, stayed some way apart from the line of boys. However, all such attempts to maintain decorum were shattered when one of the boy's wheelbarrows slipped on the kerb displaying all her belongings for the world to see. The charm of this scene is not lost on Cotton Goods, and this is extended by the penned illustration of a line of boys and wheelbarrows at the bottom of her letter (Figure 6.3). By emphasising economic necessity alongside humour in this anecdote of working-class life and spirit, Cotton Goods' writing opens up the class differences between her own life experiences and those of her fellow CCC contributors.

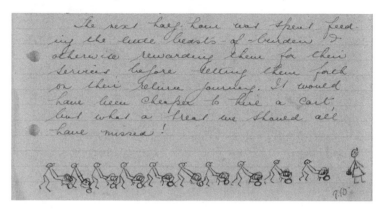

Figure 6.3 Illustrating tales of working-class life: Moving house by a wheelbarrow chain.
© *Trustees of the Mass Observation Archive, University of Sussex.*

In a piece written for CCC about her life as a teacher, recovered some time later, Cotton Goods' writing style documents the language and situation of her class-related experiences of life. With the title *FIRST DAYS AT SCHOOL* she starts her story in this way:

> Over the hills and far away stretch the rolling moors of the Pennines. The valley below, dotted with factory chimneys testifies to the industry of its people. The little Infant School, perched on the slope of the Coppice opens its doors to the thirty two new children expected for their first day at school.
>
> It's 8.30 a.m. and I, as 'baby-class' mistress, have everything in readiness – a cosy fire behind the huge fireguard, tiny chairs and tables, rocking horse, doll's house, sand-tray, trucks, blocks, engines, tricycles and innumerable smaller toys.
>
> I hear the sound of tiny, pattering clogs and a voice calling, 'Here we are, luv, what a big boy you are now you've come to t' schoo'. The mother approaches, while a tiny, shy face hides in her skirt. Other mothers and children arrive, each child carrying some familiar toy as a link with the babyhood he is shedding. […] Many of these mothers work in the factories from 9 am. to 4 p.m., these times having been arranged so that they can take the children to school before themselves going to work and collect them at the end of the afternoon school.

Evident here is a high level of writer's craft in the details of local dialect recorded in speech, 't' schoo' and practices such as the factory hours of the mothers. Accomplished writing engages her readers' interest in working-class experience, adding local colour and translating where necessary, and explaining that 'jinnies' is the local name for spinning jennies and that if a boy was promoted to 'bigger jinnies' he earned more money. However, potential deprivations such as the conditions of factory and home, health of the children and size of families, are subjects avoided, perhaps in order not to make CCC members feel uncomfortable. So Cotton Goods both retained a sense of herself as working class and related her Lancashire background to fellow CCC members.[42] She was educated and evidently skilled at writing, and knew how to present her working-class situation as interesting to others. She did not limit her tales to the CCC, and went on to publish 'many articles all about Lancashire Life, accepted by various papers'. Thus her writing for CCC was not the end of her writing career, encouraged by the appreciation of this private audience, she found a wider market for her interpretative tales of northern working-class life.[43]

Letters emulating magazine articles

Whilst it is possible to conceive of the *CCC* magazine as apart from other media forms, as a private, intimate space for female expression of confidential ideas and feelings, as a secretive set-up and as a non-commercial venture, supported only by subscriptions, this does not give quite the full picture. All of this is true, but many of the letters demonstrate influence from other media forms, and some even a keen engagement. For these were not women isolated from the world or from the media, they were highly literate, and sufficiently engaged with their interests and circumstances to make this correspondence commitment. Besides writing for their magazine, some women had engaged with media in other ways, ranging from Hacker's writing of non-fiction and local journalism, to 'Cotton Goods' published accounts of working-class life, to 'Angharad's' (Elaine Morgan's) plays for television, written in fact initially to earn the money to buy a television.

When 'Sirod' was invited to talk on the BBC radio magazine programmes, *Farmer's Wives* and *Farm Woman's Hour*, about agricultural life, her letters recount the difficulty of trying to sound as good on air as the non-rehearsed pre-broadcast chatter; and she illustrates the hilarity of trying to make conversation sound natural whilst crouched around a microphone.[44]

A few letters demonstrate direct engagement with the broader media. However, many more show the influence of other media forms in content and delivery styles. This is particularly the case regarding women's magazines as evidently they were mostly all magazine readers. One way letters subtly emulate the content of women's magazines is to focus on interests of perceived interest to women, and to report on items and events in a way that both places women at the centre of things and evokes a sense of women's cultures. 'Sirod', for example, set up the National Association of Flower Arranging Societies and in one letter relates her tale of the day the Queen visited the flower festival in Westminster Abbey. One small personalised moment shows Sirod's writing capabilities and relates the event through the writing technique of 'telling it slant', through a small humorous detail: Sirod was spoken to by one of the Queen's attendants, 'It was in the cloisters the Lady in Waiting spoke to me and asked if I was caught red-handed. I was still holding a beautiful white stock flower so I suggested "White-handed" and was so pleased to tell her that the next garden she was to see was a Dorset garden [...].' Her enthusiasm leaps off the page, and the detail both conceals and reveals her central role in the organisation. Women's cultures in magazines were emulated in other ways too, such as the incorporation of wartime recipe cuttings from women's magazines, in order to share helpful techniques and methods of coping with food rationing and shortages with the whole group.[45] This indicates that commercial magazines still functioned as an understood form of communication amongst members. Similarly to commercial magazines too, there was even some recycling of material, but this time from other correspondence magazines: 'Cornelia' produced recipes she had sent to another magazine saying, 'Old Phoenix members will laugh to see this feature again!'[46]

The holiday letter was another mode which borrowed design and format techniques from mainstream magazines; this time the travel articles. These were often produced with great care by correspondents: they attached photographs, or more often picture postcards, to illustrate an account of a holiday and frequently wrapped their text around the postcards, relating text to illustration, emulating a travel page in a magazine (Figure 6.4). The postcards bring descriptions of far-flung places to life, whilst also fulfilling the requirement of bringing new experiences to the group. One particularly artistic member illustrated her letters with small watercolour paintings, bringing her own interpretations to the gondolas of Venice or the ruins of Greece. These, whilst borrowing from magazine layout also have something of the crafted appearance of scrapbook entries too.[47]

Even the mode of the magazine questionnaire/survey was emulated, with one member showing a particular interest in body weight and appearance of the group. She attempts a survey of heights and weights of the members. 'I'd

 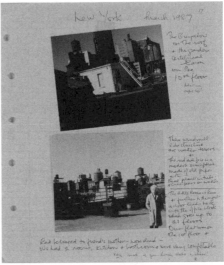

Figure 6.4 Travel pages of the *CCC*: Writing about travel to Tunisia (a) and New York (b).
© *The Hacker family, Rose Hacker Archive, Mass Observation Archive, University of Sussex.*

like to know some weights and measures of CCC, for comparison and if you are not bashful about giving this information. I should appreciate the filling in of the attached list.' Members had to give age, weight, height and measurements. Just before this, in discussing relative weights of husbands and wives she says, 'Then, too, consider the effect of a fat *couple*, each enhances the heaviness of the other, yet a thin husband with a fat wife – mustn't be too thin, else he will look henpecked.' Moreover, there seems to be a detailed interest in the 'perfect figure' of Tony, Roberta's husband. Some members did respond, and in this fact-finding project there was a sense of being shielded by the agreed terms of privacy of the CCC. This brings to mind the ways later women's health magazines operate for their readers, allowing them to critically engage with mainstream discourses about health.[48]

Some readers interpreted their remit at times to give 'news' of their local area, again emulating a magazine feature on a specific place, a common enough article type in women's magazines. Vignettes of local life were elaborated into letters, and one such by 'Ad Astra', entitled 'Our Railway', discusses disruption on her local Dengie Peninsula line in Essex and offers humorous tales of local colour. She authenticates her tale by including a cutting from the local newspaper:

The last sentence sums up the attitude of our local station masters: if you 'can't account for the trouble' you can't be responsible for it. Anyway the fault was not in the track, nor in the train, so some human was at fault I guess, but of course it wasn't anyone between Wickford and Southminster.

In this letter, some trouble has been taken to provide a hand-penned illustration of the area, including a map of the line, with an enlargement in one corner (Figure 6.5).[49]

Lastly, there was also the sense of the group readership relayed through occasional letters, a metanarrative perhaps that drew attention to the group, just as a magazine sometimes addresses special offers or meetings to a semi-select group of readers who have paid regular subscription of acknowledged loyalty to the magazine in some other way. As CCC friendships developed beyond the page, the writerly connections expanded when the group decided to officially meet up once a year, either in London at 'Elektra', Rose Hacker's house, because it was central, or in Essex at 'Ad Astra's' large house in Essex. There was great excitement at meeting up at the annual lunches and the effort some women made to make the journey heightened the occasion. One of Ad Astra's letters goes into great detail about hats, skirts and colours of outfits, and very much plays down her own part in hosting the event, expressing her 'pure pleasure' in the day. This letter, the author acknowledges, was written especially descriptively for the benefit of those who could not attend, and the explicit intention is to paint a picture in words, to allow those not present to join in the experience.

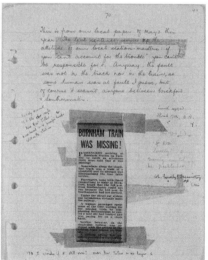

Figure 6.5 Snippets of local news: 'Our Railway', The Dengie Peninsula Line.
© *Trustees of the Mass Observation Archive, University of Sussex.*

A range of media genres, styles and techniques, especially from commercial women's magazines, can be seen to have influenced the production of some letters to the CCC. Writing skills and attention to presentation are plain to see, and through this may be discerned a high level of engagement with different aspects of media, even though this was a private magazine removed from the public gaze. The very reason for starting this correspondence club was to have an alternative mode of discourse to the dominant ideologies of femininity and domesticity for women: there is no editor or editorial board accepting or rejecting articles, no agony aunt dictating the moral parameters of personal dilemmas or choices, no domestic science team giving advice about running a home. The narrative threads created through the letters were sometimes ongoing and not just one-off writings; the letters refer to each other, acknowledging joy and sadness in the events of each other's lives. It is an assemblage of different aspects, a patchwork, of the stories of women's lives; there are narratives, but all are necessarily incomplete. In many ways all these aspects disrupt the hierarchies of knowledge and power of a commercial magazine. In place of more regular magazine constructs of femininity, other aspects of women's lives, ingenuity and talents rise to the surface.

There was one further and important way in which written communication amongst the CCC extended beyond the commercial magazine, and that is the offering of responses to articles. This may have some equivalence in letters to editors in commercial magazines, but for the readers of CCC, the input of other readers was a key factor to the enjoyment of the magazine. As the magazine content, the letters of CCC operate as text to be read and received, but unlike a commercial magazine, reception of those texts invited written response. This manifested as writing comments on each other's letters, making comments about content, or offering opinion, expressing sympathy and understanding. The comments from other readers are often appreciative of the sharing of personal information, and this acknowledges the confidences to be kept as part of the intimacy of the group. Besides engaging with the topics, readers also commented in other ways on the texture of the writing perhaps congratulating the writer on the delivery of a tale. Comments were sometimes provocative and elicited further responses to the comments as well as the original article. Sometimes these additions were so extensive that other members complained that the comments obscured the original or were sufficiently interesting to have become the subject of a separate letter. Other readers complained that because of their position in the roster, they had missed out on all the comments and remarks and they wanted to engage with the total discussion. Readers towards the end of the roster may have had to wait some days or even weeks for the magazine to arrive, but they benefitted from the overlaid comments from the other previous readers. There was a further mode of appraising letters too, established as a grading or rating system, where up to four dots could be given in the hollows of a cross, looking like a star with one, two, three or four points. Occasionally, there were double stars recording especially enthusiastic appreciation, as in A Priori's controversial letter about 'Religion in Schools'. Readers felt very free to make their responses, whether they agreed or not, and in this way, the letters became discussion pieces, with immediate responses and further letters with different points of view (Figure 6.6). Readers were prepared to admit their limitations too in these comments, for instance, 'S' says of Robina's laborious enquiries for *Baconiana*, 'Please do go on arguing it out. I find it the most interesting thing in CCC for a long time but I am not intellectual enough to join in.' All the responses on the

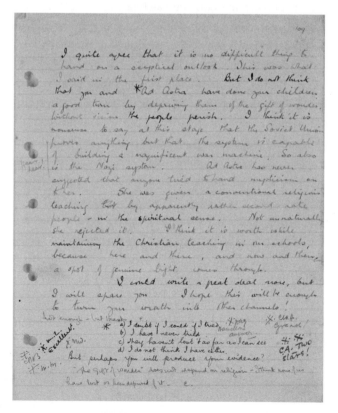

Figure 6.6 The systems of reader response to letter-articles.
© *Trustees of the Mass Observation Archive, University of Sussex.*

articles facilitated a mode of written conversation, albeit with a time delay and this process of writing back, answering, contradicting and generally continuing the conversation was a highly valued aspect of the magazine, with some calls for magazines to be circulated twice so that all the contributions could be read, no matter where one appeared on the roster. There were disagreements, sometimes quite heated, so much so that some conflicts had to be resolved out of the spaces of the magazines and using other modes of communication, such as telephone calls, involving, at times, the diplomatic skills of the editor, as suggested above by Ad Astra.

The comments operated as a dialogue of comment, offering the potential of giving opinion as marginalia and having it heard. This may be compared with the twenty-first century facility of online magazines and blogs, but has never been a part of mainstream magazines. The only opportunity for comment and response has been in the letters pages: a more formal structure subject to the external factors of editorship and commercial production. A conventional magazine claims to offer friendship and companionship through its familiar structures, textual devices, reader address and content, but it can only do so at a distance, not knowing its target reader personally. The CCC, where writers and readers and magazine editor all knew each other well, sheds light on the magazine form and on the complexities of the intimate and personal relationship between a magazine and its reader in interesting ways.

In many ways then, the *CCC* magazine has its similarities to any woman's magazine: its content are varied; it offers information of interest to women; it provides insight into the lives of other women through letters and confessionals and, generally speaking, it tells women's truths in the manner of familiars sharing confidences and observations of life. And yet it offers more: the *CCC* magazine was an unfolding narrative, with articles not standing alone, but developing with each issue; it built familiarity as well as giving information, but this time between readers and writers who knew each other; and there was an element of participation and exchange, making the magazine communication dynamic and real rather than imagined.

'True letters'

The question remains why this magazine was such a success, why it lasted for over half a century and why the women of the CCC continued to write in this way for their magazine. Having looked at the particular circumstances of the magazine, the intimate space it created for women to express themselves, the function of magazine letters and the letter of the CCC, this last section draws together potential reasons for the magazine's longevity.

One letter, written about 1960 by Ad Astra, ruminates on why, in an age of telecommunications, and when members of the CCC know each other so well, they still write letters:

> Who writes a letter with a telephone to hand? Who under thirty writes a long letter to a friend in the same county or, eve, country? A picture postcard on a holiday, a get-better card, an urgent notelet about an appointment, a hasty letter to fix times, to ask for information (or money), to send an invitation, but not a gossipy letter that paints the sender's surroundings, gives current news, comments on interests personal and public, indulges perhaps in jest or anger or cattery or affection en passant, those items come in true letters and the over-thirties or forties write those if anyone does today.[50]

Understood here is the privilege and importance of both writing and literacy, and in many of the letters of the *CCC*, there is a confidence in written expression, perhaps born of class and certainly of education, indicating an engagement with words and their meaning, and a delight in the written word as a form of communication. However, also understood is a qualitative difference between many forms of letter and the 'true letters' of the CCC.

In a similarly reflexive mode, when Hacker considered the effect of the magazine on members, she wondered how these women, 'who, on the surface, seemed to have so little in common' formed such a close and caring network. She points to similarities in having to do housework, bringing up children and, in some cases, making marriages work, and differences in types of home and location, with 'endless ways of living' suggesting that 'a lively curiosity and non-judgemental attitude were essential'. Their different situations were of interest to one another, and this interest brought them closer and that new experiences, written about honestly and frankly, led to sympathetic responses and that 'honesty begat honesty, so that people felt they knew each other better than even close friends or relatives'. This closeness, where friendship becomes conflated with kinship, is reflected in the title of her manuscript, taken from Rudyard Kipling's 1896 poem 'The Ladies',[51] where 'the Colonel's lady, and Judy O'Grady are sisters under the skin'.

To return to Granovetter's notion of bridging, in the context of this chapter understood as women making connections to other women of different circumstances, Granovetter questions whether 'something flows *through* these bridges' [emphasis in original] and that this 'actually plays an important part in the social life of individuals'. The connections of the group were certainly strongly felt, and these deepened with time, becoming the 'living vein' described by one member. As friendships developed through the letters, and then annual group meetings, there were individual visits, phone calls, kindnesses in need and evacuation of children to other member's homes, but still they wrote for the magazine. What flowed through the letters of the *CCC* was initially information and interest, even inquisitiveness, into the difference and variety of other women's lives.

Some of this inquisitiveness was based in a class curiosity. Many of the women of the CCC were of the middle classes, and it has been argued that middle-class friendships are easier to maintain because there is more 'time, space, energy and material resources' within bourgeois routines to keep friendships going.[52] In the case of the *CCC* contributors there are many signifiers of middle-class status, such as help in the home, a husband in a professional job and education and leisure time to pen letters. But there are other indicators too of financial constraints; many also found it difficult to squeeze letter writing into their day due to family and domestic commitments, mentioning sitting down at midnight or alluding to difficulties in finding privacy to write, an important observance for contributions. The *CCC's* desire to encompass class difference into the mix, naturally led to variations in personal circumstances and this brought some material problems, with calls for additional stamps to help out those on lesser incomes, and after the war, the prospect of meeting up for a meal became too expensive for some. However, these issues, rather than hinder production, seemed to provoke a determination to continue to contribute to a magazine which offered them the opportunity to share the 'truth' of their lives in letters.

As well as class curiosity then, was a determination to subvert social norms of discretion about circumstances and private life, and in expressing a desire to build this network of women founded upon 'true letters', Ubique and others were acting autonomously, subversively even, voicing dissatisfactions with their lives as defined by 1930s British ideological expectations of domestic femininity. At the outset of CCC, the gathering imperative was one of railing against the limitations imposed on women in Britain in the 1930s, including the marriage bar for working women and inter-war expectations of domesticity and motherhood. It was to mainstream magazines that many women turned to solve their dilemmas in their private lives, or to learn what society expected of them, and to seek an intimate space, a woman's culture. Whether commercial magazines provided this, and gave women the answers they sought, has been the subject of much enquiry. But women have always turned to their magazines to provide answers and so it is hardly surprising that in constructing their letters for the CCC, members often chose to emulate different facets of the commercial magazine form.

CCC members wrote out of habit, out of commitment to the CCC and to keep in touch with what became a long-term friendship group. But they also wrote because they had a willing audience, and just as they were interested in one another's tales, so each woman in her particular window onto the CCC had her own tales to tell and had found a group of confidants, receptive and attentive to the detail and stories of her life. This was a valued forum for expression: and contact was kept up through major changes such as divorce and death of husbands, and women told these stories in their 'true letters', receiving emotional support from fellow writers through their responses and their telling also. There was a kind of 'inclusive intimacy'[53] to the letters, whereby although husbands and children were not involved in the CCC, if they were people important to the letter writer, then they became important to the group. The letters, dealing as they were, in private and personal information, were significant in that they proffered 'fulfilment of friendship' within the rules of the group.[54]

Recent writing has challenged assumptions about heterosexual female friendships being secondary to the married relationship.[55] In discussing contemporary middle-class female friendships, Harrison has suggested that '"Identity work" between women is one of the achievements of women's talk.'[56] A major reason for writing for the CCC was to achieve and maintain a sense of identity at a time when it was difficult to find friends willing to express dissatisfaction with their roles as wives and mothers. Allan has argued that personal circumstances and class are influential on regular friendships.[57] However, the CCC was not based upon regular friendships, as we have seen through their letters, for this group, difference was crucial to membership. And seeking friendship which has nothing to do with obligation or social group patterns, in order to expand one's own experience of life, is an autonomous act and has been linked to the modern Western notion of the, mostly middle-class, autonomous self.[58] Autonomy and individual agency, regardless of class or circumstances, is what bound these women together at the outset, and was also their motivation to keep writing even when friendships had been established in other ways. In questioning why women read commercial magazines, reflection, empathy and identification are considered key themes.[59] The CCC offered this and as time wore on, it offered even more and what flowed between the members was a deeper friendship and intimate network of support. It was this that helped to make the group into one of 'strong ties' that lasted as a family until the end of their lives.

***

The work of this magazine was initially to facilitate the introduction of women to other women in different circumstances in order to enlarge their life experiences, but it became the writing of lives through letters to a trusted group of women. As the magazine developed, and the contributors knew each other better through accounts, opinions and tales so the involvement, interest and interaction in each other's lives heightened and intensified. The magazine itself, whilst so physically different to a commercial women's service magazine of the mid-twentieth century, in fact had many more esoteric similarities to a regular magazine than might appear and in many ways, the genuine friendships and concern expressed between contributors truly delivered the emotional support that could only be superficially and generically offered by professional editorial guidance and advice. Advice given, if any, by members of the CCC was from a basis of experience and not assumed authority and although there were differences in terms of lifestyle and to some extent education and wealth, however, within the CCC they were equal: what counted was the quality and sincerity of their magazine contributions. There was no commercial imperative and no intention of conforming (within the contributions to the magazine at least) to an ideology of femininity; however, there was a lifelong interest in other women's lives, and an opportunity for confidence through correspondence. In many ways, CCC was more magazine than magazines, achieving a heightened level of personalised communication, relevance and interaction. It provided the level of intimacy, friendship and communication that, in truth, women really crave from their magazines.

'Make the Women Feel That They Are Important': Developing the Radio Magazine

Discovering how to produce radio magazine programmes with a wide and genuine appeal for women was a long learning curve for the BBC in its early years of broadcasting. There was argument, contestation, reflection and experimentation regarding form and content; and at the same time, there was increased consideration of how to respond to the perceived needs of women and how to address an anticipated female audience. Whilst the term 'magazine' has been used for a very long time with regard to radio programmes of mixed content, deep understanding of the dynamics of such a programme, beyond the notion of two or more items, proved quite elusive, and there was no formula, format or even outline design of an early presentation style. Early attempts at magazine programmes had to experiment with different ways of speaking to women, developing in success and stature only through trial and error, listener feedback and astute decisions by producers who were prepared to experiment and remain alive to what worked and what did not. This chapter discusses in detail some of the innovative and influential programmes for women that came before the re-launch of *Woman's Hour* in 1946 and that culminated in the present sophisticated and embracing format of *Woman's Hour* (BBC R4 1946–ongoing). The majority of research for this chapter has come from the BBC Written Archive Centre and the often extensive memos sent between employees of the corporation. The discussion weaves together ways in which producers and presenters developed a mode of talking to women on the radio, progressing from a straight lecture to an engaging conversational style.

Woman's Hour: Contemporary radio magazine form

Woman's Hour has long been acknowledged as an archetypal radio magazine programme for women. It is usually dated back to October 1946 when it was transmitted on the Light Programme, firstly with a male producer Norman Collins and male presenter, Alan Ivimey, succeeded by Joan Griffiths, then Olive Shapley, Marjorie Anderson, Sue MacGregor and others including Jenni Murray from 1987 and Jane Garvey to the present. Its hugely successful format, familiar to millions in Britain, comprises a range of journalistic presentation including reports, interviews, reviews and discussions as well as the delivery of fictional texts as dramatisations, adaptations or abridged readings. Content ranges across a full spectrum of subjects of potential interest to women, including news items and political and current affairs. Advertised as 'The programme that offers a female perspective on the world', it comments on life at home and abroad, on domestic and working spheres of women's lives, often including articles on family, household, fashion and health. A focus on women's history is not unusual, often discussing remarkable women and their achievements, contextualising women's social history. In this way, *Woman's Hour* moves between serious journalistic enquiry, sometimes with an intellectual tone, and a more down to earth and light-hearted mode; it can assume prior knowledge and interest or provide information. The format is complexly and robustly structured: it is intimate and inclusive, with a lead presenter opening the programme, introducing what is to come and in effect advertising the articles to follow. Other presenters may participate with interviews or reports, perhaps from outside the studio, while the main presenter holds the programme together. Sometimes the programmes are themed, but often they are a mixed bag. The *Woman's Hour* umbrella also extends to other special programmes of specific research and more in-depth analysis, and some of these individual enquiries have been particularly influential and educational.[1] Programmes engage women at different levels, consolidating what they know and sharing a broader context, introducing new topics, both of specific and general interest, and retaining engagement with existing interests, both inside and outside home life; at once it is lively and serious, educational and affirmative. In short it is a collation held together by experienced broadcasting professional announcers, as a magazine programme of variety and specificity aimed at an audience of two-thirds women, and one-third men. Furthermore, the *Woman's Hour* web page enables listeners to catch up on missed programmes, references and current themes and projects.[2]

Yet this high standard of multi-layered radio magazine production and presentation took years to achieve and although *Woman's Hour* has famously been running continuously since 1946, it did not start at that point. The BBC had been broadcasting directly to a female-gendered audience since its very early days, and it took some time to learn how to speak inclusively to a broad range of women. Moreover the concept of the magazine programme took some time to evolve, with early women's programmes slowly developing an appropriate broadcast style and content of interest to the listening audience. The precursors to *Woman's Hour* varied in their approach to their listeners and consequently in their levels of success. They owed a large debt to the pattern established by women's pages in newspapers and in women's print magazines. However, perhaps the greatest assets in the development of the BBC radio magazine formula were the innovations of early radio programmes and the listener-attuned acuity of the programme producers.

The first *Women's Hour*: Imagined and real interaction with the audience

On 2 May 1923, *Women's Hour* opened at 5.00p.m. with H. R. H. Princess Alice, Duchess of Athlone, giving a talk on 'The adoption of Babies', and Lady Duff Gordon on 'Fashions'. It was in fact only a half-hour programme with *Children's Hour* following on directly. The following day, Mrs C. S. Peel offered 'Recipes, Kitchen Conversations', and Madame Edith Baird talked on 'Dancing Games'. The early days of *Women's Hour* went on to offer quite a range of talks on gardening, child welfare, cookery, beauty, tennis, shopping and household hints. Mrs Peel became one of the regulars as did Margaret Dyer with her 'In and Out of the Shops'. But besides a domestic focus, there were also talks in these very early days on issues of broader concern: Musgrave Watson on 'Current Topics' and The Lord Mayor of London on 'The need for development of Maternity Work of London', and Mrs H. A. L. Fisher on education.[3] An attempt at a range of interests, concerning both the home and the outside world, was evident from the outset. However, the title *Women's Hour* was dropped less than a year later, and the material for those talks was absorbed into other programmes.

Women's Hour of 1923 was amongst other audience-specific transmissions with *Children's Hour*, which has been described as an impromptu 'nightly romp' with 'uncles' and 'aunts',[4] and *Men's Hour* or sometimes the half-hour

Men's Talks which had started a day earlier on 1 May 1923, the very day that the Savoy Hill Studios opened. The first talk was given by the Earl of Birkenhead, and it soon settled down to a repertoire of talks on motoring, business and a range of sports such as cricket, fishing and golf, with sporting fixtures as a regular feature. The records give only the title and the presenter's name, and whilst the contents of P. S. Turner's 'Carburetta Troubles' and Capt. Birley's 'How a Business Man can Keep Fit' may be easily imagined, Major Christie's 'The Gentle Art of Snaring Unicorns' remains more enigmatic.[5] *Men's Hour* had only a short life, possibly because 'few speakers were prepared to turn out on cold winter nights to make their way to Savoy Hill to broadcast at 10p.m. for a purely nominal fee'.[6]

Ella Fitzgerald joined the BBC in April 1923 to be in charge of both the *Children's Hour* and *Women's Hour*. Initially, *Women's Hour* usually consisted of a talk and a music item. The London programme was advertised in the *Radio Times* from September 1923 onwards though there was a different offering for provincial stations. Whilst the music in London would be performed by a minor concert artist, in the provinces the music was often a piano solo 'by the Station accompanist and occasionally a singer'.[7] Similarly, the manuscripts for the talks were typed in London and syndicated to the various stations to be read by 'the chief "aunt" or some other woman'. The often well-known figure presenting from the London studio would be printed in the *Radio Times*, while the talk in the provinces was only selected from these manuscripts at the last moment, and so remained unadvertised.[8]

Fitzgerald set up the Women's National Advisory Committee in 1924 to suggest speakers and material and cover women's interests generally, not only in the *Women's Hour*, but throughout the programme. At their first meeting on 18 January 1924, it was suggested that a debate be broadcast between two members of the committee to ascertain 'listener's opinions on the timing and subject matter for the *Women's Hour*'. It seems these women were set up as opponents: Mrs H. Earle who had worked for the Ministry of Food represented women's vocations, housing and home, faced Miss E. Evelyn Gates who worked in publishing and represented professional women's interests. These two women then, both of whom had in fact entered public life and worked, were set up to represent two sides of women's occupations: the home and the professional world. The debate was broadcast on Saturday 2 February 1924, recorded as 'Discussion, The Women's Hour'. This was the second of two talks scheduled for 5.00p.m., the first was 'A Barrister-at-law: Why you should get your Husband to make a Will.' Listeners were invited to respond to the *Women's Hour* discussion and to suggest preferred timing and content. After the debate, 326 women wrote in. One hundred and eighty-seven letters (over half) supported Miss Gates (with her emphasis on professional interests), and fifty-two supported Mrs Earle (representing the interests of the domestic sphere), and the remainder wanted either no change or a 'general compound' of domestic and non-domestic subjects. Most wanted no cookery, market prices or household hints. Resulting from this early reader response, it was suggested that two days would be given over to home and children, whilst four days would focus on entertainment, travel, literature and educational items.[9]

Subsequent decisions about the talks led to ambivalent outcomes for women listeners to *Women's Hour*: Lady Denman, the Chairman of the National Federation of Women's Institutes, had already raised the question whether talks should be delivered by their author, considering that: 'women's voices were rendered definitely unpleasant by the microphone'.[10] At this same meeting Admiral Carpendale, the chairman, suggested that 'Women's Topics' should be given in conjunction with the afternoon concerts and that the term 'women's' should not be used in order to achieve a wider appeal. Lady Denman agreed and at the second meeting of the committee she suggested that the word 'Women's' should gradually be dispensed with, and that the titles alone should indicate the subject of the talk. Consequently, the title '*Women's Hour*' was dropped, although in abolishing the term '*Women's Hour*' and generally getting rid of 'Woman' as a mode of address in programme listings, the committee rather negated its own purpose, a point noted in a letter on the subject of the Women's Advisory Committee:

> The objects of this Committee were, we think you will agree, considerably modified by the Committee's recommendation that the title 'Women's Hour' should be abolished and with it the majority of subjects essentially domestic in character, talks upon subjects of general interest being substituted.[11]

The upshot was that the timing was changed to 3.30p.m., and the material went out within broader groupings of *Household Talks* and *Women's Talks*.[12] The abbreviation 'W.H.' does not appear in programme listings after Saturday 22 March 1924, although talks clearly targeted at a range of women's interests continue: 'Spring Cleaning', 'The Art of Conversation', 'Notable XVIII-Century Women', 'Some Ways with Ribbons' and 'A Magic Working Mother', to name but a few. These titles indicate the intention to continue the delivery of content identified as interesting to women even if it is not specifically labelled as 'Women's Hour', but given the abbreviation 'W.T.' (presumably Women's Talks). The Women's Advisory Committee, then, had complained about women's voices on the air and abolished the title 'Women's Hour'. In so doing, it had voted itself, and the focus provided by 'Women's Hour', out of business and off the radio.

The problem of the all-important timing of the *Household* and *Women's Talks* was an issue set to rumble on for quite some years. The initial change to 3.30p.m. was only conceded on the understanding that when the talks became 'programme obstructions' or interfered with other talk-heavy programmes, they would be moved to a morning slot.[13] There was, it seems, much experimentation with the timing of the programme, but by the early 1930s a morning slot was decided upon with an accompanying rationale:

> 10.45 am was chosen with the idea in mind that many women would turn on their sets for the weather forecast and morning service and leave them running whilst they were busy about the house, and would therefore be edified by a discussion on, e.g. paint-washing.[14]

It had become clear that daytime programmes targeted at the female listener had to fit in with a housewife's domestic routine: gaps in her daily round of housework, cooking, shopping and childcare needed to be identified. Indeed, from early on there was an important area of confluence in the organisation of time between daytime radio for women and women's domestic work. Just as radio schedulers needed to fill the hours of transmission appropriately and interestingly, so the housewife had to organise her day to keep on top of her domestic chores (chores that were more extensive lower down the social scale, where there was less money available for appliances and domestic help), while taking care of her children and retaining some sanity and connection to the outside world. Listening to the radio whilst completing housework became an integral part of the housewife's day and Michael Bailey has suggested that 'Broadcasting reinforced and rationalised the housewife's timetable of work.'[15]

This focus on the housewife's day, alongside technical developments in radio home sets, increasingly identified the radio as an important media form for women. Originally, radio had been seen as a male-gendered technology and only gradually became a domestic media form.[16] 'After all', said one commentator, 'women had to learn how to switch on the receiver to get the best signal'.[17] By the 1930s, however, the radio was an expanding media form in middle-class and upper working-class households and with the increased supply of electricity to homes and the addition of the loudspeaker to radio sets, listening to the radio could become a family activity.[18] The stay-at-home tradition of many 1930s married women led to the anticipation that daytime radio would have a female audience. Michael Bailey suggests that women listeners were interpolated as housewives and mothers, and that the introduction of the radio to the home along with the presentation of daytime radio programmes meant that 'Women could go about their everyday domestic chores while simultaneously being educated in issues of political and social importance.'[19] These easily identifiable Reithian ideas may have been the intended mode of affect of early radio programmes for women, but as I argue below, such didactic intentions were undercut and undermined by programme makers and listeners alike.

Household Talks: Conversation, participation and magazines

One of the appeals of the magazine format is the notion of listener participation; the idea, real or imagined, of a conversation. The conversation might be through the spoken word or a letter, or it might be more esoteric and remote in the sense of providing food for thought and later reflection in the mind of the listener. Furthermore, despite the authoritative even instructional tone of many print magazines which might lead to a sense of one-sided communication, the personal nature of the content can give a sense of intimate exchange rather than pronouncement, and an interesting problem of magazines of all genres is how to manage and deal with audience participation.

Household Talks were not magazine programmes as such, but the producers learnt a good deal about how to address the female radio listener from their delivery and from the listener feedback received. The name 'Woman's Hour' might have been dropped, but much of the content continued from 1928 under this title of *Household Talks*, which encompassed a range of speakers on a range of topics, from within the BBC Talks Department, headed up by Hilda Matheson as Talks Director. Originally, they included a range of items such as travel and politics, with a variety of items, experts and amateurs in this broadcasting slot each weekday from 10.45 to 11.00a.m. However, Maggie Andrews has suggested that these talks became increasingly focused on domestic matters, including childcare and cookery.[20] Miss Sprott, for instance, in charge of the series of 'Daily Household or Practical Talks' requested more air time for her programmes, explaining the limitations of one weekly talk. The scheduling of the programme to suit the housewife's day was significant, 'when housewives are about their work' and 'early enough not to interfere with the shopping hours', as was the broadening of subject matter to appeal to a range of social classes.[21] There were many series of talks aimed at women on a broad range of subjects, some programmes overlapped and some had eventual difficulty in finding new speakers. Andrews has remarked upon the significance of radio in giving advice to women and has noted the 'competing ideas about domesticity' given by experts of the *Household Talks* programmes.[22]

The participatory or listener response aspect of radio certainly proved a challenge from the very early days of the popular *Household Talks*. A BBC internal circulating memo to Hilda Matheson entitled, rather amusingly, 'Marmalade Talks etc.' reports minutes from the Control Board where this very issue of replying to listener requests was discussed (Figure 7.1). The problem of follow-up replies, a task already refused by one department, had resulted in thousands of 'Roneoed' copies (an early form of photocopying) of recipes being sent out to listeners in response to their postal applications. The principle, if not the recipe, is important here: the process of listener follow-up is seen as an integral part of the programme and the report states that these particular *Household Talks* only had 'value if followed up by written recipes, etc.'. However, the BBC, apparently, did not have the capacity to handle the mail it received over the marmalade recipe, and the prospect of dealing with a mass written communication to individual listeners resulting from the broadcast had clearly not been anticipated in such numbers. The solution to demands for this level of listener communication was to put 'advance annotations in the "Radio Times"' and to suggest that the listener take careful notes at the time of broadcast.[23] This is a very early example of the use of a print media magazine to reinforce listener participation and loyalty to a pre-magazine broadcast programme.

A couple of weeks later, a different solution was proposed: and this time a complex system with different departments performing different aspects of the task, involving loose stamps and unstuck envelopes, with one department slitting open the reader envelopes and another department extracting the listener-supplied return envelopes.[24] These unanticipated problems of

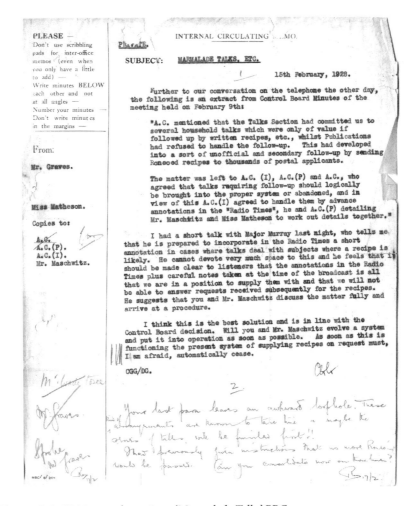

Figure 7.1 Writing up the recipes: 'Marmalade Talks' BBC memo.
© *BBC Written Archives Centre.*

overwhelming audience participation did not go away and without a clear process, secretaries, the post room and the accounts department were all involved in trying to maintain listener communications. This problem continues in memos in the records, raising issues of staffing and profitability, and it becomes clear that the infrastructure of the BBC had been set up in the assumption and anticipation of radio broadcasts as one-way communication. When it was clear that this assumption was incorrect, and that listeners were responding in their thousands, it caused difficulties within the internal workings of the BBC.

Print media became increasingly important as a backup to the *Household Talks*. The talks' success led to proposals for the production of pamphlets,[25] and subsequently the publication by the BBC of a range of books and pamphlets to accompany the *Talks*; its paperback book, *Home, Health and Garden* (1928), had sold over 15,000 copies by October of that year.[26] It cost one shilling and contained extracts and excerpts from talks (with dates) given by various speakers: Julia Cairns from the magazine *Woman's Journal* on 'Decorating Your Own Home'; Mrs Clifton Reynolds on 'Planning an Ideal Kitchen'; 'Jam Making for Summer and Autumn' by Mrs Cottington Taylor (director of the 'Good Housekeeping' Institute) and extracts from the fortnightly talks 'Round the Year in the Garden' by Marion Cran in 1927. Of particular importance are the illustrations, including drawings and sketches as well as photographs.[27] The photograph of the ideal kitchen with small worktops and few appliances appears modest but modern with clean lines and gingham check curtains. Undoubtedly, the photograph accompanying 'A Corner of Mrs. Cran's Garden at Coggers', encompassing pond, lawn, trees and historic house would have given listeners a good deal of pleasure in bringing to life the much-discussed garden. These visual images no doubt illustrated and augmented the content of some of the talks, as did the recipes and transcripts of instructions on bee-keeping and so on. The following year, another booklet, *BBC Household Talks 1928* (BBC, 1929), was produced in a similar vein, links with Empire Shopping were maintained, followed by Furniture and Furnishings, Cooking (perhaps with *the* marmalade recipe reproduced on page 41), Keeping Fit, Bee-Keeping and others (Figure 7.2). Smaller individual leaflets from the 1930s programmes carry the titles of the talks such as *Shopping and Cooking*, *The Wise Penny* and *Economical Cookery* (Figure 7.3). As if this need for communication with listeners beyond the programmes needed further proof, an experiment with recipe leaflets printed by the Empire Marketing Board in the year following the marmalade fiasco, 1929, resulted in over 5,000 applications for the leaflet on the rather homely subject of 'various ways on cooking cheese!'[28]

Thus, the demand for two-way listener communication and its associated problems emerged out of *Household Talks* from the earliest days. Recipes, needing detailed ingredients and weights, pushed the boundaries of the delivery of talk broadcast information and, in an era long before web pages, the need for printed details was clear. It seems that as these talks became increasingly successful – and there was one single request for 500 copies of a talk on casserole cookery[29] –

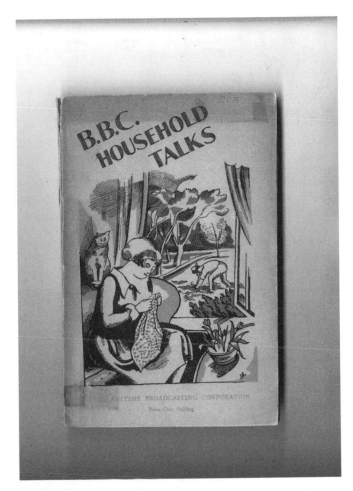

Figure 7.2 Producing talks in print: BBC 'Household Talks' leaflet.
© *Estate of John Northcote Nash, Bridgeman Images.*

the *Radio Times* became keener to publish the recipes, and indeed started to offer a household page, 'Home Pages'. Meanwhile, *The Listener* (1929–1991) had had a regular 'About the Household' section from the late 1920s, efficiently reproducing talks. An early talk, 'Bright Ideas for Dull Houses' by Lucy Yates in the 3 July 1929 issue was reprinted from talk given only in the previous week, 29 June 1929. The bottom half of the page is taken up by Mrs Stephenson's talk, given only the day before, on 'An Easy Way to Bottle Fruit'. The need for print reinforcement and the continuation of communication beyond the talk proved that there was still a very large audience eager for radio programmes that related to listener's daily lives.

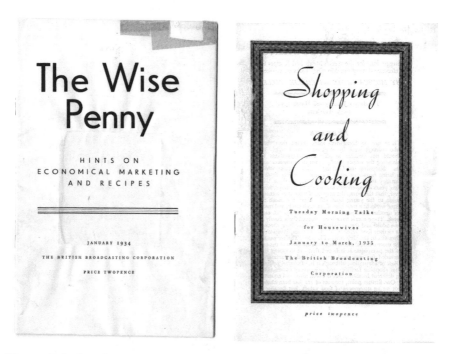

Figure 7.3 Complementing radio talks: 'The Wise Penny' and 'Shopping and Cooking' leaflets.
© *BBC Written Archives Centre.*

As listener participation became a permanent aspect of radio broadcasting there were special series of *Household Talks* where listeners were invited on to the programme to give talks. This caused a series of problems regarding voice and content, such as the working-class housewives who frequently wanted to mention the Co-operative Store dividends as a way of saving money and supplementing a meagre family income. Whilst some parties at the BBC wanted these potential endorsements removed, others saw them as throwing light on 'the psychology and methods of the working-class housewife'.[30] The records kept about the various series that were broadcast to women under this general term of *Household Talks* reveal important developmental aspects of the radio magazine format. Undoubtedly lessons were learnt as the style of programming became more sophisticated and progressive. Radio talk had always been important, but increasingly radio professionals started examining the processes, social significance and dynamics taking place in those talk programmes.

Developing talking styles

The early radio magazine was approached and developed in a number of overlapping ways from within the BBC: there was interest in the actual construction and delivery of a talk; there were experiments and new styles of talking personally to a listener, as in a conversation rather than a lecture; and there was increased interest in the needs of the listener and the potential impact that radio might have on women's lives. Some radio professionals helped to develop the form by pushing boundaries of broadcasting technique, whilst others reflected on style and format.

An early article in *The Listener* (1929–1991) demonstrates a high level of institutional interest in the process of construction behind radio talks. 'The Making of a Talk' (1929) discusses various aspects of the planning behind an effective radio talk in the light of the increased interest in the spoken word on the radio. Speakers, the writer claims, must of course be knowledgeable on their subjects, but must also have a voice suitable for the microphone, as experience at public speaking is not always 'a certain passport to successful broadcasting' and speakers may need to master 'the necessary technique of broadcast delivery'. The article points out that male voices tend to come out better than female voices in the voice tests. In this time of live broadcasting, the outline of the talk was agreed through conversation and then written by the speaker. More than just preparing the talk, the speaker must also 'indicate to the B.B.C. what his needs are in the way of supporting the appeal to the ear by the appeal to the eye; that is, by use of the B.B.C. publications to help listeners make the best possible use of his talk'. This meant publishing in magazines or pamphlets the notes, pictures or advice that the speaker deemed necessary for the listener. Significantly though, this preparation should have no impact on the spontaneity of the talk at the moment of delivery.

The article continues that the manuscript itself would be worked on and perhaps adapted to a broadcast talk by professionals at the BBC as well as the speaker. There are things that work well in broadcasting that the speaker or lecturer might not be used to, such as putting at least one of his most striking points at the beginning so as to attract interest quickly. Long sentences and too many facts were also to be avoided for fear of dryness in the talk. The speaker would also rehearse his talk, to learn where to pause, how to pace his speech, handle the papers and so on. Rehearsal also helps the speaker become familiar with the atmosphere of the studio and to help speakers 'lose that trace of nervousness'. It is in a course of lectures that a speaker may improve, particularly when he becomes aware of his audience after the second or third week. Such careful attention was being paid to talks because of their popularity and audience demand. In an insightful concluding remark, the article considers that as well as straight talks:

> Broadcast discussion and dialogue are also finding their place alongside the 'straight' talk, and may even in time to some extent supersede it. ... We are now only sharpening a blunt tool which the next generation may be expected to bring to a fine edge.[31]

Hilda Matheson, in charge of the Talks Department from 1927 until 1932, was a significant force behind the originality and breadth of the talks in these early years. At the time she took the post, talks were seen as an inferior form of entertainment, but Matheson's great interest in the potential of talks, her enthusiasm for talks and her willingness to experiment had a tremendous impact on the development of talks as a genre. She was concerned to reach the individual listener on a personal level, and to develop a tone that was intimate and conversational rather than that of a lecture.[32] Matheson also showed great discernment regarding authenticity and naturalness in broadcasting and was able to foresee the potential for personal rather than formal communication on the radio. She understood the paradox at the heart of broadcasting talks, where for a mass communication medium, talks of a specific interest worked best of all, 'the larger the audience, the less general in their appeal can programmes remain'.[33] She reflected on radio as a great force for good in the lives of women at home:

> It is difficult to exaggerate what broadcasting has done and is doing for women. The world at large stands to gain much from the wider outlook, greater interest, and more up-to-date practical knowledge which wireless has brought into their homes. ... The evidence from women, particularly of the poorer classes, as to what a wireless set may mean to them, is one of the most remarkable and encouraging results of broadcasting.[34]

Matheson saw women wanting to be better informed, but that their domestic duties held them back, and she felt that radio talks could help give advice and educate women in running their homes, but they could also respond to the:

> equally strong demand for talks outside the common round of household drudgery, on travel, on books on play producing, on current events, on how

people live in other countries, which may be given in simple terms at hours of the day when busy women can most easily afford a pause.[35]

In these ways, Matheson felt radio could help the housewife feel less disadvantaged.

Matheson has been credited with changing the mode of address at the radio microphone from a formal manner to a more intimate way of talking, as Hugh Chignell has argued, by developing a style of 'writing for the ear'. She also experimented with unscripted talks, a radical even potentially dangerous mode as it questions who has the right to speak,[36] and whether they would represent the views and outlook of the BBC.[37] Although it has been suggested that there was always 'more to radio talk than the straight talk' including 'the discussion, the debate and the magazine format',[38] these perhaps became more common as the BBC lifted its ban on controversial issues in 1928 and sought to appeal to a wider audience, not limited by solely middle-class tastes. As the single-subject talk was increasingly seen as dated, there was a move towards the magazine programme.[39]

Nigel Balchin in a 1953 article for *The BBC Quarterly* on 'The unscripted discussion' discusses the problems of conversations on air. He argued that broadcasting should 'make it possible for a large audience to hear conversation that is brilliant and entertaining, but which retains the spontaneity and intimacy which are only possible in a small group'. He accepted that organised public entertainment could not ever really be spontaneous, but that even an unscripted discussion would need to be rehearsed in some way, often by a preliminary talk to determine the shape of the talk to come, although this was often better than the eventual discussion. He suggests a compromise between freedom and order, by 'using a tape recorder, to record a truly unscripted and unrehearsed discussion, complete with all its hesitations, repetitions, irrelevances, and verbal and mental woolliness; and subsequently to cut and edit it so as to retain most of what is valuable and entertaining and remove most of what is not'.[40] Olive Shapley, working in the more flexible Manchester branch of the BBC, had already been 'making programmes in which recorded actuality was mixed, through the panel [Dramatic Control Panel], with studio presentation and commentary'. Making use of the mobile recording van, she travelled all over the Manchester region talking to ordinary people about their lives. The content and technique of her programmes are credited with breaking new ground.[41] It was clear from some of the poignant interviews with working-class people that not only was there room for this style of broadcast, and that it was popular, but that interesting material and voices did not need a high level of education or training in broadcasting. Shapley used the mobile unit, not for the women's magazine programme that she was supposed to be making, but for documentaries about human stories.[42] She wrote articles about the people she met for *Modern Woman*, a print magazine, thus extending her work into another media outlet. So, whilst she avoided making a magazine programme, Shapley was in fact pushing the boundaries of techniques and approaches which, later on, would benefit the women's magazine programme. Indeed, Olive Shapley took her skills to *Woman's Hour* under the control of Noman Collins after the Second World War; she was the programme's third presenter and was associated with *Woman's Hour* for over twenty years, where she frequently, amongst the articles on keeping house and childcare, interviewed women and broached new adventurous topics.[43]

There was increasing interest within the BBC about the nature of talks and how they appealed to various groups, according to the standard of education, intelligence and prior knowledge of the listener.[44] The Talks Department sought to develop appropriate modes of address for different kinds of talk, to find content and presentation methods that would enliven the delivery and reduce an authoritarian, class-based tone.[45] Hilda Matheson understood the power of radio to educate women in affairs beyond the domestic, and that in itself would provide impetus to a progressive feminism. This dissemination of important information to women via the medium of the radio has been noted in early German radio too. Kate Lacey has argued that women in Germany acted as 'mediatrix' in the 1920s for a number of important issues.[46] In Britain too, the large audience for programmes relevant to everyday life had been witnessed by the massive response to the *Household Talks*, but audiences needed programmes targeted at them to be broadcast at appropriate times. In magazine programmes of the 1930s, there was a degree of experimentation with types of discussion, subject matter and audiences, and also with types of chairmen for discussion programmes, to 'mediate between speakers'.[47]

Development of radio talk was taking place across a number of programmes at this time and a very early suggestion for what we might consider a prototype women's magazine programme came in 1935 for 'Domestic Talks in the Evening'. Although this was a similar expansion of domestic interests as in the *Morning Talks*, it was to be aimed distinctly at working men and women who could not listen in the mornings because of work commitments. The memo reveals a very keenly felt class and income issue, with expensive recipes and talks about 'decorations, furniture, etc.' to be omitted because they require 'a certain expenditure of money'. Of significance to the discussion here is the suggestion for a 'composite programme consisting of two or three talks', and this was suggested not just because it would allow an increase in breadth of subject and therefore interest a wider audience, but also because it would also allow from time to time, a discussion.[48]

Permission was requested to experiment further along these lines in the programme *Men Talking*:

> I have been discussing this series with Miss Quigley and we want to put up several tentative suggestions for its latter half. We think our experience has shown that on certain subjects the inclusion of unrehearsed discussions in the main evening programme would be useful, and we should now like to experiment a little further with a view to finding out what happens over a slightly different line of country and with rather more varied speakers.[49]

In the development of the radio magazine programme, these small shifts are significant. The memos from this early period of experiment and development make it possible to discern changes in broadcast style and programme presentation. In a detailed set of notes on *Men Talking*, there is careful description of the use of two studios to facilitate a 'fade in/fade out' technique over a conversation already in progress, to avoid 'heavy beginnings and pompous ends'. It was decided, through trial and error, that pre-discussion of topics was a failure and that what worked best was to have the speakers feel at ease with each other. These, along with comfy chairs causing problems with differing heights of speaker at the microphone, were some of the many minor issues under consideration in order to give the listener a sense of lively but relaxed conversation on air.[50]

A memo from Janet Quigley, about another programme, *Mostly for Women*, reveals a desire to bring in discussion on public questions such as the 'Women for Westminster' movement. What she wants to do is to give:

> women listeners on Sunday mornings something that at the time appears to be relaxation, i.e. they are interested and carried away by the speaker, but that afterwards leaves them something that is food for serious thought.[51]

This indicates the level of very careful attention paid to the needs of the woman listener, and even to her psychological make-up. Serious topics need to be presented engagingly, by skilful presenters, and even disguised as relaxation on a Sunday morning, and this technique of disguising broad political engagement as entertainment is a significant step in the thought processes behind the development of a broadcast magazine programme.

Women at War: Rapid response and shifting perceptions of the female listener

The Second World War accelerated the development of the radio magazine programme. Along with many other broad developments in science, medicine and food technology, the war had an impact on developments in radio, partly because needs changed and partly because of increased urgency. Certainly the national perception of women's roles shifted from early on in the war, both in the home and in the workplace. For some women the perceived changes became realities and certainly for all women, their relationship to home, family and society was changed by the onset of war. Women's radio magazine programmes had to learn how to respond to those changes.

Women at War was a weekly programme for women in the services, started on 6 October 1941 and broadcast at 8.15–9.00p.m. on the Forces Programme, intended for servicemen from January 1940 that soon became more popular than the Home Service. *Women at War* was targeted at a highly specific audience of uniformed servicewomen, and the very title of the programme was intended to stand for the three women's services in order of seniority: W.R.N.S., A.T.S. and W.A.A.F.[52]

Women at War was an innovative venture in both management and structure: intended as a collaborative effort from the outset between the Variety Department, the Talks Department and the Programme Planning Department. Archie Campbell of Variety was to be in charge and Janet Quigley of Talks was to coproduce. This collaboration permitted the programme's contents to be more varied than usual as the Variety Department already had contacts with bands, singers and stars from the Forces prepared to take a guest slot. Variety knew how to manage the process of guests and performers and in fact had already booked the band in advance of the programme. They were also able to handle the general knowledge competition.[53] In a similar vein, the Talks Department presumably were able to offer their experience of speakers and scripts, and a list of contacts, from the many and varied series of talks programmes over the years.

The programme's contents were to be varied with: a talk on appearance and self-respect called 'Beauty in Battledress'; another talk called 'Straight from the Shoulder' on personal problems of women in the services, perhaps to be based on letters received; a competition between opposing teams from the women's services comprising general knowledge questions and a musical crossword puzzle; a male guest star from stage or film and Carroll Gibbons and his band to play popular music and the signature tune 'Women at War'. Moreover, there was to be a live audience drawn from the three services, with double tickets given to servicewomen, and a two-minute opening speech each week by a principal officer from a service.[54]

Women at War might have seemed a promising initiative in its management across different departments, but the programme was troubled in a number of ways, not least of which was the sense that it was acting as a recruitment drive for the women's services.[55] Serious problems soon emerged with the format and presentation style, such as an overly determined audience definition which became an issue within months of its inception. The initials of *Women at War* may have stood for the three most established women's services, but these were not the only women doing service for their country in the Second World War. It is quite evident from the archives that the Land Army and the Nursing Services thought they should be included in the programme, but there was a determination at the BBC not to extend the programme 'to include all the various categories of women that might well consider themselves to be called "women at war".[56] This exclusiveness was far from the only reason that the programme ran into difficulties: the 'Beauty in the Battlefield' talk, for instance, was criticised for being dull and patronising, and so the format was changed from a talk by an expert, to a round-table discussion with the intention of covering a wider range of subjects. The name of this item was changed to 'Forces Forum' and books, hobbies, dancing partners and 'Service Slang' were proposed subjects (Figure 7.4).[57]

Women at War was the only women's magazine programme on air at the time and perhaps as such it attracted critique: an extensive internal feedback report four months after the programme started identifies some major problems. The report is highly critical and starts with a damning statement: 'The basic fault with this programme is that it has no women's features whatsoever.' It continues, '"Women at War" should justify its title and adopt a feminine character by having at least two essentially women features.' The report does not stint on its criticism of the compère, who, it was claimed, 'appeared to have

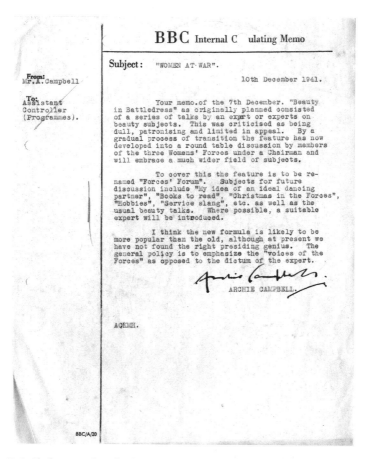

BBC Internal C ulating Memo

Subject : "WOMEN AT WAR".

From:
Mr. A. Campbell

10th December 1941.

To:
Assistant
Controller
(Programmes).

   Your memo of the 7th December. "Beauty
in Battledress" as originally planned consisted
of a series of talks by an expert or experts on
beauty subjects. This was criticised as being
dull, patronising and limited in appeal. By a
gradual process of transition the feature has now
developed into a round table discussion by members
of the three Womens' Forces under a Chairman and
will embrace a much wider field of subjects.

   To cover this the feature is to be renamed "Forces' Forum". Subjects for future
discussion include "My idea of an ideal dancing
partner", "Books to read", "Christmas in the Forces",
"Hobbies", "Service slang", etc. as well as the
usual beauty talks. Where possible, a suitable
expert will be introduced.

   I think the new formula is likely to be
more popular than the old, although at present we
have not found the right presiding genius. The
general policy is to emphasize the "voices of the
Forces" as opposed to the dictum of the expert.

ARCHIE CAMPBELL.

AC/MH.

BBC/A/20

Figure 7.4 Shifting modes of radio address to women: 'Women at War' BBC memo.
© *BBC Written Archives Centre.*

under-rehearsed' and was considered, 'not spontaneously funny, and unless he has a better script than this one, he would be wiser to play straight'. The layout was considered 'straggly', the production 'lacked pace and polish' and the game 'lacked suspense', moreover, there was considered to be a dearth of ideas, and 'Fresh ideas' were urgently needed. The advice given is that, 'A little thinking (and a glance through a few women's magazines) would produce dozens of good features.'[58] This deliberate linking of the magazine format across media genres reveals an intended closeness in subject matter, with one genre leaning heavily on another for content suggestions.

Criticism came from the listeners too and a series of points from a Petty Officer in the W.R.N.S. were fed back about the programme. This starts with an

utterly damning statement about the current programme being a positive insult to every woman's intelligence, but nonetheless the list goes on to make detailed and pertinent points. It is suggested that *Woman at War* 'should be compèred by a woman' to avoid a male compère patronising the listeners, and importantly this should be a woman who is currently serving in the forces. A further suggestion is that another woman who has seen active service should give a talk, indicating a need for a woman of authority and one whom this listening group would respect. It is clear that 'feeble and facetious jokes' are not wanted, and it was considered that 'lately some of the questions grossly underrate women's intelligence'.[59] The feedback from this listener, who was thought to be fairly representative, was that a tone of male silliness should be replaced with a more serious-minded woman. Not that the programme should not have its light-hearted moments or items, but that a wider range of women in uniform, as suggested, would relate better to a woman who understood the forces herself, this is also asserted in another memo from Norman Marshall in which it was his view that the programme should have 'a certain amount of "dignity" and "guts"'.[60]

In response, William MacLurg now in charge of this programme and having had success with *Ack-Ack, Beer-Beer*, a Forces programme of mixed items, points out some problems with *Women at War*: it is a programme 'directed to a minority at a majority time'; the audience definition is too narrow and that the remit is for a 'purely entertainment programme'. This identifies a number of mismatches between intended audience and actual audience and between title address and content instruction for *Women at War*.

MacLurg recognised the need to increase the scope of the programme to include all 'Women at War', and to make it 'a real specialised programme for women'. He knew that the tone would have to be changed and that it would need to be not dull and heavy, but would need to cover serious topics observing how women's lives have been changed by war, with a presentation that would 'have charm and be original, friendly and happy'. The presenter might also offer a maternal air of tolerance and genuine interest, and in this MacLurg understands that tone is important and aligns the potential appeal of a radio magazine to women's print magazines. He was impressed that print magazines have maintained both sales figures and influence during the wartime period:

> In times of peace, women's magazines had a strong influence selling as they did something like 10 million copies per week. Under conditions of war this sale has been maintained and their influence is probably even stronger now.

MacLurg acknowledges the sophistication of this radio magazine target audience as already 'a ready-made audience with a well-developed taste', and goes on to list some potential items for the show, acknowledging clear and direct links to aspects of women's regular print magazines. These include that adaptation to radio of print magazine contents such as stories that would become radio sketches; craft items could become hints from well-known dress designers; questionnaires that might be serious questions to show listeners 'that women really are thinking' and an adaptation of the 'appeal to the "mystic"' in women's magazines, usually astrology and palmistry, might be physiognomy, 'simple character reading from facial construction'. MacLurg was not afraid to suggest that the radio magazine take a lead from women's print magazines, he knew they had a winning formula and saw no problem in adapting their stock in trade, across media genres, from print to radio broadcasting material.

Just as importantly, MacLurg understood that the key to providing a successful radio magazine for women was in the editing and presentation:

> Women cannot be appealed to through the ways that work with men, they do not automatically react to war or calls to patriotism. They are much more interested in the smaller and in many ways the more important things of life. It is probably true that they are much less idealistic and at the same time much more practical than men.

He goes on to discuss in detail how the tone of the radio magazine must appeal to women:

> It is important to make the women feel that *they* are important. One must make them feel that those running and presenting the programme are friendly characters, with a genuine interest in them. It must build up confidence and interest so that the women have an automatic desire to listen to it, are entertained by it, and feel safe and happy taking any advice which, in the most oblique or disguised way, may be offered through it.[61]

Demonstrated here is a clear missive to put women at the centre of *Women at War* which until now had struggled to do just this, where although the initial items were potentially interesting to women, dullness of material and patronising, unfunny men had meant that women were simply not interested. MacLurg in identifying differences between male and female listeners still has a tendency to patronising comment, such as women needing to feel 'important' and 'safe and happy', but nonetheless is trying very hard to emulate the very successful formula offered by women's print magazines at this time. In his

memos he proposes a woman-centred environment, which will respond to women's acuity and discernment in what is important, and will talk of things of interest to women.

The new series of *Woman at War* did make some significant changes and was to be much more focused on the individual stories of women working for the services or in factories.[62] It was broadcast on Mondays at 8.15p.m. starting on 20 April 1942 and in a release for the press, MacLurg outlined the items for the first programme. They included an account of the work of the Land Army; a 'True Stories Page' of a girl now doing war work; introductions between women munitions war workers and men of the forces using those munitions and a problem section with Hilde Marchant of the *Daily Mirror*, all adding up to a much more inclusive programme than before. MacLurg's ideas of widening the prospective audience and dealing in an amenable way with serious war issues for women are evident in this newly fashioned line-up.

Once the new format was established, Janet Quigley asked to be released as one of the formal editors from the programme as she did not see the need for a Talks Producer and was busy developing her own programmes.[63] In his reply, thanking Miss Quigley for all her help, MacLurg speculates as to whether the programme will come back in the Autumn, but should it not, he remarks: 'I can't say I shall drop any tears over this!'[64] The development and evolution of *Women at War* had been a troublesome journey, but an important one in the history of the radio magazine.

It seemed that this wartime programme intensified the problems of the development of the radio magazine. A number of difficulties with this programme had been experienced and addressed: there were problems in trying to define the audience too closely, despite the reality that the Forces Programme, with its lighter feel, was extremely popular with general audiences too; there were difficulties over how to address women and what tone to adopt to avoid being patronising, a particular problem emerged with silly-sounding male presenters; there was an acknowledged need to avoid insulting the intelligence of both the woman listener and the women who participated in the programme and there were also serious reconsiderations over content and subjects that actually engaged and interested women listeners. External influences and interested parties had to be dealt with and managed, as did the internal workings and free-flowing criticism from within the BBC; little wonder Bill MacLurg felt he would shed no tears, but these are the problems of experimentation and development. Once the straight scripted talk or the tightly controlled discussion was left behind, and different departments collaborated, and unpredictable entertainers were used to compère, things could go wrong, and it was easy to criticise a less than perfect broadcast. But looking back, it is the imaginative efforts and experimentation of producers such as Matheson, Shapley, Quigley and MacLurg that were the building blocks towards the radio magazine programme for women we now see in the current *Woman's Hour*. These producers have to be admired for their determination to improve their craft.

Woman's Page: Identifying and understanding the woman listener

One of the programmes Janet Quigley was developing at around this time was *Woman's Page* which was broadcast on Fridays at 6.30p.m. from 1 December 1943. In a request for publicity, Quigley describes *Woman's Page* as 'a programme of short talks on a variety of subjects addressed primarily, but not exclusively to women listeners'. The subjects of those talks have been extended to include 'women and politics, in which current questions will be discussed with particular reference to their significance for women both in the home and outside it'. As Siân Nicholas has suggested, the programme avoided domestic topics and it was aimed 'neither at the career woman nor the housewife, but sought to inform and broaden the outlook of each in a way that would also interest the other'.[65] This shows a deeper identification with the women listener than before, it anticipates a later understanding of the multi-faceted aspects of many women's lives. The range of speakers was also an expansive one, with some names familiar from women's magazine journalism, but also to include 'women members of Parliament and others prominent in public life'.[66]

To this extent the programme sounds as though it might be a progression from *Women at War*, with a wider political remit and a broader pool of contributors, though otherwise with many similarities. However, in some notes prepared by Janet Quigley, radical differences in target audiences may be discerned. For instance, the new *Woman's Page* was,

aimed at reaching women who have few opportunities and little inclination to interest themselves in public questions or to realise that what they dismiss as politics affects their personal lives. [...] Unfortunately this is not an audience which readily listens to talks so in trying to attract it very careful though has been given to finding speakers who will sound sympathetic and friendly and will in no way alarm them.[67]

These notes have a sense of encouraging a new, hard-to-reach audience, normally inured against political discussions, to become interested or even participate in subject areas beyond their usual range. This has an air of improvement about it, but also a desire to bring the world outside the home to women whose interests have been, for whatever reason, mostly limited to the domestic.

Facilitating a personal touch of listener familiarity with a few friendly speakers was seen as a necessary gateway to tackling subjects that otherwise this listener group might avoid. The idea of a sympathetic speaker referred to a range of qualities, it could refer to accent and the timbre of the voice, the personality-driven mode of delivery and of course the subject matter. To this end, one feature of *Woman's Page* was to be 'Mary Fergusson's answers to problems from women war workers.' In a rare surviving radio recording there is a sample of Mary Fergusson's 'Women's Wartime Problems' section from *Woman's Page*, dealing with three specific wartime problems. The recording opens with a clearly spoken female voice with a pronounced Scottish accent, and with little preamble, Fergusson goes straight into her talk, 'Good evening. People who live on their own have special problems in wartime ... '. Fergusson then summarises the letters she has received into a question, giving the name of the letter writer, and proceeds to give authoritative and well-researched responses. The first letter presents the problem of a listener wanting to have her milk delivered in half-pint bottles; the second is an issue over whether looking after two Land Girls constitutes war work and the third question is asked on behalf of a listener's sister, due to immigrate from Jamaica, and querying whether she will be able to take a course in nursery nursing or whether she will have to undertake war work. The responses, especially to the first query about half pints of milk, are exceptionally thorough. The first answer, delivered in a very serious tone, includes ways of dealing with the milk girl, reminders to all housewives to return the half-pint milk bottles, now in short supply, and reference to the Ministry of Food's directive that single people need to have their milk in half-pint measures. This reference to the relevant Ministry continues into the responses to questions two and three, where remarkably definite responses of yes to the lady looking after Land Girls, and no to the woman seeking to do a course rather than war work are given. Little emotion and little opinion are offered in these fulsome responses. However, at the very end of the recording, there is an appeal to the young woman who wrote in anonymously, Fergusson asks for her name and address so she can help this misplaced person, indicating a problem-solving role that continued beyond the official broadcast and in letter form.[68]

Woman's Page also developed ideas from the *Mostly for Women* series (1942–1943), by now at an end, using some of its already-familiar speakers and their subjects. Quigley had paid close attention to feedback on this earlier programme and in a memo to her Director of Talks, she saw *Mostly for Women* as a 'kind of forum' as:

> considerable evidence has come in both by letter and verbally since this series started to suggest that discussions on public questions affecting women would be more welcome than anything else.[69]

Speakers for *Woman's Page* had to have a sympathetic approach to people perhaps borne out of their own life experiences, such as Minnie Pallister, a member of the socialist movement,[70] whose career as a promising young political speaker was cut short through ill health. However, those with a cold, intellectual approach or hard, grating voice such as Mary Stocks (writer, educationalist and suffragist) were less suitable, no matter how brilliant. Although Quigley speculated that if the series 'gets a steady and faithful audience, we can be bolder and occasionally risk an unsympathetic speaker if the subject matter is interesting enough'.[71]

Later memos reveal a class distinction in this audience, claiming that the programme is 'addressed to the large audience of factory workers and others who have had to leave home to live in Government hostels and lodgings'.[72] *Woman's Page* was seen as a 'new venture', and there was a sense of 'trying to do the right thing by this audience', with development and ongoing modifications of the programme.[73] Later that year, Janet Quigley was able to report that the 'Listener figures are fairly good for such a new programme', with success demonstrated through listener percentage, with the most recent at eleven and a half per cent, despite broadcasting at what was considered 'an impossible hour for women to listen'.[74] There was a keenness to prove both the success and the promise of the programme, but achieving high ratings took discernment and good judgement and Quigley had to pick her way through topics offered, as not all were suitable or original, and some, she considered would work better with a different format. For instance, she asked for an additional ten minutes to broadcast a feature on the Women's Voluntary Service, saying that 'the prejudice against them has faded considerably' and that to do a feature rather than a talk was more interesting and also 'an opportunity of exhibiting flexibility between Depàrtments' within the BBC.[75] However, she was less keen on an item about the 'Churchill House' because it had already received a fair amount of publicity.[76]

Woman's Page was enough of a success to warrant an extension of time. With one fixed item already and a new series of regular talks, the time slot of twenty minutes was seen as too short. Notably, a longer time would also permit an occasional discussion where the programme had 'several speakers expressing their views on one subject' such as Equal Pay, the Education Bill and married women's nationality. These topics, important to women and serious in content, were to take their place alongside talks on personal relations, book and film talks, advice on hygiene and looks and some domestic talks, as well as items anticipating the end of the war, such as careers for women on demobilisation.[77] The request for time was opposed by the Director of Talks because he did not feel that 'we yet know how to support 30 minutes of spoken word divided into snippets', he was concerned about the 'dreadful block' of talk this would create alongside a thirty minute news programme.[78] The assistant director C.V. Salmon was, however, more convinced by the programme's past success but also impressed by something intrinsically to do with the programme format itself: 'it does not try to introduce an artificial fusion of subject by links, but is content to put out each item as something which can stand on its own legs'.[79] This suggests a quality and integrity within each item, each of interest and worthy of its own air time and not just as supporting items for other aspects of the programme. The return of the new *Woman's Page* was announced in the *Radio Times* on the front page letting listeners know it was a longer programme of twenty-five minutes.[80]

Publicity memos indicate the range of items to start off the new series in September 1944, to include: an Indian woman doctor, talking about female doctors in India; an item on new houses; Minnie Pallister talking about a biography of Agnes Hunt (nurse and hospital founder) and Marian Cutler talking to the wives of service men.[81] Letters from listeners to the programme were a good indication of the popularity of the programme, and Quigley had paid close attention to subject matter as well as presentation style. Her intention had been to concern the programme with mostly non-domestic subjects because the domestic topics had been covered in other programmes like *Kitchen Front*, but now that *Woman's Page* was established, talks about 'food or housekeeping or care of children' could be included. Subject matter had also been dictated by the war, and there was a time when 'the war was too serious to make it likely or desirable that listeners would be interested in talks about "clothes and looks"', but now they could be reintroduced as monthly talks.[82] Programmes, as well as leading women to new interests, had to reflect shifts in women's concerns: and the prospect of the end of the war led to an optimism about availability of goods and fashions, so that as well as offering guidance, magazine programmes had to demonstrate their cultural competence by following trends too.

As Quigley became more experienced, she could discriminate between what worked on this women's magazine programme and what went down badly with the listeners. For instance, there had been a problem over a controversial talk by Jeanne Cooper-Foster on 'Women on the Land in Ulster' which had offended some women, consequently it was suggested that the programme put forward the 'opposing' point of view in a later talk. Potentially contentious issues, later on, were dealt with in a group format crucially enabling different points of view to be put forward at the same time, and therefore appearing to carry the same weight. Different groups of listeners with different opinions would then feel that their views had been catered for and appropriately presented.[83] As well as offering balance in issues comprising opposing opinion, Quigley also had to show discernment and discretion: a suggestion to feature a village pie scheme in the Spring of 1945, where women of Langstone and Penhow Women's Institute baked pies for sale to hungry workers of their villages, had to be rejected because so many villages, perhaps as many as 5,000, had done this, and it would be wrong to single out just one.[84] Material about Burma was rejected because it was potentially contentious. Also rejected was the formally written farewell from the council of Czechoslovakian women war workers, on the grounds that listeners to the programme 'expect and like a much more intimate approach and would always prefer to hear an individual Czechoslovakian woman speaking from her own experiences than to hear a formal message of this kind'.[85] In this rather tough rejection, the interesting point is made about the listener that, no matter however many are listening overall, the programme is actually received by a lone listener, or perhaps two people, and so radio broadcast needs a personal mode of address. Even as she left the programme, Quigley was keen to ensure the quality of the talks remained high. In anticipation of the new producer, she returned all substandard scripts and left only a few scripts and suggestions for her successor to consider.[86] Little surprise that Quigley who had been instrumental in many developments of the magazine programme for women went on to edit *Woman's Hour* and to be an early editor of the *Today* programme.

***

Radio magazine programmes did not spring to life as an already-established format, as a sound medium there were particular ideas and politics about how material should be delivered as well as about the actual material itself. The upper-class agenda and voice of many presenters who gave talks in the style of lectures on the very early *Women's* and *Men's Hour* of the 1920s gave way to a more mixed and less formal way of speaking and this offered a more intimate approach to the listener. However, getting to this point had been a struggle and various aspects of radio broadcasting for women were only learnt through experimentation, reflection and feedback. Some early talks had already needed the support of written backup information, and some of these talks were reproduced for their informative value. Closer links with print magazines for women are revealed in their adaptation to radio content and an understanding of the print magazine assisted in the development of the radio form. Sharp feedback was given at times, particularly about women's tolerance of male condescension, but huge lessons were learnt by responsive producers who were open to criticism and so improved their offerings, and format and content expanded as the woman listener became better understood. Lessons were learnt about how to speak to women and how to engage their interest; inclusiveness was key, for instance how to appeal to all classes and how to include amateur listener-speakers. At the outset of *Woman's Hour* in 1946, there were still lessons to be learnt: with its male presenter, it had a shaky start. It was a magazine programme, building on previous experience and experiment, but still in development. However, one of the major developments in radio magazine broadcasting for women had been a shift from an obsession about fitting radio into her domestic schedule, to a broader consideration of how to approach women's minds, sometimes as part of a reforming rhetoric and sometimes as a way to engage her interest and listening loyalty. Magazine radio for women moved in its consideration of its audience, from what she was doing, to what she was thinking.

Magazines Working for the Feminist Cause

The historical relationship of women to the media, including magazines, has been seen as problematic at the very least. James Curran, for example, has argued that the 'dissemination and acceptance' of a gendered division of spheres, with women at home and men in the 'external world' has been 'greatly assisted by the rise of women's media'.[1] However, this account of media history has been criticised for, amongst other things, seeing media as nothing but oppressive towards women. Maria DiCenzo has suggested that Curran's approach pays no heed to women's politicised media: 'The disproportionate emphasis on the adherence to two-sphere ideology and the oppressive nature and effects of media on women, renders women's politicized media – which have a long and consistent history – invisible.'[2] This last chapter, rather than focusing on an individual magazine, draws attention to a number of feminist magazines, across forms of media production, and reflects upon how magazines have remained a very popular vehicle of political expression. Despite differences in form, magazines have, in important ways, been consistently used by feminists as expressions of, and in working towards, different feminist causes.

Political involvement and the desire to improve the lot of women in a patriarchal society have been the guiding principle behind many of the feminist magazines produced in Britain from the nineteenth to the early twenty-first century. Feminism as a movement has branched out, fought itself and had some success. Through all this, the magazine format, in its broadest definition, has been a dependable and regular tool in feminism's political development. The political movement of feminism is not of course limited to its magazines. Women have striven towards feminist goals of equality in public and political spheres, in the workplace, in trade unions and in educational and counter-cultural environments; there has been feminist protest in public places and domestic spaces, individually and collectively; feminism has been expressed in the writing of feminist novels, journalism, testimonials and memoirs; as well as in music, art and film. The magazine, however, has been a persistently present form, addressing and commenting upon all manner of inequalities and feminist activities. No single feminist magazine can represent the sum of any one feminist movement, cause or wave of feminism of the last century. However, a feminist magazine can engage and sustain the major debates of the moment and can report on women's resistance and activism. In expressing opinion, attitude, anger and humour, it can give a voice to the views and ideas of its contributors and its members. A single magazine can be a kaleidoscopic representation of feminism, with different elements appearing, merging, overlapping and contradicting, in relationship to the other activities of the movement beyond the magazine. Nonetheless, a representation it remains.

Feminist magazines have played their part in developing the movement too, and movement media have been seen as crucial in communicating with like-minded people and in developing networks beyond an immediate group: Sidney Tarrow has suggested that whilst 'primary associations and face-to-face contacts provided solidarity among people who knew and trusted each other', what movements needed to be successful was, amongst other things, 'the experience of reading the same journals' in order to build necessarily expansive or weak ties across strong movements.[3] Discussing an earlier period, Tarrow considers that subscribing to a journal, 'linked readers to an invisible network with unknown others with similar views in communities whose amplitude could only be imagined and could easily be exaggerated'.[4] This sense of belonging to, and building a network of unknown women through a journal or magazine is, I believe, part of the impetus to produce and engage with feminist magazines; the participation is crucial, as is the dissemination of information through the movement; it builds confidence and involvement allowing women to name themselves, and to advance the cause.

However, while the relationship between the feminist movement and its magazines is complex and varying, still the movement has relied upon magazines to communicate guiding principles and political objectives to a wide audience. Magazines have identified issues of gender inequality in society through articles and reports, drawing attention to national and local problems by setting them down in writing. They have articulated potential solutions by making written demands and claims, and campaigned towards those goals through calls for activism, meetings and rallies. At the same time, through letters and testimonials, feminist magazines have given members a personal forum for airing individual opinion and experience. In acting for both individuals and the broader movement, feminist magazines must at times serve conflicting, even oppositional functions: both pedagogic and evangelistic. Whilst educating members regarding the movement's rationale, objectives and campaigns, in ways sufficiently engaging to keep the reader following the periodical, a feminist magazine must also spread the word and attract new membership. This has proved a demanding and challenging task for editors: on the one hand offering a forum for debate, even dissent, whilst on the other, trying to produce a publication that functions to make the movement unified, and, in addition, working towards both national and individual aims. Such a magazine must try to operate on a number of different levels. Yet despite the shifting of feminist aims and all these potential problems of mixed content and varied audience, the expression of feminism through magazines has persisted.

The format of the magazine lends itself to women's political engagement in accommodating the expression of diverse opinion and disparate voices. The production of the artefact of the magazine itself, no matter how home-made and humble, announces a group's formation. Making a statement of its shared intentions and, through the setting down in print of its views, lends the group authority. Magazines allow feminists to enter the discourse. Discourse, discussion and disagreement have been the roots of much progress in Western feminism, and the magazine format has enabled the expression of diverse argument, vital to the progression of movement, to be expressed, solidified and understood. Indeed, as discussed below, although this process has taken its toll on editors and publications, the magazine or *magazin* has proved the perfect storehouse for these important, and necessary, conflicts.

Feminist magazines are different to other magazines for women, be they minority interest or commercial glossy publications, in appearance, content and communication strategies. Janice Winship has argued that:

> To compare *Spare Rib* with commercial magazines is like evaluating the appeal of a spartan wholefood diet by reference to the rich diet of junk food. It is found, inevitably, to be lacking: no layers of sugary icing between the editorial cake and no thick milk chocolate as palliative to the 'hard nuts'.[5]

Feminist magazines are often visibly different: less advertising and commercial backing lead to a more spartan appearance; their observations of and commentary upon patriarchy and sex discrimination give them the focus of a protest periodical and, most importantly for this discussion, they have a self-consciousness about their status in representing the feminist cause. This emerges in a number of ways. Working for a feminist magazine is a politically committed activity, a political statement in itself, but often also one informed by a history of feminism and often by other feminist magazines too. Furthermore, because feminist magazines deal in current news of the movement as well as contemporary cultural representations of women, they are always in some way more connected than commercial women's magazines to mainstream news processes. This self-consciousness is the focus of the following discussion: firstly, there is the acknowledgement of an act of political engagement within the very production and distribution of the magazine as artefact; secondly, there is the linking with other mechanisms and outputs of the print media industry and thirdly, there is an awareness of and involvement in the dialogics and historicity of feminism.

The following discussion, therefore, does not offer a chronology or history of feminist magazines. That is a history still waiting to be written. Rather this chapter considers how the magazine has worked for the feminist cause in three ways: firstly the opportunity to act politically that magazines have always offered feminists; secondly how feminist magazines have maintained various links with other print and written media forms and thirdly how feminist magazines convey the sense of history of the movement. I suggest that as part of a print media succession, feminist magazines have long expressed an awareness of their place within the continuum of the development of feminist consciousness. Although a number of feminist magazines from their earliest publication (though very far from all) are mentioned in this chapter, my four key examples come from the different moments or 'waves' of feminist history from the early twentieth century: *Votes for Women* (1907–1918), a periodical in newspaper style; *Spare Rib* (1972–1993) perhaps Britain's best known feminist magazine; *the F-Word* (2001–ongoing) and the *Feminist Times* (2013–2014), both online feminist magazines. Evidently, different media forms are adopted, and each magazine speaks to its feminist era and represents specific feminist priorities, but each magazine, in its different way, can be seen to respond to a need for feminist political action in the very business of production, retain some relationship with print culture presses and convey a sense of history of the movement and its publications, all as part of its political engagement. In essence, I am raising the question of what makes a feminist magazine.

Publishing as a political act

Feminist magazines operate at the chalkface of the movement, as malleable vehicles for feminist political expression, whatever the particular politics of the movement at any given time. The implications of this, and there are often numerous magazines riven by conflicts within the movement, are that the very act of creating the magazine, writing copy, editing, funding the production demonstrates political commitment just as much as other forms of activism. Simone Murray has argued, when discussing British feminist presses that:

> While varying enormously in their political priorities [...] all of these imprints were united in their perception that the act of publishing is, because of its role in determining the parameters of public debate, an inherently political act and that women, recognising this fact, must intervene in the processes of literary production to ensure that women's voices are made audible.[6]

In a similar way to the later feminist presses, the publication of early feminist papers and magazines also demonstrated a desire to have an impact upon the public debate, to enter the discourse. The *Nonsense of Commonsense* (1737–1738), a short-lived weekly political essay paper launched by Lady Mary Wortley Montagu, denounces the excesses of wealthy society and champions education for women, influenced by the pioneer feminist, Mary Astell.[7] The first explicitly feminist magazine mentioned in Doughan and Sanchez' annotated bibliography of feminist periodicals is *The Waverley Journal* (1856–1858), with the subtitle '*the cultivation of the honourable, the progressive, and the beautiful*', and the contents include 'Social reform, including much of feminist interest'.[8] Another early magazine, *The English Woman's Journal* (1858–1864), provided essays on early feminist theory and issues, and is described as 'The theoretical and practical source of organised feminism'.[9] The debate on social inequality was a general political theme, but also prominent was the desire to educate women regarding politics and society and periodicals. *The English Woman's Journal* and its successor *The Englishwoman's Review* (1866–1910), for example, proposed feminist reforms in society before the women's suffrage movement. The working woman's journal, *The Woman Worker* (1907–1921), was affiliated to the all-female trade union,[10] and there were also journals for women entering the world of work, such as *Women and Work* (1874–1876), and for those joining established and developing professions, such as *Nursing Times* (1905–ongoing). The *Woman's Penny Paper* (1888–1890) was vigorously feminist in its outlook, interviewed prominent feminists and reported on a variety of women's organisations,[11] and the working-class *Shafts* (1892–1900) sought to open up the array of new and sometimes complex writings on social and political issues and bring them to the attention of a broader group of women readers, including the middle classes. Combining ideas of social progression with some higher creative powers, '*Shafts* functions as a medium for enlightenment, then, in a dual sense: as an agent both of intellectual emancipation and of spiritual elevation.'[12] By publishing and entering into public debates, all these early feminist periodicals are able to emphasise the importance of education as a means of political empowerment for women. The very production of the magazine is testament to a commitment to the participation of women in society and in the world of print media, as well as the magazine offering itself as a place of mediation in that process.

The political significance of the feminist periodical was reinforced by its extensive use in the years of the suffrage campaign. The suffrage movement with its splinter subdivisions, differing factions, diverse interests and oppositional groups was far from a coherent enterprise. However, one thing many of the suffrage and feminist groups did have in common was the use of a periodical paper to represent their particular approach to suffrage and feminist politics, as well as to campaign for the cause of women's enfranchisement, and bring other social and political issues for women to the fore.

The periodical *Freewoman* (1911–1912) (later *New Freewoman*, then *The Egoist*) rejected the single-minded concentration on the vote and broadened its concerns to explore other personal and social aspects of emancipation.[13] Other journals highlighted social issues, such as Sylvia Pankhurst's *The Woman's Dreadnought* (1914–1924), the periodical of the East London Federation of Suffragettes, which was concerned with socialism and the living conditions of the poor. Moving into a different kind of political engagement at the outset of war, *Dreadnought* expressed pacifist views in opposition to the paper of Pankhurst's mother Emmeline and sister Christabel. *The Common Cause* (1909–1920) was particularly concerned with the wider issues of reform for women and less supportive of violence in the cause of women's suffrage, while the *Anti-Suffrage Review* (1908–1918), as part of the Women's National Anti-Suffrage League, opposed giving the vote to women at all.[14] The flexibility of the feminist magazine met the needs of all these differing factions, with their varying views and opinions (including dissenters), and was even able to accommodate a complete *volte-face* when the editors' political views changed completely. At the onset of the First World War, when Emmeline and Christabel Pankhurst, of the most ardently militant group, took a 'fervently patriotic stance', they renamed their official WSPU organ *The Suffragette* (1912–1915), as *Britannia* (1915–1918) in order to support the war effort.[15] In sum, the suffrage journals were connected not only through their common feminism but also through their engagement in arguments about how to achieve the vote and, more generally, how to pursue feminist goals. The complex and competing relations between different suffragette organisations, their leadership dynamics and their official organs have a fascinating history,[16] but for the present discussion there are two distinct modes of political commitment to be observed in the processes of the best known suffrage journal: the level of dedication to producing *Votes for Women* demonstrated by its editors, and the methods of distribution of the paper by the suffragettes themselves.

Votes for Women (1907–1918) was the longest lasting suffragette periodical and was initially the organ of the Women's Social and Political Union (WSPU), the militant suffrage organisation. It was started and funded by Emmeline and Frederick Pethick-Lawrence and at its height achieved a circulation of 40,000–50,000 a week, with secondary reading by many more.[17] Its style was forceful and journalistic and of all the suffrage periodicals it was perhaps the most single minded in its pursuit of the vote, reporting on WSPU leadership and militant activities. Even so, it still included articles on more general issues such as politics, work, legal commentary, reviews and short stories. The opening editorial section, 'The Outlook', explains that the paper is 'wanted' in order to fulfil, 'the growing desire for knowledge on the part of the outside public to learn what it is that women are really striving for and how far the agitation is progressing'.[18]

Firstly, the editorship of *Votes for Women* stands as an example of uncompromising dedication to the feminist print media cause in that the level of the Pethick-Lawrence's political commitment to reporting on the movement was such that despite being arrested for conspiracy, and calling upon Evelyn Sharp to edit the paper at very short notice, they continued their work fully believing in the power of their paper to influence public opinion.[19] Furthermore, even when they were abandoned by the WSPU, which created its own paper, *Suffragette*, they still continued to fund and produce the paper, keeping their message going, eventually handing it over in 1914 to the United Suffragists, a mixed-sex society and another organisation of the suffragette movement.[20]

Secondly, association with the paper through its distribution was seen as a political act in itself: *Votes for Women* was advertised and sold by members of the suffragette organisation on the streets in London and also distributed by members on their holidays and in train station waiting rooms.[21] Street selling of the suffragette periodicals by the suffragettes themselves involved wearing a sandwich board, enduring a fair amount of public heckling and verbal abuse and standing in the gutter to avoid charges of obstruction; all were considered necessary for the cause. Performing this task of distribution, often revealed in private diaries as onerous and demoralising, was understood to be a feminist act in itself.[22] (It was also largely responsible for the impressive sales figures of *Votes for Women*.) The political commitment of the suffragettes, in enduring imprisonment and force-feeding, is undeniable, but commitment to the cause of enfranchisement is also evident in the Pethick-Lawrence's story and the supporter's work in the buying, reading and distribution of *Votes for Women*.

As feminism shifted its focus from suffrage and social rights to issues of individual sexuality, family life, social status and the workplace, a new kind of counter-cultural feminism emerged in the Women's Liberation Movement (WLM),[23] on both a national and a local scale. National conferences heralded the new movement, as well as local groups of women who gathered to address neighbourhood issues or engage in feminist consciousness-raising. As Sheila Rowbotham remembers:

> Three permanent groups started, one in Essex and two in London, including the Tufnell Park Group. The first newsletter came out in May. The next was called *Harpies Bizarre* and reported response from leafletting [sic] the equal pay demonstration, and the formation of a group in Peckham. [...]
>
> The third newsletter was called *Shrew* and the name stuck, with the principle established that the editing should pass from group to group. This issue reflected the disparate influences which went into the London Workshop. It included accounts of meetings with older feminists and a vehement denunciation of the Maoists in the Revolutionary Socialist Students Federation. [...]
>
> When the Tufnell Park group produced *Shrew* in October 69 they raised questions which have continued to be discussed by many other groups since. They presented them in conversational form. They hinged on the old problem of how explicit the aims of any organisation should be.[24]

Along with feminism's re-emergence as a political force came a range of newsletters, magazines, pamphlets and women's newspapers, each supporting their group members through a central source of information and sense of connection, as well as hoping to attract new members. This new era brought a range of publication possibilities and a marked change in the type of magazine produced by feminists. Magazines were often created collectively in domestic environments and appeared as small, localised newsletters, typified by low-key, low-cost, home-produced, photocopied material, sometimes stapled together and often comprising handwritten work with line illustrations and collages alongside typed articles. These publications exude a sense that contributions were welcome from all comers, combined with an appearance of non-professional or small press production, both important ways in which such newsletters and magazines conveyed their democratic and inclusive impulse.

One of the earliest magazines to reflect this emergent grassroots feminism was *Shrew* (1968–1978), which was written and compiled by different women's consciousness-raising groups across London. Others like *Red Rag* (1972–1980) were more radical politically or, as with *Bread and Roses* (1975–1977), focused on a contentious theme each issue. Numerous other newsletters and newspaper-style publications supporting women's groups in major cities and regions had more localised style and focus, such as *Move* (1974–1980), the Bristol gay women's group newsletter, and *Country Woman* (1974–1981) for feminists in rural areas around Britain.[25] Whilst some magazines were home-made, others were printed by a number of successful feminist publishing houses in Britain, many of which emerged in the 1970s.[26]

Spare Rib (1972–1993) was the best known and most widely distributed magazine of the WLM in Britain. Started by Marsha Rowe and Rosie Boycott, both of whom had been involved with the journalism of the counter-cultural movements of the 1960s, it became, as Winship says, 'a key national institution where the terms of the women's movement are set out'.[27] It was direct, questioning and illuminating, bringing a whole range of issues of women's inequality to the fore and offering a critically feminist perspective to its readers. It highlighted direct action, offered commentaries on sexism and the sexist portrayal of women, such as in advertising,[28] and engaged with female culture, such as the women's section of the Edinburgh festival.[29] *Spare Rib* set itself apart from mainstream women's magazines in its consistent and thorough promotion of the feminist cause, and especially in the humour and irony that it directed at patriarchy and norms of femininity. However, unlike many of its predecessors, this was a feminist magazine that adhered to a more conventional, commercial magazine format and content, especially early on, with beauty, cookery and craft features, albeit with an ironic twist.[30] In its exposure of inequalities, *Spare Rib* may have been more strident, more thorough and more wide-ranging, but it also, on occasion, trod the same ground as some more conventional magazines, such as *Cosmopolitan* and *Woman's Own*, which were themselves, after all, not entirely blind to feminist debates and social taboos on women's sexuality, women's health and women and children's welfare.[31]

Rowe and Boycott made their address to feminism in a number of ways. In their first editorial, they emphasised their commitment not only to spreading the word, but to welcoming contributions from their readers:

> It was startling to realise that we could not buy any publication which discussed what we felt to be vital issues and so Spare RIB is a Beginning. We have tried to create a magazine that is fluid enough to publish work by contributors who have not written before as well as by women and men who are successful journalists and writers.
>
> We are waiting with bated breath for your reactions.[32]

From the outset, then, contributions beyond readers' letters were anticipated from women who were not professional journalists and writers. *Spare Rib* also reported the activism of women and women's groups and how it was making a difference to their lives and the lives of their fellow women. The very first issue of *Spare Rib* carried an article with the title, 'The First Cow on Chiswick High Road'.[33] The punning humour of the title, potentially referencing feminists behaving badly, and then the realisation that a real dairy cow did lead an actual protest about the loss of school milk, organised by the Chiswick women's liberation group, reflects the tone of *Spare Rib*. The eye-catching title leads the reader into a serious article about the welfare needs of women in the local area and the setting up of a community house through the efforts of the Chiswick women's aid group to offer a refuge and support to destitute and battered women.[34] Political involvement in this complex movement might take various forms, its contributors might be diverse and its modes of communication multi-layered, but it was possible to demonstrate political commitment and be involved with *Spare Rib* in a number of ways. The magazine sought to combine the work of its editorial team, with other writings about feminism, to include reports of feminist activism and direct action, as well as describing personal life histories and experiences by women new to feminism.

The splintering in understanding of the feminist project decisively changed, and the realisation of the exclusion of groups of women brought difficulties for the editorial team. *Spare Rib* struggled to withstand that shift.

The closeness of the commitment to feminism between editors, writers and readers was made clear in the statement of 1983 over race and racism. By this time, the editorial team had become a committee and the policy of the magazine now embraced a wider politics across class, race and sexualities as well as other oppressed groups. Winship discusses the stormy arguments at the heart of *Spare Rib*.[35] In these tensions over prejudices around race and sexuality, the politics of the committee represented the politics of the women's movement. The arguments within *Spare Rib* were echoes of the accusations towards second-wave feminism in general of being concerned primarily with white, middle-class women and having those editorial arguments, and risking the readership of the magazine by making them public, demonstrated the extent to which involvement in the magazine was a political act.

There were important shifts in feminism in the late 1980s and 1990s, to what is variously called postfeminism, indicating a deliberate break with second-wave feminism, or more helpfully, third-wave feminism, a movement known to accommodate ambiguity and multiple identity. Shelley Budgeon explains the motivations of third-wave feminism thus:

> The aim is not to develop a feminism which makes representational claims on behalf of women but to advance a politics based upon *self-definition* and the need for women to define their personal relationship to feminism in ways that make sense to them as individuals. This is evident for instance in the D.I.Y. ethic of Riot Grrrl which promotes self-empowerment and independence as the motivating force behind its pursuit of a politics that will allow women to develop an understanding of the personal realm focusing 'more on the individual and the emotional than on marches, legislation, and public policy'.[36]

Even though there were, by this time, fewer nationally distributed feminist magazines in Britain than in the United States, the concept of the feminist magazine in Britain did not disappear from view; rather, it was adapted to a different form. The political impetus of feminism had altered radically from collective to individual engagement with society, but the form of the magazine remained pertinent to the cause. The Riot Grrrl movement from the United States emerged out of disaffection from the sexist punk rock music scene, including the 'mosh pit',[37] and the essence, values and rhetoric of punk were appropriated into a new feminism, distinctive from what was regarded as outdated 1970s feminism.[38] It was embraced by young women, often in their early teens who sought to create new social systems that empowered women, rather than being a part of the disempowering patriarchal systems already in existence. Alongside music bands, zines and comic books were a very strong creative feature of this movement, and used politically to communicate this new mode of feminism. Shelley Budgeon has suggested that Riot Grrrl culture was a template for third-wave feminism in a number of ways: firstly, women became active and independent producers of music and print media; secondly, women were able to seek identity through self-expression; and thirdly, the nature of this home-made democratic participation enabled resistance to formalised organising structures.[39]

Many Riot Grrrl activists produced small-sized, non-commercial 'zines' – a term derived from the fanzine – to express their views. Written in individually expressive styles, and often stridently feminist in tone, zines offer personal and unconventional outpourings of views and anger at sexism and patriarchal dominance of the music industry and the world. They are often handwritten, with doodles, drawings, photos and collages, and are creative assemblages, celebrating a single feminist voice. Such individualised feminist political mode has been criticised for rejecting many of the tenets of second-wave feminism and yet benefitting from all the advancements made by those feminists.[40] Nonetheless, the production of the zines, in all their polemical feminist identity and self-definition, clearly constitutes a political act, and, despite frequently having only a very limited distribution, these zines form part of the wider Riot Grrrl argument with sexism.[41] Sometimes the zines were compiled by a group or chapter, such as the one surrounding Karen Ablaze, who started *Ablaze!* in Leeds, which had as well as a rape crisis information point, a number of different workshops including ones for putting on gigs, song making and creating zines.[42] Here the very production of a zine is being used as a political act of communication for the Riot Grrrl movement. Not only were these zines an attack on conventional modes of beauty and femininity in regular fashion magazines, but they also had an influence on other feminist magazines such as *Bust* (1993–ongoing) and *Bitch* (1996–ongoing).[43] Many found their way onto the Internet. The easy availability and low cost of production of web-based magazines suited the individually expressive nature of this magazine form and third-wave feminist ethics.

The move to the blogosphere for wider feminist commentary, and the broadening of the scope of the feminist discussion on the World Wide Web, has encouraged an entrepreneurial, creative spirit, already present in the Riot Grrrl production of zines, offering new ways for women to communicate their feminism online. The rapid spread of computer literacy has seen a concomitant multiplication of online magazines, and researchers have been interested to question whether this would mean increased prominence of women.[44] This democratisation, accessibility and availability of magazine production on the Internet have led to a range of outputs, using a variety of platforms.[45]

With Catherine Redfern as founder and initial editor, followed by Jess McCabe, the *F-Word* has offered a forum for feminist debate since the start of this century in 2001, keeping readers up to date with current feminist issues and observations, whilst also housing an archive of past debates going back to the start of the site, indicating a keen political engagement. Visitors to the site can access the special features of a web magazine: reviews, blogs, events, resources, a shop and an opportunity to make donations, as well as opportunities for the reader to contribute, including the problem page 'Ask a Feminist'.

The influence of the Internet on third-wave feminism, however, did not mark the complete disappearance of feminist print magazines. In 2007, there was something of a resurgence of feminist print magazines in Britain. A number of new feminist magazines had been started, 'sprung out of a wider movement that has seen activist groups launching in cities across the UK'. Jess McCabe, by then editor of the *F-Word*, suggested in a *Guardian* article that these young feminists 'have focused on creating an alternative that doesn't simply avoid everyday sexism, but actively confronts it'. Similarly, McCabe continues, with online blogs adding to the resurgence of feminism and activism, these magazines are able to echo the same issues as previous magazines, they collect feminist commentaries, they act against pornography and they satirise the soft porn of Lads' Mags.[46]

KnockBack (2006–2013) was one of these magazines, producing five print issues and launching with the tagline: 'The magazine for women who aren't silly bitches on a diet', and sought to humorously occupy a 'middle ground between political feminism – which is all female circumcision and rape statistics – and women's pop culture, which is all deodorant and celebrities'.[47] When Marie Berry, the co-founder of *KnockBack*, was asked about continuing in the print media format in an age of the Internet, 'Why is a print magazine still an effective tool for getting your message across?' she replied:

> People enjoy the tactility of magazines, they last longer than websites (it's harder to click away). Magazines, or 'zines' more specifically, are diverse, they are still pushing boundaries (with thanks to people like Stack). For me having a printed product represents that idea of actually doing things instead

of talking about doing things or criticising other people who have done things. It's about making things and holding them and giving them to other people. Also I don't know any web developers, but I know a ton of printers (all called Alan, bizarrely).[48]

This makes a serious point about the magazine: it speaks of the experimentalism possible within print media, of the print magazine's tactile and enduring qualities and, above all, of the important ways in which magazines share information. Moreover, Berry regards the construction of a magazine as a creative act, and most significantly, as an act of committed activism in itself. However, by 2013, the following was posted on the website:

> KB has been in existence since 2006. 5 issues in 6 years is not a terribly impressive track record and when it came to the making of issue 6 (which was, for the duration, called the DIY issue) we just couldn't find the time, the energy or the passion. Life took over and KB fell away[49]

However, by using the Internet to advantage, this magazine has not totally disappeared from view. The *KnockBack* magazine issues and other writings still coming in, have now been collected onto the website. The print issues are still for sale, and also available as files on the webpage, as a 'tool for other people interested in feminism done funny'. In the end, the web page has proved enduring when the energy required to produce print magazines fell away. *Uplift!* for example, has become a website, while still selling its first (and only print) issue.[50] Many of these new feminist magazines then, originally intended to be printed publications, were either short-lived or ultimately resorted to web-based platforms.[51] The Internet permitted an enduring political commitment for these feminists, when producing in print media became too onerous.

The web has proved a very productive place for feminist concerns, for individual expression, such as craftivism, and for group presence and new activism too, whilst also bringing many existing feminist groups such as Southall Black Sisters or the Fawcett Society to greater attention. This shift in the use of magazine attributes on web pages has proved a swift and low-cost enterprise for smaller concerns, individuals or non-commercial groups with a minority interest or specialised readership.

In 2013, there was an increase in feminist websites as well as a surge in feminist activism, and one of the things that caught attention was Charlotte Raven's announcement that she planned to relaunch *Spare Rib*,[52] and at the same time, a more politically engaged feminist movement:

In the email Raven said she and her supporters have raised the £6,000 needed to launch phase one of the Spare Rib website in May. She is seeking to raise another £20,000 to launch a bi-monthly print magazine this Autumn. 'We're proud to be part of a continuum of feminist thought, and up front about our desire to revive the passionate spirit of the original SR', she wrote.

Raven added that she was looking for a £100 commitment from supporters who are 'as frustrated as we are by the PR and celebrity-filled women's magazines and long for an alternative'. […][53]

The intersection of the printed format and the online potential for feminism was noted by Reni Eddo-Lodge in her article, 'Let *Spare Rib* reflect all the richness of online feminism.' Excited by the prospect of the relaunch, she praises the accessibility and diversity of feminist opinion and discussion available online. Feminist activism has moved to the sphere of the Internet, but Eddo-Lodge makes clear the connections with the feminism of a previous era:

Consciousness raising, the cornerstone of 1970s feminist activism, can now be found online. It's never been easier to tap feminism into Google and find a cacophony of voices bringing home that jarring realisation that gendered inequality is a worldwide phenomenon. It's what I did four years ago when I first stumbled across *the F Word*, a website with content that would change my perceptions of gender forever.

[…]

The beautiful thing about feminism online is that you don't just hear from the same people who have somehow unofficially been crowned feminism's official representatives. Online feminism means the people in the mainstream media no longer get to set the perimeters of debate. Instead, there is a rich melting pot of voices who have never before been given a platform.

However, Eddo-Lodge is clear about the advantages of a printed version too, because of the power of the printed word, and because 'feminist politics aren't often found in women's magazines'.[54]

Charlotte Raven mentions Nina Power's *One Dimensional Woman*, an anti-capitalist and anti-consumerist critique of contemporary feminism, and Caitlin Moran's *How to Be a Woman* as sources of inspiration.[55] Part of Raven's motivation in reinventing the magazine, echoes Power's 'frustration with modern feminism'.[56] Raven's mission is to get feminism back on course and leave behind a 1990s form of feminism, where 'you could just be as superficial as you liked, and you could call yourself a feminist, and still be obsessed with shoes. I think you've just got to draw a line under that and say it's better not to be obsessed with shoes, actually'.[57] Raven, aligning herself with a number of different aspects of feminism, web feminism, popular feminism and activist feminism, announced her vision as 'more than just a magazine, but also a grassroots movement'.[58] Raven used the resources and contacts at her disposal to announce and project her feminist political intentions into the public domain through her media links. And although this caused problems, in so doing she was following a long line of feminist magazines.

Feminist magazines, representing all kinds of feminism, serve multiple aims and ambitions. The very act of creating, editing, selling and buying and generally being involved with a feminist magazine provides an outlet for feminist activity; it is feminist activism. Also, the engagement of others through education, encouragement and on the ground activity through the content of the magazine is a significant way of furthering the cause.

Feminist publishing: 'Not a separatist activity'

Sheila Rowbotham has recognised the part that journals have played from the turn of the twentieth century in acting as intellectual hubs as well as providing stimulation and support for those intent upon social change: 'Journals acted like hives around which rebels and trouble-makers buzzed away with their dreams and schemes.'[59] Specifically, Maria DiCenzo has argued that suffrage magazines are 'part of a long tradition of other presses'.[60] Suffrage periodicals owed a debt to feminist journals before the time of women's fight for the vote; they also had important press relationships with other competing, suffrage periodicals during the same period, being closely inter-related, often through their associated or affiliated organisations, through the leadership of those organisations and through editorial teams and contributors.

A constant of feminist activity and discussion, as well as academic critique, has been the commentary on how women have been portrayed in the media. From very early days, feminist periodicals and magazines have paid close attention to the representation both of women and of the feminist movement in the mainstream press. As Brian Harrison has suggested, it has been the silence and/or indifference to a cause in the mainstream press that has often provided a catalyst for reforming groups to 'create a periodical under their own control'.[61] This is a helpful way of understanding 'pressure-group periodicals',[62] and their complex relationship to other print media products. For those already associated with the print industry in some way, the extension of a feminist commitment into an independent publication, utilising existing publishing or writing skills, contacts and industry know-how, is an obvious outlet for political expression. Feminists, whilst frequently critical of the patriarchal dominance of the media industry processes and outputs, have always understood the media's power to promote (or ignore) the cause of women. This section, then, explores how feminist magazines maintain connections with, and, in some cases, continue to emulate the style of the mainstream press and media, whilst still understanding the media as a vehicle for women's oppression.

This is not just a matter of content, as in feminist magazines' responses to the mainstream press' reporting of politics and general opinion, but of continuing diverse and dynamic connections with the print media. Feminist magazines have always maintained closer links in style, presentation and communication strategies with other print media than commercial magazines for women. The politics of feminist magazines necessitates and invites this closer relationship; it operates both as a means of political engagement and as a way of answering back and railing against patriarchal dominance and the gender injustices of society. Simone Murray has discussed how feminist publishing is not a separatist activity, stating that any 'attempt to define feminist publishing activities by reference to a would-be separatist criterion of fully autonomous female endeavour must fail at the outset'.[63] This section regards the production of feminist magazines as activism in itself, despite engaging with industry processes and maintaining mainstream media connections. *Votes for Women* had a particularly close relationship to the mainstream newspaper press: even the front cover came from another paper (Figure 8.1), as was remarked upon in the first issue:

> In presenting this first issue of *Votes for Women* to the public, we should like to draw special attention to the pages of the cover. The cartoon which appears on the outside was originally published in the *Daily Chronicle* in April last, and attracted attention for the strength, beauty, and subtlety of its design; it is by the courteous permission of the proprietors of that paper that it is reproduced here. The flag on which the words 'Votes for Women' are inscribed typifies the fight which women have to wage before their victory will be won.[64]

The editorial and journalistic talents of Frederick Pethick-Lawrence and Evelyn Sharp made further newspaper connections apparent, and Pethick-

Figure 8.1 The front cover of the first issue of *Votes for Women*, 1907.

Lawrence's previous involvement with publishing various left wing newspapers meant that he brought the techniques and strategies of the newspaper world to *Votes for Women*. From the outset the journalistic element was clear. The magazine was to be 'a bulletin of the doings of the Union which shall keep them [the ranks] in touch with all the ramifications of the movement and enable them to devote their work in the most profitable manner to the furtherance of the agitation'.[65] John Mercer has noted how, 'over the period it acted as official newspaper of the WSPU, *Votes for Women* gradually adopted a journalistic manner, visual style and promotional strategy modelled on the popular press'.[66]

Accounts of the activities of middle-class suffrage leaders and supporters were balanced by the use of the deliberately popular tone and lively visual style of the newspaper, as well as shopping guides for the middle-class readers. These shopping guides meant negotiating with the commercial world of department store advertising, and then encouraging readers to patronise those stores. *Votes for Women* also reviewed and recommended books as well as carrying advertisements from booksellers promoting 'Important books relating to women.' Books and printed ephemera were very important to *Votes for Women* and indicate an extensive engagement with other printed forms. Not only did these items earn additional income to further the political cause,[67] but central to the magazine's founding aims was to educate its readers and cater for their demand for information. This was indicated from the outset: 'The magnitude of this demand may be gauged by the fact that already during 1907 the W.S.P.U. has effected a sale, exclusive of leaflets, of 80,000 books, pamphlets, and other publications.'[68]

Frederick Pethick-Lawrence was not the only one to bring his newspaper skills to *Votes for Women*. Evelyn Sharp, novelist and newspaper journalist, became assistant editor at dramatically short notice when the Pethick-Lawrences were arrested and charged with conspiracy, and did so to great acclaim.[69] Her involvement with the movement started after being sent by the *Manchester Guardian* to report on the annual conference of the National Union of Women Workers.[70] Sharp, who was imprisoned in Holloway for smashing War Office windows, recorded her experiences as a suffragette in sketches about selling *Votes for Women* on street corners wearing cumbersome sandwich poster boards and working in the suffragette shop.[71] Sharp's journalistic skills, her experiences as a committed suffragette and her writing from life experiences all combined to produce an engaging quality and wide appeal in her writing, shifting her perspective to a class-based analysis of society.[72] Such direct experiences made the news in themselves, and a broader understanding of society and brought *Votes for Women* into a different kind of conversation with the mainstream press, both supplying and commentating upon the news.

Like *Votes for Women*, *Spare Rib* owed an intellectual debt to the print industry, but this time to a different sector: the vibrant underground press which had produced counter-cultural magazines such as *Oz* (1967–1973), a satirical magazine originally from Australia, and *Friendz* (also *Friends* 1969–1972), originating in the music scene. Elizabeth Nelson, whilst explaining that the output of the underground press must be viewed cautiously, nonetheless indicates its significance:

> it is primarily within that press that the documentary record of the social history of the counter-culture lies. The underground press was more than a mere documentor of events and attitudes within the counter-culture: its other role – that of articulating and shaping the new lifestyle – was equally important.[73]

This dual function of the underground press of both documenting the counter-culture and reflecting back new opinion is an approach that can be seen in the editorial management of *Spare Rib*. Both Rosie Boycott and Marsha Rowe's experience of the underground press, notwithstanding its sexism, may be discerned in the counter-cultural ironies, mocking illustrations and attacks on establishment practices and thinking, as well as offering more enlightened visions of potential gender equality.

Besides borrowing from the underground press, *Spare Rib* also took cues from the newspapers, borrowing the style of the daily papers and included this as a special section within the overall format. This was an element not found in commercial women's magazines and added to the political weight of *Spare Rib*. This news section, with coloured pages in columns, newspaper style, kept readers up to date with events and with items in the mainstream news of concern to feminists and all women.[74]

Spare Rib also had some parallels with commercial women's magazines, borrowing from their format in having distinct and regular sections in areas that overlapped with the mainstream agenda of femininity. However, part of its genius was to parody more commercial offerings: for instance, the inclusion of a men's page, as Marsha Rowe has commented, was a 'joke on the tokenism of women's pages in the national newspapers'.[75] Mainstream magazines, whilst mocked for their excessive devotion to femininity, were also emulated in some early *Spare Rib* articles on cookery, fashion, craft and DIY, where familiar subjects within women's magazines were reworked into a feminist formula. Adverts projected an anti-mass consumption ethic.[76] These conventionalities of format gave *Spare Rib* broad appeal, helping to achieve a national distribution, whilst also exposing the oppressiveness of femininity. In this sense, *Spare Rib* both colluded with the format of women's magazines and criticised their outlook at the same time.

Many of the online feminist websites and magazines have closely followed a newspaper visual format in structuring their web pages and their material, with headings in larger type, columns and text wrapped around images; in some aspects they emulate the physical appearance of newspapers. Moreover, they have integrated themselves within the wider media world, not just in arguing back but in utilising tactics to promote campaigns, and employing the full range of modes of communication in the blogosphere, such as The Everyday Sexism Project where anyone is free to add their story, and Vagenda, which comments on sexism in the current media. The *F-Word* is a case in point and not only reports on feminist issues and issues of interest to feminists, but encourages reader responses to those ongoing debates through writing features or reviews and posting on the blog.

However, few online magazine launches could have utilised the mainstream press as astutely as Charlotte Raven, who situated what she then envisioned as both web and printed new '*Spare Rib*' amongst other magazines already available. This magazine would not be worthy but desirable, sitting 'alongside Cosmo on the newsagent's shelf, instead of on those carousels in Whole Foods alongside Green Parent'. It was to be funny and like a 'girls' club', not a boys' club like *Private Eye*.[77] Others also positioned new '*Spare Rib*' in a magazine context, but related this to the online feminist world too, describing their aims thus:

> to take the existing sparks of stimulating online feminist discussion and produce a monthly glossy that can compete with *Glamour* and *Grazia*. […] if *Spare Rib* can emulate the thriving diversity of feminism online – interactive, creating debates, democratising the creation of content – it will have a bright future.[78]

Demonstrating further connections, it was announced that Rosie Boycott, *Spare Rib's* original co-founder and journalist, was to join the team planning the magazine's relaunch as a contributing editor, making issues of copyright to the name 'fine'.[79] Raven's links with Boycott, now a mainstream journalist and feminist, were significant to the launch, 'I'm thrilled that Charlotte Raven is relaunching Spare Rib: there is a great deal to do,' said Boycott, adding her feminist voice: 'Feminism, for me at least, is about trying to make the lot of all women better: to value what women do and to afford it the same status as what men do, whether that be work, child-rearing or keeping a family together […] Feminism is not about a single individual climbing up the ladder.'[80]

Raven continued utilising the media to puff, and to try and fund, the new '*Spare Rib*'. A small flurry of newspaper articles revealed activism, immersive theatre and consciousness-raising groups, as ways of rekindling a whole movement, not just the magazine. Emails to 'rich friends' brought in the launch purse of 20,000 pounds, with the result that Raven, who argued that feminism had become ' "a marketing device", felt she was avoiding the current trap of the commodification of feminism'.[81] Newspaper articles continued to drip-feed information about the relaunch, until newspaper coverage reached another dimension, with both Marsha Rowe and Rosie Boycott threatening legal action over the use of the name.[82] 'Spare Rib is not a brand' claimed Rowe, who objected to the proposed business plans. Rowe reflected on the relationship between the magazine and online feminism:

> The web offers a different opportunity today for women and for feminism. It is a marvellous opportunity. But that does not alter the fact that, by definition, a movement is not something that you pay to join. We were therefore keen to clarify, with Charlotte, that part of her venture that she was calling the 'Spare Rib Movement'.

She also commented on how the new movement commodified feminism:

> The name *Spare Rib* has an emotional and a commercial value, but to us it was never a brand. It became iconic because of the energy, commitment and time of the many women who contributed to the magazine, who worked on it tirelessly. If this name were to be revived, co-founded Rosie Boycott and I want to ensure that, as a web magazine or in print, it would not fall at first base.[83]

Raven decided to drop the name as it would be 'an "ugly and entirely wrong note" on which to launch a magazine'. So, in another media-savvy move, Raven announced a competition for the new name to take place on the web with a commentary on Twitter, with a shortlist including:

The Other Woman – the movement aimed at women who think differently
The Purple Notebook – Doris Lessing in suffragette colours
Speculum – the punk option, but will it make voters wince?
The Feminist Times – pleasingly literal minded, like calling a dog Rover
Monstrous Regiment – a John Locke quote reclaimed by a 70s theatre company

The naming process twisted and turned, presumably generating more followers; some suggestions had to be taken off the list: 'Riberation', 'Hip Bone' were too close; 'Redstocking' was already in use in America,[84] finally deciding upon 'Feminist Times'.[85]

This argument amongst feminists, productively rehearsed in the full glare of the national press, raised questions and generated further articles. 'How many feminists does it take to relaunch a magazine?' one asked, explaining that 'the sisterhood is not a many-splendid thing of female encouragement. It tends to be a horrid bitch-fest'. Rosie Millard, noting that twenty years on, Marsha Rowe decided to trademark the name, interprets the problem as one of communication strategies:

> According to a statement from Raven, widely circulated on Twitter, what really stuck in Rowe's (and presumably Boycott's) craw was the 'grassroots movement' character of 21st-century Rib. Well boo-hoo. So nobody was online back in the medieval era of the 1970s. So what? Rowe and Boycott have, it seems, dumped their support in favour of legal threats, which would, if carried out, squander the financial resources of the new magazine.

Millard wondered if this might work in feminism's favour:

> It means a generation of younger women won't know about *Spare Rib* and what it was. But maybe that doesn't matter. Perhaps a phoney notion of the 'sisterhood' needs to be replaced by a more general encouragement of working women who are already beset by issues such as lower pay rates and anxieties about ageism and parenting. Who don't necessarily feel themselves as politicised, and feel uneasy about calling themselves a feminist, but would just like to get on, in equal terms.[86]

There was an impressive online posting in response to this article, and one respondent was pragmatic about feminism: 'There is a general consciousness raising around regarding women's issues at the moment and the Raven project reflects this. Increasingly using the full social media toolkit.'[87]

As the argument over the *Spare Rib* relaunch continued in the press, helpfully advertising the new feminist magazine, the discussion became one of current feminism's need to draw on the most imaginative and the most relevant communication strategies available to the cause. With Raven commenting that: 'This project began as a series of conversations around my kitchen table – and broadened into a dialogue with hundreds of members and supporters. I'm proud that we are able to use the tools of the digital age to facilitate these conversations.'[88]

The links to the mainstream press remain important for feminist magazines because, unlike commercial magazines, political engagement, protest and commentary, often upon the media itself, are central to their existence and interventionist ambitions. Feminist magazines do not offer a 'whole world' of being to their readers, they necessarily engage with political and public spheres and utilise print media and mainstream communication networks to achieve impact. Instead of retreating from patriarchy and creating a world away from politics and sexism, feminist magazines must engage in dialogue from a position of being within that world of production of meaning.

Conveying an understanding of feminist history

Feminist magazines speak to the ongoing history of feminist politics, explicitly acknowledging current activity as part of a longer feminist history. This is a significant part of their political message. One of the strategies common to feminist magazines is to build and raise feminist consciousness in their members through strengthening bonds with past feminisms. Feminist magazines can utilise the magazine format to accommodate a variety of different materials, including historical articles. This might include reminiscing about the lives of exceptional women, sharing previous writings, illuminating historical contexts and exploring accounts of activist moments and campaigns. These are all strategies employed to foster a sense of political cohesion and purpose. In employing historical content, feminist magazines deliberately situate themselves as part of feminist historical progression, and sometimes also consciously situate themselves within the history of feminist magazines, starting from at least the mid-nineteenth century.[89] Building a collective memory of activism, people and past protest periodicals within a social movement authenticate and empower the present membership. Feminist periodicals and magazines have always done this.

Liesbet van Zoonen has discussed feminist scholarship as an integral part of the women's movement,[90] while Maria Mies argues that:

> The appropriation of women's history can be promoted by feminist scholars who can inspire and help other women to document their campaigns and struggles. They can help them to analyse the struggles, so that they can learn from past mistakes and successes and, in the long run, may become able to move from mere spontaneous activism to long-term strategies. This presupposes, however, that women engaged in women's studies remain in close contact with the movement and maintain a continuous dialogue with other women.[91]

This section considers the relationship of feminist magazines with feminist history. Many early feminist magazines emphasised the importance of reading and education in order to build knowledge and further the cause, seeing reading feminist history as a feminist activity. The suffrage movement in general placed great significance on educative reading, and *Votes for Women* in particular leant heavily on historical writings and the history of feminism and feminists. Kate Flint has argued that reading feminist history was central to the establishment of a gender identity not formulated by men. Discussing *Votes for Women* specifically, Flint describes how:

> the publication itself provided information with which to argue one's case; for gaining a historical awareness of the social and political contributions made by generations of earlier women; for reliving contemporary history with the knowledge that one is recording the struggles of the current movement as an inspiration for future generations of women readers; and which acknowledged that reading could provide relaxation.[92]

She continues: 'To this end, as well as reporting current events, it published articles on earlier women's history. *Votes for Women* concentrated, although not exclusively, on those nineteenth-century developments which paved the way for the current suffrage campaign.'[93]

Votes for Women provided this historical strand in a number of ways. Sylvia Pankhurst, for example, in a series of extensive and detailed histories, started 'The History of the Suffrage Movement' with 'Chapter 1 – The Battle of Peterloo':

> In a history of the suffrage movement it is not necessary to go back further than the agitation which preceded the Reform Act of 1832. Before that time women possessed and exercised, as is well known, the same voting rights as men. These were, however, almost entirely confined to the rich and influential classes, and as women are seldom property-owners, only a very small percentage of them could in those days be qualified to vote.[94]

Written with authority, readers were clearly encouraged to accept and digest this information in order to better understand and support the cause. Besides this regular educational feature on the history of the suffrage movement, there were other ways in which the paper looked for a historical context for its present campaign. Emmeline Pethick-Lawrence's 'What the Vote Means to the Woman as Wife', for example, starts with a discussion of women's status in the nineteenth century. She opens with a statement of the rights granted to slaves in England: 'From the date of that judgement the right in this land of ours of a human being to personal freedom has never been questioned, except in the case of the English wife.'[95] This transhistorical overview positions the reader, with the writer, at the centre of the debate, giving clear rationale for the cause.

Another use of history was to find heroines for feminism, as in the following review, possibly by Emmeline Pethick-Lawrence, of Douglas Murray's *The Story of Jeanne d'Arc*:

> Jeanne, the peasant maid in the lowly home of Domremy, Jeanne the dauntless leader, always at the front, always where the fight is thickest, bearing her uplifted sword which never fell to kill, may well be the chosen saint of the woman's movement of today.[96]

All these historical inclusions, adopted within this periodical, intentionally foreground women's history as a way of building a knowledge base and elevating confidence and conviction in the reader.

Spare Rib also mobilised feminist history to bolster the cause, paying tribute to Emily Wilding Davidson in its very first issue. 'What Emily Did' by Antonia Raeburn, author of *The Militant Suffragettes* (1975), considers the suffragette movement in order to disprove the myth that those involved were 'merely a bunch of hysterical women.'[97] Davidson, who died under the King's horse, has been memorialised for her sacrifice, and Raeburn, in reminding readers of this earlier period of heightened feminist struggle for equality, initiates a critical strain of discussion for this most important of second-wave feminist magazines. In this same first issue, Sheila Rowbotham delves further back in history to look at women in the fourteenth and fifteenth centuries: 'Adam's Knobby Rib: Some amusing anecdotes about the situation of women in the 14th and 15th centuries.'[98] Humorously referencing the magazine's title, Rowbotham, feminist historian, uses historical detail in this and later articles on women's history to capture the reader's interest by finding new examples through which to situate the reader within a long-standing history of women.[99]

Feminist magazines have been central players in the circulation of, and inter-textual reference between, feminist texts in their recording, recovery and analysis of feminist history. Despite being very much of its moment of 1970s women's liberation, *Spare Rib* leant upon an earlier feminism to add weight and resolve to the new feminist causes. It was interested and invested in the previous 'wave' and, as a protest periodical, was conscious of the history of the movement and of contributing to that history. This investment in writing history remained even when the magazine had started to broaden its feminist reach to include minority groups and international feminism. The front cover of one issue, May 1978, is dominated by an illustration of two Edwardian suffragettes furtively posting Bills on Parliament walls by H. M. Paget (1857–1936) (Figure 8.2).[100] The

Figure 8.2 Suffragettes and second-wave feminism, *Spare Rib*, May 1978.
© *Spare Rib collective; permission kindly given by the Fawcett Society.*

same principle of steadfastness to the cause underpins the reprinting of the short story by Evelyn Sharp from *Votes for Women*: 'Shaking Hands with the Middle Ages'. Taken from her *Rebel Women* collection, the piece describes a political meeting where a woman never previously involved in politics finds her voice and calls for the vote:

> 'Then give all that to the women,' she said, in a voice she never seemed to have heard before. 'If you think so much of justice and freedom for men, don't keep it any longer from the women.'

For a little space of time, a couple of seconds, probably, her eyes went on seeing nothing, and her ears drummed. She thought she had never known what it really meant to be alone until that moment. She was a woman who had known loneliness very early, when it came to her in an uncongenial nursery; she knew it still, in some houses, where everything was wrong, from the wall-papers to the people. But the meaning of utter isolation she had never learnt until that moment when clamour and confusion reigned around her and she saw and heard none of it.

Then her senses were invaded by the sound and the look of it all; and to her own perplexity she found herself on the point of smiling.[101]

This admirable choice explored the challenges of standing up for justice and acknowledged that feminist activism was never an easy option. Its inclusion in *Spare Rib* in the late 1970s sounded a call to those women not yet involved to come forward and join, a call from the suffragist moment and the time of *Spare Rib*, compressing that time span into a single continuum of feminist activism.

Feminist histories exist in other ways in *Spare Rib* too. Marsha Rowe's anthology, *The Spare Rib Reader*, includes an interview with Hazel Hunkins Hallinan of the Six Point Group, a successor to the women's suffrage movement, entitled: 'Decades: Talking across the Century.'[102] Hallinan, denied employment as a qualified chemist in America on the grounds that she was female, devoted herself to the feminist cause:

I came to England in 1920, just after Lady Rhondda had established the Six Point Group. Lady Rhondda's idea was: We've got the vote, now we've got to do something with it. But the Six Points were welfare matters, they were not universal freedom causes. Along in the 1930s we changed the aims to 'Equality for women politically, occupationally, morally, socially, economically and legally.'[103]

This interview, reflecting upon the period just after the first wave of feminism, first reprinted in *Spare Rib* in November 1980, generated Dale Spender's discussion of how women such as Hallinan, who had made a feminist contribution throughout the century, challenges a narrative that makes women absent from cultural history.[104]

History is no less important to the *F-Word*, where the link 'herstory' contains a range of articles on former and recent history of feminism, including a series on British Punk by Cazz Blase, articles on Emily Davidson, suffragette and Boudicca, Queen of the Iceni. In addition, the significance of the preceding activity of Riot Grrrl movement is keenly felt: 'What has Happened to the legacy of Riot Grrrl?'[105] Apart from indicating the importance of the Riot Grrrl movement and the revolutionary aspects of female punk music,[106] this indicates the influence of the Riot Grrrl movement on later feminisms. Once again history remains important, this time in an online feminist magazine, radically different in media presentation.

Reclaiming the F-Word (2010), written just before the emergence of the fourth wave in 2013,[107] provides an interesting retrospective. Redfern considers that the debt to earlier feminism is strongly felt by those who have responded to third-wave feminism: 'in our experience younger feminists are quick to acknowledge their debt to older feminists.'[108] In the same vein, *Pirate Jenny* zine admonishes those who think they owe nothing to previous feminists:

> Let me have a moment here with those of you who have no idea the price your First and Second Wave Sisters paid so you could enjoy the benefits of saying you are not a feminist. Need I remind you that LESS THAN 40 years ago a woman could not get a credit card unless her husband cosigned for it. It has been LESS THAN 30 years since women have been admitted to graduate programmes ... sister, someone cleared that path for you and paid dearly for it.

Charlotte Raven, too, has stressed that her feminism recalls an earlier era: originally the *Feminist Times* was to be called *Women's Journal* after the old suffragette newspaper. In the end, '*Spare Rib*' was chosen as the title because 'we love the 70s version of Spare Rib and didn't want to fall prey to the female compulsion to reinvent the wheel'. It was intended that, 'SR will revive the spirited and soulful vision of feminism that SR once embodied not the timid liberal one that dominates the mainstream media.'[109] Feminist history featured strongly in Raven's motivations for relaunching a grass roots movement and her research in the Women's Library left her inspired by the '"wonderful, countercultural" tone' of the early *Spare Rib*. She embraced a sense of feminist history, wanting 'that continuity with the past'.[110] Accordingly, the first wave was also referenced when Raven considered protesting at the Epsom Derby on the centenary of feminist heroine, Emily Wilding Davison's death, and again in *Feminist Times'* Christmas gift to all readers: a printable image of Davison to be cut out and put on the tree as an anti-consumerist declaration.

The recycling of second-wave feminism has taken numerous forms. For instance, third-wave American feminist magazines have reclaimed and repoliticised crafting activities, and as Elizabeth Groeneveld has pointed out, despite claims for a new feminism, this in fact recalls second-wave feminist DIY cultures.[111] Reni Eddo-Lodge, writer and campaigner, reminisced that the old *Spare Rib* served as a 'noticeboard for feminist events and activism', and she described her copy of *Spare Rib* September 1981:

> With a front page dedicated to black women rising against racism and police harassment, articles about sex workers on hunger strike, and coverage of working class female factory workers challenging their employers with the Sex Discrimination Act, the magazine was nothing if it wasn't intersectional.[112]

Finally, Catherine Redfern's response to the controversy over new '*Spare Rib*' was to post a blog and some images on her site with the title: 'Controversy in feminism & Spare Rib: Nothing new', where she writes:

> A few years ago, I found this in an old issue of Spare Rib, from September 1980 and took photos of it, to share with the F Word collective when some controversy or other was raging about something on the site and we were all feeling pretty down about it (I can't even remember what the issue was now).
>
> The recent announcement about Spare Rib being re-published made me remember this.
>
> Sorry for the bad photos but I think it's pretty interesting. Arguments about feminism in the media; the responsibility of magazines like Spare Rib to represent the movement and not discriminate; how collectives are run; censorship; political splits; conflicts; class issues; what terminology/language to use; all these debates are not new.[113]

Redfern's blog, which also references Eddo-Lodge's Guardian article, includes images of the published editorial argument and ensuing reader's letters from her own copy of *Spare Rib* September 1980. It is the editorial controversy discussed by Winship (and cited earlier in this chapter) and Redfern, a magazine founder herself, comments on *Spare Rib*'s style at the same time: 'I love the jauntiness of this font, considering how awful the whole fall out must have been for everyone involved. Woo! Controversy!'

Redfern uses her own website, mostly about her 'Crafty, arty creative life', to post a blog about the current *Spare Rib* controversy, electronically embedding a *Guardian* article, and using the Flickr facility to upload photographs of *Spare Rib*'s original pages. She draws parallels between feminist magazine editorial arguments of the second and fourth waves. She notes the responsibility of representing a movement, the problems of running a magazine by a collective and the political issues at stake, not least of which is language, all feature. This reaching back to previous feminist magazines for reference and reassurance for new feminist magazines, now presented in new media formats, enfolds a history of the feminist magazine into current debate. This circulation of feminist historical experience, endeavour, debate and publication centres on the feminist magazine. This is not just a use of the magazine as a vehicle for purveying feminist principles, but, crucially, an insistence on feminist magazines as part of feminist history.

***

Magazines are highly suited to the feminist cause: the very flexibility of the format enables a mode of expression that centres on female experience.[114] The increased flexibility of the Internet has served to enhance the communicative reach of the magazine for feminist journalism, comment and responses. Feminism remains reliant upon its magazines, and in this chapter I have pointed to some of the preoccupations that have shaped generations of feminist magazines. Feminist magazines historicise, record and recall, in order to educate, encourage, inspire and amuse their readerships. I have argued that the very creation, contribution, distribution and even the reading of a feminist magazine may be seen as a feminist act, as well as the contribution of articles, news and commentary. Feminist magazines have always retained connections with mainstream media in terms of format and processes: newspapers, books, conventional women's magazines and the Internet. Recalling feminist histories of all kinds, including previous feminist magazines, is an important resource for new feminist magazines, appreciating feminist causes of the past and validating present. In all these ways, feminist magazines anchor the movement.

Afterword

All women's magazines are not the same. Making this argument has led my discussion in various directions, and into distinct areas of study and critique. The chapters in this study have followed diverse paths across print, television, radio and the Internet, and each has adopted a particular approach to exploring the content and communication strategies of women's magazines, as well as reflecting on their cultural valency. My aim has been to broaden the study of women's magazines and to explore the varying ways in which magazines approach and address their intended, but often imagined and unknown, audiences. The question of what unusual, non-commercial magazines might mean to women remains unanswered and is perhaps unanswerable in full, as indeed it is for mainstream magazines.

It is certainly quite possible to define the magazine as a collection of items assembled in a media package, aimed at an interested audience. However, it is much more difficult to describe how magazines communicate their essence, how they retain their audience and how they work for both producers and recipients. The magazine's malleability is, as I have argued, beyond question.

Women's magazines, especially those that perform different kinds of personal, social and political work for women, should be considered as agents of women's engagement with modernity. Marshall Berman, writing about the experience of modernity, has this to say about the 'contradictory forces and needs' that 'inspire and torment us':

> our desire to be rooted in a stable and coherent personal and social past, and our insatiable desire for growth – not merely for economic growth but for growth in experience, in pleasure, in knowledge, in sensibility – growth that destroys both the physical and social landscapes of our past, and our emotional links with those lost worlds; our desperate allegiances to ethnic, national, class and sexual groups which we hope will give us a firm 'identity,' and the internationalization of everyday life – of our clothes and household goods, our books and music, our ideas and fantasies – that spreads all our identities all over the map; our desire for clear and solid values to live by, and our desire to

embrace the limitless possibilities of modern life and experience that obliterate all values; the social and political forces that propel us into explosive conflicts with other people and other peoples, even as we develop a deeper sensitivity and empathy toward our ordained enemies and come to realize, sometimes too late, that they are not so different from us after all.[1]

Such forces and needs, pulling individuals in different directions, help to explain the ways in which magazines for women function. Women's magazines are contradictory media forms: they recall women's history and a sense of women's past occupation and lifestyle whilst also offering opportunities for development and growth in understanding, in general knowledge and in self-awareness. Many of the women's magazines illustrated in the present volume pay close attention to identity formation through ethnic group, social class or sexuality, and yet they also look further afield to establish that identity and to promote interpretation of the self. Women's magazines promote their values to a willing audience, but many, simultaneously, urge women to embrace the contemporary world. Finally, magazines, while they seem to be targeted to an exclusive group, naturally excluding other groups, offer valued insight into other women's lives. Contradictory forces lie at the heart of women's lives as they learn to negotiate gendered roles within societies and cultures not set up to suit women's needs. Magazines recognise and reflect these ambiguities: they offer empathy with women's situations.

In considering the magazines discussed in *Magazine Movements*, it is possible to see how each one reflects, adopts or partakes of contradictory stances regarding women's experience of modernity. *Housewife* for instance, starts as a class-bound advice handbook for suburban women, but becomes fully engaged with a contemporary female modernity, both inside and outside the home, embracing not just a shifted focus on the housewife over the war, but also anticipating a new set of empowered and elevated roles for women after the war. This is a magazine that changed dramatically over the period in question, embracing a new modernity. As *Housewife* twisted and turned to represent the role of the housewife variously, so early radio magazine programmes also had to twist and turn, to experiment and develop in learning how to address women over the radio. Such early developments meant that *Houseparty*, another broadcast magazine, was able to use formal structures to move beyond the medium of television to deliver its message of companionship. By the 1970s, the *Houseparty* team had learnt to speak to a generation of women, for whom many private and political tensions had been made apparent by the Women's Liberation Movement, and it strove to help women to navigate those contradictions.

The magazines *Mukti* and *Arena Three*, with the distinct purpose of assisting women to form positive identities through their publications and associated meetings, set about this in different ways. *Arena Three* encouraged women to identify positively as lesbians and provided a group forum to enable this and also mobilised resources to form a social movement organisation, and yet concomitantly sought to demonstrate the very 'everydayness' and ordinariness of those women in the national press. These are not incompatible aims; it is the tension between these two states that points to the ways the magazine can comprise the conflicting desires of the modern condition. *Mukti* too tried to conflate the notion of an inward, private space for individual expression of the inner self, with an outward-facing British-Indian subcontinental feminist approach and outlook, accommodating a paradoxical situation of conflict and empathy. The CCC, constructed by women who felt buffeted by modernity, 'embraced' its 'possibilities' in secret. In contrast, feminist magazines, which have always understood the conflicted position of women in society, have tried to deal head-on with various contemporary 'social and political forces' of women's oppression, whilst maintaining links with the very mainstream press which has often played its part in women's oppression.

All these magazines for women acknowledge and even embrace the contradictory forces pressing upon women's experience of modernity within their pages. It is the very format of the magazine as an assemblage of items that permits this various and conflicted engagement with society and culture. It is this negotiation that is the work of women's magazines, brought to life by the participation and conversations women have with their magazines in pursuit of narratives through which to reflect upon their lives.

Notes

Chapter 1

1   Merja Mahrt, 'The Attractiveness of Magazines as "Open" and "Closed" Texts: Values of Women's Magazines and Their Readers', *Mass Communication and Society*, 15 (2012), pp. 852–874.

2   Janice Winship, *Inside Women's Magazines* (London: Pandora, 1987), p. xiii, identifies herself as a feminist closet reader of magazines; Amy Aronson, 'Still Reading Women's Magazines: Reconsidering the Tradition a Half Century After *The Feminine Mystique*', *American Journalism*, 27 (2010), pp. 31–61, p. 48, argues that women are not dupes.

3   Aronson, 'Still Reading Women's Magazines', p. 32.

4   See Chris Atton, *Alternative Media* (London: Sage, 2002).

5   For example, Betty Friedan, *The Feminine Mystique* (1963) (London: Norton, 1997); Marjorie Fergusson, *Forever Feminine: Women's Magazines and the Cult of Femininity* (London: Heinemann, 1983).

6   Friedan, *Feminine Mystique*, p. 83.

7   Friedan, *Feminine Mystique*, chap. 3.

8   Fergusson, *Forever Feminine*.

9   Ros Ballaster, Margaret Beetham, Elizabeth Frazer and Sandra Hebron, *Women's Worlds: Ideology, Femininity and the Woman's Magazine* (Basingstoke: Macmillan, 1991).

10 Winship, *Inside Women's Magazines*.

11 Winship, *Inside Women's Magazines*, p. 23.

12 Joke Hermes, *Reading Women's Magazines: An Analysis of Everyday Media Use* (Cambridge: Polity, 1995).

13 Hermes, *Reading Women's Magazines*, p. 143.

14 Brita Ytre-Arne, 'Women's Magazines and the Public Sphere', *European Journal of Communication*, 26:3 (2011), pp. 247–261, p. 252.

15 Rebecca Feasey, 'Reading Heat: The Meanings and Pleasures of Star Fashions and Celebrity Gossip', *Continuum: Journal of Media and Cultural Studies*, 22:5 (2008), pp. 683–695.

16 Cynthia White, *Women's Magazines 1693–1968* (London: Michael Joseph, 1970).

17 Brian Braithwaite, *Women's Magazines: The First 300 Years* (London: Peter Owen, 1995).

18 Brian Braithwaite and Joan Barrell, *The Business of Women's Magazines: The Agonies and the Ecstasies* (London: Associated Business Press, 1979).

19 Anna Gough-Yates, *Understanding Women's Magazines: Publishing, Markets and Readerships* (London: Routledge, 2003).

20 Trevor Millum, *Images of Woman: Advertising in Women's Magazines* (London: Chatto & Windus, 1975).

21 Judith Williamson, *Decoding Advertisements: Ideology and Meaning in Advertising* (London: Boyars, 1978).

22 Ellen McCracken, *Decoding Women's Magazines: From* Mademoiselle *to* Ms (New York, NY: St Martin's Press, 1993).

23 Lesley Johnson and Justine Lloyd, *Sentenced to Everyday Life: Feminism and the Housewife* (Oxford: Berg, 2004).

24 Rosalind Gill, *Gender and the Media* (Cambridge: Polity, 2007).

25 Margaret Beetham, *A Magazine of Her Own?: Domesticity and Desire in the Woman's Magazine, 1800–1914* (London: Routledge, 1996).

26 Margaret Beetham and Kay Boardman (eds), *Victorian Women's Magazines: An Anthology* (Manchester: Manchester University Press, 2001).

27 Maria DiCenzo, Lucy Delap and Leile Ryan, *Feminist Media History: Suffrage, Periodicals and the Public Sphere* (Basingstoke: Palgrave, 2001).

28 For instance, see Laurel Brake, Bill Bell and David Finkelstein (eds), *Nineteenth-Century Media and the Construction of Identities* (Basingstoke: Palgrave, 2000); Peter Brooker and Andrew Thacker (eds), *The Oxford Critical and Cultural History of Modernist Magazines* (Oxford: Oxford University Press, 2009–2013).

29 Angela McRobbie, *Feminism and Youth Culture: From* Jackie *to* Just Seventeen (London: Macmillan, 1991).

30 Penny Tinkler, *Constructing Girlhood: Popular Magazines for Girls Growing Up in England 1920–1950* (London: Taylor and Francis, 1995).

31 Noliwe M. Rooks, *Ladies' Pages: African American Women's Magazines and the Culture That Made Them* (New Brunswick, NJ: Rutgers University Press, 2004).

32 Erin A. Smith, *Hard-Boiled: Working-Class Readers and Pulp Magazines* (Philadelphia, PA: Temple University Press, 2000).

33 Adrian Bingham, *Gender, Modernity, and the Popular Press in Inter-War Britain* (Oxford: Oxford University Press: 2004), p. 27.

Chapter 2

1 Friedan, *The Feminine Mystique*, pp. 103–104.

2 Friedan, *The Feminine Mystique*, p. 105. Friedan's motivations for writing this book have been discussed by Lesley Johnson, ' "Revolutions Are Not Made by

Down-trodden Housewives": Feminism and the Housewife', *Australian Feminist Studies*, 15:32 (2000), pp. 237–248, p. 240, who also cites Friedan's political activism as discussed by Daniel Horowitz, 'Rethinking Betty Friedan and The Feminine Mystique; Labor Union Radicalism and Feminism in Cold War America', *American Quarterly*, 48:1 (1996), pp. 1–42, p. 2.

3   It was only perhaps when female editors and writers started addressing themselves also as readers of their magazines, that major changes in this mode took place, see Gough-Yates, *Understanding Women's Magazines*, pp. 118–131.

4   Fergusson, *Forever Feminine*.

5   Catherine Hall, *White, Male and Middle Class* (Cambridge: Polity Press, 1992), p. 44.

6   Hall, *White, Male and Middle Class*, p. 50.

7   Hall, *White, Male and Middle Class*, p. 43.

8   Hall, *White, Male and Middle Class*, pp. 44–50.

9   Hall, *White, Male and Middle Class*, p. 43.

10 Beetham, *A Magazine of Her Own?* pp. 59–70.

11 White, *Women's Magazines*, p. 103 and chap. 3.

12 Deirdre Beddoe, *Back to Home and Duty: Women between the Wars 1918–1939* (London: Pandora, 1989), p. 89.

13 Alison Light, *Forever England: Femininity, Literature and Conservatism between the Wars* (London: Routledge, 1991), pp. 113–155.

14 Gail Finney, *Women in Modern Drama: Freud, Feminism and European Theater at the Turn of the Century* (Ithaca, NY: Cornell University Press, 1989), cited in Rita Felski, *The Gender of Modernity* (Cambridge, MA: Harvard University Press, 1995), p. 3.

15 Felski, *Gender of Modernity*, p. 8.

16 Felski, *Gender of Modernity*, p. 8, following Adorno and Horkheimer's *Dialectic of Enlightenment*.

17 Felski, *Gender of Modernity*, p. 8.

18 Martin Pumphrey, 'The Flapper, the Housewife and the Making of Modernity', *Cultural Studies*, 1:2 (1987), pp. 179–194.

19 Felski, *Gender of Modernity*, p. 28.

20 Judy Giles, *The Parlour and the Suburb: Domestic Identities, Class, Femininity and Modernity* (Oxford: Berg, 2004), pp. 5–6.

21 Following Marshall Berman's, *All That Is Solid Melts in Air: The Experience of Modernity* (London: Verso, 1983).

22 Giles, *Parlour and the Suburb*, p. 6.

23 Giles, *Parlour and the Suburb*, p. 22.

24 Bingham, *Gender, Modernity, and the Popular Press in Inter-War Britain*, p. 16.

25 Ballaster et al., *Women's Worlds*, pp. 118–125.

26 David Cannadine, *The Rise and Fall of Class in Britain* (New York, NY: Columbia, 1999).

27 White, *Women's Magazines*, pp. 95–96.

28 White, *Women's Magazines*, p. 99.

29 For example, Bernard E. Jones, *The Practical Woodworker: A Complete Guide to the Art and Practice of Woodworking* (London: Cassell, 1920).

30 Beddoe, *Back to Home and Duty*, p. 18, discusses the housewife 'fantasy' of pretending to be richer than is really the case.

31 Judy Giles, *Women, Identity and Private Life in Britain, 1900-50* (Basingstoke: Macmillan, 1995), pp. 78–85.

32 Roger Silverstone (ed.), *Visions of Suburbia* (London: Routledge, 1997), p. 7.

33 Giles, *Parlour and the Suburb*, pp. 47–64.

34 *Housewife*, February 1939, pp. 4–5.

35 Beddoe, *Back to Home and Duty*, pp. 129–130.

36 Maggie Andrews, *Domesticating the Airwaves: Broadcasting, Domesticity and Femininity* (London: Continuum, 2012), p. 33.

37 Christopher Stone, 'Christopher Stone Introduces *Housewife*', *Housewife*, February 1939, pp. 4–5.

38 McCracken, *Decoding Women's Magazines*, pp. 13–37.

39 Marjorie Fergusson, 'Imagery and Ideology: The Cover Photographs of Traditional Women's Magazines' in Gaye Tuchman, Arlene Kaplan Daniels and James Benet (eds), *Hearth and Home: Images of Women in the Mass Media* (New York, NY: Oxford University Press, 1978), pp. 97–115, p. 100.

40 Giles, *Parlour and the Suburb*, pp. 65–70.

41 John Corner, *Theorising Media: Power, Form and Subjectivity* (Manchester: Manchester University Press, 2011), p. 67.

42 *Housewife*, February 1939, pp. 7–10.

43 Corner, *Theorising Media*, p. 66.

44 *Housewife*, February 1939, p. 22–23.

45 Fiona Hackney, '"Use Your Hands for Happiness": Home Craft and Make-do-and-Mend in British Magazines in the 1920s and 1930s', *Journal of Design History*, 19:1 (2006), p. 26.

46 *Housewife*, March 1939, pp. 40–42.

47 *Housewife*, February 1939, p. 48.

48 *Housewife*, November 1939, pp. 36–39; *Housewife*, December 1939, pp. 52–55.

49 *Housewife*, February 1939, pp. 16–21. By Nora Baston, Formerly Head of Domestic Department, County Technical College, Newark, Notts.

50 Leonora Eyles, *Cutting the Coat* (London: Hutchinson, 1941), p. 10.

51 Eyles, *Cutting the Coat*, p. 9.

52 *Housewife*, February 1939, pp. 14–15.

53 Jane Waller and Michael Vaughan-Rees, *Women in Wartime: The Role of Women's Magazines 1939–1945* (London: Macdonald Optima, 1987), p. 12.

54 *Good Housekeeping*, October 1939, p. 5.

55 Sonya Rose, *Which People's War?: National Identity and Citizenship in Wartime Britain 1939–1945* (Oxford: Oxford University Press, 2003), pp. 107–150.

56 James J. Kimble, 'The Home as Battlefront: Femininity, Gendered Spheres, and the 1943 Women in National Service Campaign', *Women's Studies in Communication*, 34 (2011), pp. 84–103, p. 87.

57 *HM Queen Elizabeth Speech* (tx 11 Nov 1939 BBC Home Service). http://www.bbc. co.uk/archive/ww2outbreak/7930.shtml [accessed 16 June 2010]. All punctuation is added.

58 Caitriona Beaumont, *Housewives and Citizens: Domesticity and the Women's Movement in England, 1928–64* (Manchester: Manchester University Press, 2013), pp. 135–164, for a discussion of women's groups during the war.

59 Hall, *White, Male and Middle Class*, p. 51.

60 As Andres has also noted, this aspect was brought to life by Victoria Wood, *Housewife*, 49 (ITV 2006).

61 Mark Donnelly, *Britain in the Second World War* (London: Routledge, 1999), p. 42.

62 Waller and Vaughan-Rees, *Women in Wartime*.

63 Andrew King and John Plunkett (eds), *Victorian Print Media: A Reader* (Oxford: Oxford University Press, 2005), pp. 4–5, discuss cultural transmission in the context of Victorian periodicals.

64 Waller and Vaughan-Rees, *Women in Wartime*, p. 13.

65 Author of various books on interior design such as Roger Smithells, *Make Yourself at Home* (London: Royle Publications, 1948) and Roger Smithells (ed.), *News of the World Better Homes Book* (London: News of the World, 1954).

66 *Housewife*, January 1940, pp. 11–14, 71.

67 *Housewife*, January 1940, pp. 8–10.

68 *Housewife*, November 1939, pp. 10–11.

69 *Housewife*, November 1939, pp. 20–23.

70 *Housewife*, November 1939, pp. 43–47.

71 Rose, *Which People's War?* p. 31.

72 Beetham, *A Magazine of Her Own?* p. 2.

73 *Housewife*, November 1939, p. 53.

74 *Housewife*, August 1940, p. 27.

75 *Housewife*, August 1940, p. 3.

76 *Housewife*, August 1940, p. 36.

77   *Housewife*, July 1940, pp. 70–71.

78   *Housewife*, February 1940, pp. 83–84.

79   *Housewife*, January 1940, pp. 2–3.

80   Lesley Johnson, ' "As Housewives we are Worms": Women, Modernity and the
     Home Question' in Morag Shiach (ed.), *Feminism and Cultural Studies* (Oxford:
     Oxford University Press, 1999), pp. 475–491, 489.

81   Johnson, 'As Housewives we are Worms', p. 488, citing Michel de Certeau, *The
     Practice of Everyday Life*, trans. S.F. Rendall (Berkeley: University of California
     Press, 1984).

82   *Housewife*, October 1940, pp. 34–35.

83   *Housewife*, October 1942, pp. 40–42; December 1942, pp. 20–22.

84   *Housewife*, August 1942, p. 72.

85   *Housewife*, January 1940, pp. 78–79.

86   *Housewife*, October 1945, pp. 21–25.

87   Hackney, 'Use Your Hands for Happiness', pp. 23–38.

88   *Housewife*, March 1945, p. 34.

89   *Housewife*, August 1945, pp. 41–43.

90   *Housewife*, April 1942, pp. 59–61.

91   *Housewife*, October 1942, pp. 58–59.

92   *Housewife*, July 1942, pp. 54–58.

93   White, *Women's Magazines*, p. 129.

94   *Housewife*, February 1940, pp. 52–53.

95   *Housewife*, September 1940, pp. 55–57.

96   White, *Women's Magazines*, p. 125.

97   *Housewife*, January 1941, pp. 44–45.

98   *Housewife*, August 1940, pp. 31–33, 86.

99   *Housewife*, January 1940, pp. 78–80.

100 Penny Summerfield, ' "The Girl That Makes the Thing That Drills the Hole That
     Makes the Spring … ": Discourses of Women and Work in the Second World War'
     in Christine Gledhill and Gillian Swanson (eds), *Nationalising Femininity: Culture,
     Sexuality and British Cinema in the Second World War* (Manchester: Manchester
     University Press, 1996), pp. 35–52; pp. 39–41.

101 *Housewife*, March 1944, pp. 30–32; June 1944, pp. 28–30; February 1945, pp. 57–59.

102 *Housewife*, February 1944, pp. 21–23, 98.

103 Ping Shaw, 'Changes in Female Roles in Taiwanese Women's Magazines
     1970–1944', *Media History*, 6:2 (2000), pp. 151–160, has also suggested a class-
     specific responsiveness to changes in women's roles in magazines, p. 158.

104 Johnson and Lloyd, *Sentenced to Everyday Life*, p. 26.

105 *Housewife*, October 1943, pp. 49–51.

106 *Housewife*, November 1943, pp. 61–63.

107 *Housewife*, January 1944, pp. 21–23.

108 *Housewife*, August 1944, pp. 30–32, 100.

109 Ian McLaine, *Ministry of Morale: Home Front Morale and the Ministry of Information in World War II* (London: George Allen & Unwin, 1979), p. 1756.

110 *Housewife*, August 1943, pp. 24–27.

111 *Housewife*, March 1944, pp. 19–21.

112 Rose, *Which People's War?* p. 33.

113 *Housewife*, July 1943, pp. 26–27, 102.

114 *Housewife*, October 1944, pp. 63–65.

115 *Housewife*, March 1943, pp. 62–63, 102.

116 *Housewife*, May 1944, pp. 57–58; pp. 59–61; November 1944, pp. 27–29.

117 *Housewife*, November 1943, pp. 51–53.

118 *Housewife*, December 1943, pp. 33–35.

119 *Housewife*, July 1944, pp. 62–64.

120 *Housewife*, February 1944, pp. 66–67, 102.

121 *Housewife*, August 1943, pp. 60–61, 104.

122 *Housewife*, March 1943, pp. 44–46, 102.

123 White, *Women's Magazines*, pp. 130–131.

Chapter 3

1 BFI Special Collections Archive File No 1632 (Houseparty), 22 February 1973.

2 Les Cooke, *British Television Drama: A History* (London: British Film Institute, 2003), p. 91.

3 See, for instance, Charlotte Brunsdon, *The Feminist, the Housewife and the Soap Opera* (Oxford: Oxford University Press, 2000); Christine Geraghty, *Women and Soap Opera: A Study of Prime Time Soaps* (Oxford: Polity, 1991).

4 Jo Turney, 'Sex in the Sitting-Room: Renegotiating the Fashionable British Domestic Interior for the Post-permissive Generation' in Laurel Forster and Sue Harper (eds), *British Culture and Society in the 1970s: The Lost Decade* (Newcastle: Cambridge Scholars Publishing), pp. 263–274, p. 270.

5 Mary Irwin, 'What Women Want on Television: Doreen Stephens and BBC Television Programmes for Women, 1953-64', *Westminster Papers*, 8:3 (December 2011), pp. 99–122, p. 105.

6 'Ann's the Delia of Dresses' in *Craven Herald and Pioneer*, 10 January 2010. http://www.cravenherald.co.uk/news/4838387.Ann_s_the_Delia_of_dresses/ [accessed 4 May 2014].

7 The discussion in this chapter owes a large debt to Jean Orba, a presenter and then organiser of *Houseparty*. I was introduced by a mutual friend, Professor Sue Harper, and Jean invited us to her home in Netley Abbey near Southampton for lunch on 17 January 2012, and kindly permitted an interview which lasted a whole afternoon. That interview has contributed greatly to this chapter. Jean was not a television professional at the start of her career, she joined *Houseparty* two years after it had started, having been introduced to the programme through family connections. Jean's valuable reminiscences, insights and observations have been used throughout this discussion. The long discussion with Jean revealed aspects of the programme not necessarily knowable, or easily understood through regular research channels, and I have added many of her comments, all attributed to her, to my argument. Where I have quoted her actual words, I have used double quotation marks for speech.

8 Roger Silverstone, *Television and Everyday Life* (London: Routledge, 1994).

9 Frances Bonner, *Ordinary Television: Analyzing Popular TV* (London: Sage, 2003), p. 32.

10 Helen Wood, *Talking with Television: Women, Talk Shows, and Modern Self-Reflexivity* (Urbana: University of Illinois Press, 2009), pp. 13–30.

11 Wood, *Talking with Television*, p. 68.

12 Andrew Tolson, ' "Being Yourself": The Pursuit of Authentic Celebrity', *Discourse Studies*, 3:4 (2001), pp. 443–457.

13 BFI SCA 1632, 26 February 1973.

14 BFI SCA 1632, 8 May 1973.

15 I am grateful to the Wessex Film and Sound Archive for providing these episodes of *Houseparty*. There are no transmission dates available at the time of publication.

16 David Morley, *The 'Nationwide' Audience* (London: BFI, 1980), pp. 10–15.

17 Dorothy Hobson, *Soap Opera* (Oxford: Polity, 2002).

18 Tim O'Sullivan, 'Researching the Viewing Culture: Television and the Home, 1946-1960' in Helen Wheatley, *Re-viewing Television History: Critical Issues in Television Historiography* (London: I.B. Taurus, 2007), pp. 159–169, p. 161.

19 For instance, see the online discussion thread, http://forums.digitalspy.co.uk/showthread.php?t=1449453 [accessed 24 May 2014]. It also still gets discussed occasionally on radio chat shows.

20 Paul Peacock, *Jack Hargreaves: A Portrait* (Preston: Farming Books and Videos, 2006), p. 88.

21 Joanne Hollows, *Feminism, Femininity and Popular Culture* (Manchester: Manchester University Press, 2000), p. 29.

22 Andrea Peach, 'What Goes Around Comes Around?: Craft Revival, the 1970s and Today', *Craft Research*, 4:2 (2013), pp. 161–179.

23 Brunsdon, *The Feminist, the Housewife, and the Soap Opera*.

24 Ann Oakley, *Housewife* (Harmondsworth: Penguin, 1976) (1974).

25 BFI SCA 1632, 31 March 1973.

26 'Ann's the Delia of Dresses'.

27 Cherry Marshall, *The Cat-Walk* (London: Hutchinson, 1978), p. 130.

28 Wood, *Talking with Television*, pp. 93–95, for a detailed example of a shift in footing.

29 Andrew Tolson, 'Being Yourself', p. 448.

30 John Fiske, *Television Culture* (London: Methuen, 1987).

31 Andrews, *Domesticating the Airwaves*, pp. 183–184.

32 Gough-Yates, *Understanding Women's Magazines*, p. 121.

33 BFI SCA 1632, 30 January 1973.

34 Local viewers would have known that these were stoneware Poole Pottery cups and saucers made by the famous chinaware manufacturer on the South coast in the region.

35 Rachel Moseley, 'Makeover Takeover on British Television', *Screen*, 41:3 (2000), pp. 299–314.

36 BFI SCA 1632, 27 April 1973.

37 BFI SCA 1632, January 1973.

38 BFI SCA 1632, 28 February 1973.

39 The first series, consisting mostly of professional female presenters, was considered by Jean to be a bit 'twin set and pearls' with too didactic a tone.

40 David Gauntlett, *Media, Gender and Identity: An Introduction* (London: Routledge, 2002), pp. 167–172, the ironic tone of 'lad's mags' is a much discussed example.

41 Geraghty, *Women and Soap Opera*.

42 John Ellis, *Seeing Things: Television in the Age of Uncertainty* (London: I.B. Tauris, 2000).

43 Charlotte Brunsdon, 'Identity in Feminist Television Criticism' in Charlotte Brunsdon, Julie D'Acci and Lynn Spigel (eds), *Feminist Television Criticism: A Reader* (Oxford: Oxford University Press, 1997), pp. 114–125.

44 BFI SCA 1632, 31 January 1973; 2 April 1973; April 73.

45 BFI SCA 1632, 9 February 1973.

46 BFI SCA 1632, 6 February 1973.

47 BFI SCA 1632, 20 February 1973.

48 BFI SCA 1632, 23 February 1973.

49 BFI SCA 1632, 11 April 1973.

50 BFI SCA 1632, 31 March 1973.

51 BFI SCA 1632, 25 January 1973.

52 BFI SCA 1632, 2 April 1973.

53 BFI SCA 1632, April 1973.

54 BFI SCA 1632, 13 February 1973.

55 Liesbet van Zoonen, *Feminist Media Studies* (London: Sage, 1994).

56 Judith Butler, *Gender Trouble: Feminism and the Subversion of Identity* (London: Routledge, 1990).

57 The relationship of *Houseparty* to the Women's Liberation Movement is further developed in Laurel Forster, ' "Everything that Makes up a Woman's Life": Feminism and Femininity in *Houseparty*', *Critical Studies in Television*, 9:2 (2014), pp. 94–116.

58 Geraghty, *Women and Soap Opera*.

Chapter 4

1 Rebecca Jennings, *Tomboys and Bachelor Girls: A Lesbian History of Post-war Britain 1945-71* (Manchester: Manchester University Press, 2007), p. 134. Also see pp. 134–172 for a discussion of *Arena Three* and collective lesbian identity.

2 Ann Bruce, *Why Should I Be Dismayed?* (London: Faber and Faber, 1958). Also see Emily Hamer, *Britannia's Glory: A History of Twentieth-Century Lesbians* (London: Cassell, 1996), p. 167, who leaves room for doubt that this is autobiographical work by Langley.

3 Antony Grey, 'Obituaries', *The Independent*, 28 August 1992.

4 A fifth woman, 'Paddy' Dunkley, dropped out of the group.

5 Jennings, *Tomboys and Bachelor Girls*, p. 136.

6 John D. McCarthy and Mayer N. Zald, 'Resource Mobilization and Social Movements: A Partial Theory' in Vincenzo Ruggiero and Nicola Montagna (eds), *Social Movements: A Reader* (London: Routledge, 2008), pp. 105–117, pp. 106–107.

7 Diana E. Kendall, *Sociology in Our Times: The Essentials* (London: Wadsworth, 2003).

8 Ben Edwards and John D. McCarthy, 'Resources and Social Movement Mobilisation' in D.A. Snow, S.A. Soule and H. Kriesi (eds), *The Blackwell Companion to Social Movements* (Oxford: Blackwell, 2004).

9 McCarthy and Zald, 'Resource Mobilization and Social Movements', pp. 107, 110.

10 J. Craig Jenkins, 'Resource Mobilization Theory and the Study of Social Movements' in Vincenzo Ruggiero and Nicola Montagna (eds), *Social Movements: A Reader* (London: Routledge, 2008), pp. 118–127, p. 120.

11 Maria DiCenzo with Lucy Delap and Leila Ryan, *Feminist Media History: Suffrage, Periodicals and the Public Sphere* (Basingstoke: Palgrave, 2011), pp. 54–56.

12 Verta Taylor and Nancy Whittier, 'Lesbian Feminist Mobilisation' in Aldon Morris and Carol McClurg Mueller (eds), *Frontiers in Social Movement Theory* (New Haven, CT: Yale University Press, 1992), pp. 104–129.

13 Laura Doan, *Fashioning Sapphism: The Origins of a Modern English Lesbian Culture* (New York, NY: Columbia University Press, 2001); Rebecca Jennings, *A Lesbian History of Britain: Love and Sex between Women since 1500* (Oxford: Greenwood World Publishing, 2007).

14 Martin B. Duberman, Martha Vicinus and George Chauncey Jr (eds), *Hidden from History: Reclaiming the Gay and Lesbian Past* (London: Penguin, 1991); Lillian Faderman, *Surpassing the Love of Men: Romantic Friendship and Love between Women from the Renaissance to the Present* (New York, NY: Morrow, 1981).

15 See Hamer, *Britannia's Glory*, chap. 9.

16 London School of Economics MRG/1 Hall Carpenter Archive/Albany Trust/14/80.

17 Jennings, *Lesbian History*, p. 152.

18 Taylor and Whittier, 'Lesbian Feminist Mobilisation', p. 111.

19 Sonia Tiernan, *Eva Gore-Booth: An Image of Such Politics* (Manchester: Manchester University Press, 2012), p. 224.

20 Alison Oram, 'Feminism, Androgyny and Love between Women in Urania, 1916–1940', *Media History*, 7:1 (2001), pp. 57–70, p. 61.

21 *Urania*, May–August 1925.

22 Esther Newton, 'The Mythic Mannish Lesbian: Radclyffe Hall and the New Woman' in Estelle B. Freedman, Barbara C. Gelpi, Suan L. Johnson and Kathleen M. Watson (eds), *The Lesbian Issue: Essays from Signs* (Chicago, IL: University of Chicago Press, 1985), pp. 7–25; p. 19.

23 John D'Emilio, *Sexual Politics, Sexual Communities: The Making of a Homosexual Minority in the United States 1940–1970* (Chicago, IL: University of Chicago Press, 1983), pp. 102–104.

24 *The Ladder*, April 1965, p. 20, pp. 4–6; Tony Geraghty, *Guardian*, 15 December 1964; Monica Furlong, *Daily Mail*, 16 February 1965.

25 *The Ladder*, January 1964, p. 8.

26 *The Ladder*, July 1964, p. 23.

27 Georgina Turner, 'Catching the Wave: Britain's Lesbian Publishing goes Commercial', *Journalism Studies*, 10:6 (2009), pp. 769–788.

28 *Arena Three*, 1:1, p. 2.

29 Julian Jackson, *Living in Arcadia: Homosexuality, Politics, and Morality in France from the Liberation to Aids* (Chicago, IL: University of Chicago Press, 2009), pp. 72–74.

30 Jackson, *Living in Arcadia*, pp. 65–66.

31 Jackson, *Living in Arcadia*, pp. 87–88.

32 Jackson, *Living in Arcadia*, p. 69.

33 MRG Dec 1964 Press Release.

34 Anthony Grey makes a special note of this in Langley's obituary, Grey, *The Independent*, 28 August 1992.

35 Dilys Rowe, 'A Quick Look at Lesbians', *Twentieth Century* (Winter 1962–1963).

36 *Arena Three*, 1:11, p. 14.

37 *The New Statesman*, 26 March 1965.

38 *Arena Three*, 1:1, p. 3; 1:6, p. 2.

39 Esmé Langley, 'Editorial Notes', *Arena Three*, 1:5, p. 2.

40 LSE HCA/Albany Trust/14/80. Ron Mount, 'Women Only', *News of the World*, 13 December 1964.

41 Jennings, *Tomboys and Bachelor Girls*, p. 137, suggests this is unlikely.

42 *Arena Three*, 1:1, p. 2.

43 Marianne Cutler, 'Educating the "Variant," Educating the Public: Gender and the Rhetoric of Legitimation in *The Ladder* Magazine for Lesbians', *Qualitative Sociology*, 26:2 (Summer 2003), pp. 233–255.

44 *Arena Three*, 1:1, pp. 3–4.

45 *Arena Three*, 1:2, p. 3.

46 *Arena Three*, 1:2, pp. 6–7.

47 *Arena Three*, 1:1, p. 7.

48 *Arena Three*, 2:3, pp. 7–8.

49 *Arena Three*, 1:3, p. 9.

50 Research of the DOB was also viewed sceptically by some; see Manuela Soares, 'The Purloined Ladder', *Journal of Homosexuality*, 34:3–4 (1998), pp. 27–49.

51 *Arena Three*, 1:5, p. 12.

52 *Arena Three*, 10, pp. 12–13.

53 Turner, 'Catching the Wave', p. 770.

54 Alberto Melucci, *Challenging Codes: Collective Action in the Information Age* (Cambridge: Cambridge University Press, 1996).

55 Enrique Laraña, Hank Johnston and Joseph R. Gusfield (eds), *New Social Movements: From Ideology to Identity* (Philadelphia, PA: Temple University Press, 1994).

56 *Arena Three*, 1:1, p. 11.

57 *Arena Three*, 1:3, p. 11.

58 *Arena Three*, p. 12.

59 *Arena Three*, 1:4, p. 10.

60 *Arena Three*, 1:5, pp. 13–14.

61 Brian Heaphy, 'Situating Lesbian and Gay Cultures of Class Identification', *Cultural Sociology*, 7 (2013), pp. 303–319, suggests that lesbian and gay cultures are not post-class.

62 *Arena Three*, 1:5, p. 13.

63 *Arena Three*, 1:7, p. 12.

64 *Arena Three*, 1:8, p. 2.

65 *Arena Three*, 1:6, pp. 3–4.

66 The literary content of *The Ladder* has been noted in Soares, 'The Purloined Ladder'.

67 Kate Flint, *The Woman Reader 1837–1914* (Oxford: Clarendon Press, 1993), (1995), p. 326.

68 Sally Munt, *New Lesbian Criticism: Literary and Cultural Readings* (Hemel Hempstead: Harvester Wheatsheaf, 1992), p. xi.

69 Minorities Research Group Progress Report. Press Release December 1964, p. 3.

70 *Arena Three*, 1:2, pp. 8–9; 1:3, p. 7.

71 *Arena Three*, 1:3, pp. 6–7; 1:5, pp. 7–8.

72 *Arena Three*, 1:4, p. 2.

73 *Arena Three*, 1:5, p. 10.

74 *Arena Three*, 2:1, pp. 8–9.

75 *Arena Three*, 1:4, p. 2. Also 2:1, p. 9.

76 *Arena Three*, 2:2, p. 2.

77 One of these remains in the London Museum.

78 Elizabeth Wilson, 'Forbidden Love', *Feminist Studies*, 10:2 (Summer 1984), pp. 213–226.

Chapter 5

1   Sukhwant Dhaliwal and Pragna Patel, 'Feminism in the Shadow of Multi-faithism: Implications for South Asian Women in the UK' in Srila Roy (ed.), *New South Asian Feminisms: Paradoxes and Possibilities* (London: Zed, 2012), pp. 169–188, p. 180.

2   Dhaliwal and Patel, 'Feminism in the Shadow of Multi-faithism'.

3   Dhaliwal and Patel, 'Feminism in the Shadow of Multi-faithism', pp. 181–182.

4   Dhaliwal and Patel, 'Feminism in the Shadow of Multi-faithism', pp. 185–186.

5   *Mukti*, 1, p. 2.

6   Stuart Hall, 'The Spectacle of the "Other"' in Stuart Hall (ed.), *Representation: Cultural Representations and Signifying Practices* (London: Sage, 1997), pp. 223–290, pp. 257–259.

7   The Combahee River Collective, 'A Black Feminist Statement' (1977) in Linda Nicholson (ed.), *The Second Wave: A Reader in Feminist Theory* (London: Routledge, 1997), pp. 63–70, p. 64.

8   The Combahee River Collective, 'A Black Feminist Statement', p. 65.

9   The Combahee River Collective, 'A Black Feminist Statement', p. 66.

10 The Combahee River Collective, 'A Black Feminist Statement', p. 67.

11 bell hooks, *Ain't I a Woman: Black Women and Feminism* (London: Pluto, 1982), p. 121.

12 hooks, *Ain't I a Woman*, p. 151.

13 hooks, *Ain't I a Woman*, p. 151.

14 Rozina Visram, *Asians in Britain: 400 Years of History* (London: Pluto, 2002), pp. 9–11.

15 Caroline Knowles and Sharmila Mercer, 'Feminism and Antiracism: An Exploration of the Political Possibilities' in James Donald and Ali Rattansi (eds), *'Race', Culture and Difference* (London: Sage, 1992), pp. 104–125, p. 107.

16 Knowles and Mercer, 'Feminism and Antiracism', p. 106, quoting Hazel Carby.

17 Atvah Brah, 'Difference, Diversity and Differentiation' in James Donald and Ali Rattansi (eds), *'Race', Culture and Difference* (London: Sage, 1992), pp. 126–145, p. 127, p. 128.

18 For a detailed history see Visram, *Asians in Britain*.

19 Visram, *Asians in Britain*, p. 8.

20 Evelyn Brooks Higginbothan, 'African-American Women's History and the Metalanguage of Race' in Joan Wallach Scott (ed.), *Feminism and History* (Oxford: Oxford University Press, 1996), pp. 183–208, p. 184. Citing Michael Omi and Howard Winant, *Racial Formation in the United States: From the 1960s to the 1980s* (London: Routledge, 1989).

21 Mikhail M. Bakhtin, *The Dialogic Imagination: Four Essays* (trans. Caryl Emerson and Michael Holquist) (Austin: University of Texas Press, 1981).

22 Amrit Wilson, *Finding a Voice: Asian Women in Britain* (London: Virago, 1978), pp. 16–17.

23 Srila Roy, 'Introduction: Paradoxes and Possibilities' in Roy (ed.), *New South Asian Feminisms: Paradoxes and Possibilities* (London: Zed, 2012), pp. 1–26.

24 Sariya Contractor, *Muslim Women in Britain: Demystifying the Muslimah* (Abingdon: Routledge, 2012), pp. 1–2.

25 Contractor, *Muslim Women in Britain*, pp. 29–33.

26 Contractor, *Muslim Women in Britain*, p. 35.

27 *Mukti*, 1, p. 2.

28 *Mukti*, 1, p. 2.

29 *Mukti*, 1, p. 8.

30 'Advertise in Mukti' leaflet inserted in *Mukti* issue 1.

31 There may have also been some additional revenue for small advertisements and the actual sale of the magazine at 40p per copy.

32 At the time of writing, no record of Mukti could be found in the council's archives.

33 *Mukti*, 6, p. 2.

34 *Mukti*, 2, p. 2.

35 Heidi Safia Mirza (ed.), *Black British Feminism: A Reader* (London: Routledge, 1997), p. 3.

36 Mirza, *Black British Feminism*, citing Sandoval 1991.

37 Mumtaz Karimjee, who had also worked for Amnesty International.

38 *Mukti*, 6, p. 8.

39 *Mukti*, 6, p. 8.

40 A British global theatre group now running for over thirty years.

41 *Mukti*, 6, pp. 4–5.

42 See www.venudhupa.com [accessed 2 February 2013].

43 *Mukti*, 2, p. 10.

44 Srimati Basu, 'The Blunt Cutting-Edge: The Construction of Sexuality in the Bengali "Feminist" Magazine *Sananda*', *Feminist Media Studies*, 1:2 (2001), pp. 179–196, discusses some similar issues in a contemporary magazine for Bengali women.

45 *Mukti*, 2, pp. 15–16.

46 *Mukti*, 3, p. 3.

47 Susheila Nasta, *Home Truths: Fictions of the South Asian Diaspora in Britain* (Basingstoke: Palgrave, 2002), p. 174.

48 *Mukti*, 3, pp. 4–6.

49 *Mukti*, 3, pp. 7–10.

50 *Mukti*, 3, p. 11.

51 *Mukti*, 3, pp. 12–13.

52 Mukti, 5, pp. 7–8, p. 16.

53 Wilson, *Finding a Voice*, p. 64.

54 Wilson, *Finding a Voice*, p. 64.

55 *Mukti*, 1, p. 4.

56 *Mukti*, 1, p. 5.

57 *Mukti*, 1, pp. 6, 7.

58 *Mukti*, 1, p. 6.

59 *Mukti*, 2, p. 2.

60 *Mukti*, 2, p. 2.

61 *Mukti*, 2, p. 3.

62 *Mukti*, 1, p. 9.

63 *Mukti*, 1, p. 10.

64 *Mukti*, 1, p. 21.

65 *Mukti*, 4, p. 2.

66 *Mukti*, 4, pp. 4–5.

67 *Mukti*, 4, pp. 13–14.

68 *Mukti*, 4, p. 12.

69 Survey carried out in Brent, London, 1984, *Mukti*, 4, pp. 6, 18.

70 *Mukti*, 6, pp. 6–7.

71 *Mukti*, 6, pp. 15–16.

72 *Mukti*, 6, pp. 16, 21.

73 *Mukti*, 7, p. 3.

74 *Mukti*, 6, p. 2.

75 *Spare Rib*, 1985, 153, pp. 26–28.

76 *Spare Rib*, 1987, 183, p. 44.

77 *Mukti*, 7, p. 2.

Chapter 6

1 The letters are held at the Mass Observation Archive at Sussex University in the Small Collections, Rose Hacker Archive.

2 Jenna Bailey, *Can Any Mother Help Me?* (London: Faber and Faber, 2007).

3 Bailey extended her work on the CCC to lecture tours, web page, play and a *Woman's Hour* interview on BBC Radio 4.

4 Rose Hacker assisted by Sylvia Simsova, 'Sisters Under the Skin' (1997) SXMOA 121/53.

5 Rose Hacker on *Woman's Hour* (tx 9 September 2006, BBC R4). Hacker related stories of her life such as how from her father's fashion business situated in Oxford Street she saw the hunger marchers of the 1920s, and how she tried to send parcels to a Welsh family to help them out.

6 Rose Hacker, *Abraham's Daughter: The Life and Times of Rose Hacker* (London: Deptford Forum Publishing, 1996).

7 Brita Ytre-Arne, 'Women's Magazines and Their Readers: The Relationship Between Textual Features and Practices of Reading', *European Journal of Cultural Studies*, 14 (2011), pp. 213–228.

8 Mark Granovetter, 'The Strength of Weak Ties: A Network Theory Revisited', *Sociological Theory*, 1 (1983), pp. 201–233.

9 Published by the Haymarket Group.

10 Bailey, *Can Any Mother Help Me?*, pp. 5–22.

11 *Nursery World*, 31 July 1935, p. 325.

12 Sarah Pederson, 'What's in a Name? The Revealing Use of noms de plume in Women's Correspondence to Daily Newspapers in Edwardian Scotland', *Media History*, 10:3 (2004), pp. 175–185, has discussed women's use of pen names.

13 Bailey, *Can Any Mother Help Me?*, pp. 5–22.

14 Not all members came from *The Nursery World* readership; some were friends of original members or women writing in another journal.

15 Hacker, 'Sisters Under the Skin'.

16 Earlier magazines of the nineteenth century had encouraged women to correspond and form 'social clubs'. See White, *Women's Magazines*, p. 87.

17 Hacker states that she felt obliged to adopt the third person in her retrospective account in order to achieve some emotional distance.

18 SXMOA, Small Collections, Hacker Papers, Box 4, Ad Astra Folder.

19 SXMOA, Small Collections, Hacker Papers, A Priori folder.

20 Bailey, *Can Any Mother Help Me?*, p. 16.

21 SXMOA, Small Collections, Hacker Papers, Box 4, Ad Astra Folder.

22 SXMOA, Small Collections, Hacker Papers, Box 2.

23 Bailey, *Can Any Mother Help Me?*, p. 16.

24 White, *Women's Magazines*, chap. 3, discusses the growth and development of women's magazines in this period.

25 Bailey, *Can Any Mother Help Me?*, pp. 5–22.

26 Hacker, 'Sisters Under the Skin'.

27 Bailey, *Can Any Mother Help Me?*, p. 17.

28 Eva Moskowitz, ' "It's Good to Blow Your Top": Women's Magazines and a Discourse of Discontent 1945–1965', *Journal of Women's History*, 8:3 (Fall 1996), pp. 66–98.

29 Lauren Berlant, 'Intimacy: A Special Issue', *Critical Enquiry*, 24:2 (Winter 1998), pp. 281–288, p. 281.

30 Berlant, 'Intimacy: A Special Issue', pp. 282–283.

31 Hacker, 'Sisters Under the Skin'.

32 White, *Women's Magazines*, p. 35.

33 White, *Women's Magazines*, p. 35, chap. 3.

34 White, *Women's Magazines*, p. 128.

35 White, *Women's Magazines*, p. 128.

36 Karin Wahl Jorgensen, 'Understanding the Conditions for Public Discourse: Four Rules for Selecting Letters to the Editor', *Journalism Studies* 3:1 (2002), pp. 69–81, has discussed criteria for selection of letters to the editor.

37 Hacker, 'Sisters Under the Skin'.

38 SXMOA, Small Collections, Hacker Papers, Box 9, Roberta Folder.

39 SXMOA, Small Collections, Hacker Papers, Box 9, Robina Folder.

40 SXMOA, Small Collections, Hacker Papers, Box 9, Robina Folder.

41 Bailey, *Can Any Mother Help Me?*, p. 103.

42 Bailey, *Can Any Mother Help Me?*, p. 103.

43 SXMOA, Small Collections, Hacker Papers, Box 6, Cotton Goods folder.

44 SXMOA, Small Collections, Hacker Papers, Box 4, Ad Astra Folder.

45 SXMOA 24/1, Box 2 121/18.

46 SXMOA, Small Collections, Hacker Papers, Box 6.

47　Karina Hof, 'Something You Can Actually Pick Up: Scrapbooking as a Form and Forum of Cultural Citizenship', *European Journal of Cultural Studies*, 9 (2006), pp. 363–384.

48　Christy Newman, 'Reader Letters to Women's Health Magazines', *Feminist Media Studies*, 7:2 (2007), pp. 155–170, p. 164.

49　SXMOA, Small Collections, Hacker Papers, Box 4, Ad Astra Folder.

50　SXMOA, Small Collections, Hacker Papers, Box 4, Ad Astra Folder.

51　Rudyard Kipling, 'The Ladies' in *Seven Seas* and *Barrack-Room Ballards* (London: Methuen, 1896).

52　Kaeren Harrison, 'Rich Friendships, Affluent Friends: Middle-Class Practices of Friendship' in Rebecca G. Adams and Graham Allan (eds), *Placing Friendship in Context* (Cambridge: Cambridge University Press, 1998), pp. 92–116, p. 93.

53　Stephen R. Marks, 'The Gendered Contexts of Inclusive Intimacy: The Hawthorne Women at Work and Home' in Rebecca G. Adams and Graham Allan (eds), *Placing Friendship in Context* (Cambridge: Cambridge University Press, 1998), pp. 43–70, p. 43.

54　Marks, 'The Gendered Contexts of Inclusive Intimacy'.

55　Harrison, 'Rich Friendships, Affluent Friends', p. 113.

56　Harrison, 'Rich Friendships, Affluent Friends', p. 102.

57　Graham Allan, 'Friendship and the Private Sphere' in Rebecca G. Adams and Graham Allan (eds), *Placing Friendship in Context* (Cambridge: Cambridge University Press, 1998), pp. 71–91, p. 72, pp. 75–76.

58　James G. Carrier, 'People Who Can Be Friends' in Sandra Bell and Simon Coleman (eds), *The Anthropology of Friendship* (Oxford: Berg, 1999), pp. 26–35.

59　Ytre-Arne, 'Women's Magazines and Their Readers', pp. 213–228, p. 220.

Chapter 7

1　Kristin Skoog, *The 'Responsible' Woman: The BBC and Women's Radio 1945–1955* (Unpublished PhD thesis: University of Westminster, 2010).

2　*Woman's Hour* web page http://www.bbc.co.uk/programmes/b007qlvb [accessed 13 June 2014].

3　*BBC Programme Records 1922–1926* Vol. 1 (London: The British Broadcasting Corporation), pp. 14–16.

4　*BBC Programme Records 1922–1926* Vol. 1 (London: The British Broadcasting Corporation), p. 317.

5   *BBC Programme Records 1922–1926* Vol. 1 (London: The British Broadcasting Corporation), 7 May 1923; 3 May 1923; 2 May 1923, pp. 13–17.

6   Brian Hennessy, *The Emergence of Broadcasting in Britain* (Lympstone: Southerleigh, 2005), p. 314.

7   Such disparity of service could have led to a sense of Londo-centrism in the BBC.

8   BBC Written Archives Centre, 'Women's and Household Talks' in Talks: Women's Programmes 1936–1938 R51/646.

9   BBC WAC R6/219.

10   BBC WAC R6/219.

11   BBC WAC R6/219, 30 September 1925.

12   BBC WAC R51/646.

13   BBC WAC R51/646.

14   BBC WAC R51/646.

15   Michael Bailey, 'The Angel in the Ether' in Michael Bailey (ed.), *Narrating Media History* (London: Routledge, 2009), pp. 52–65, p. 55.

16   Bailey, 'The Angel in the Ether', p. 53.

17   Hennessy, *The Emergence of Broadcasting in Britain*, p. 321.

18   Bailey, 'The Angel in the Ether', p. 54.

19   Bailey, 'The Angel in the Ether', pp. 54–55.

20   Andrews, *Domesticating the Airwaves*, p. 28.

21   BBC WAC R51/646, 2 October 1928.

22   Andrews, *Domesticating the Airwaves*, p. 30, Ch 2.

23   BBC WAC R51/239, 15 February 1928.

24   BBC WAC R51/239, 29 February 1928.

25   BBC WAC R51/239, 16 July 1928.

26   BBC WAC R51/239, 2 October 1928.

27   *Home Health and Garden* (London: The British Broadcasting Corporation, 1928), pp. 1, 5, facing 5, 18, 103, facing 103.

28   BBC WAC R51/239, 7 February 1929.

29   BBC WAC R51/239, 6 September 1928.

30   BBC WAC R51/239, 1 October 1934.

31   'The Making of a Talk' *The Listener* 3 July 1929, p. 12.

32   See Paddy Scannell and David Cardiff, *A Social History of British Broadcasting: Volume One 1922–1939 Serving the Nation* (Oxford: Blackwell, 1991), pp. 153–167 for a more detailed account of Hilda Matheson's work on talks.

33   Hilda Matheson, *Broadcasting* (London: Thornton Butterworth, 1933), p. 188.

34   Matheson, *Broadcasting*, pp. 188–189.

35   Matheson, *Broadcasting*, p. 190.

36   Hugh Chignell, *Public Issue Radio* (Basingstoke: Palgrave, 2011), p. 12.16. Also see Scannell and Cardiff, *British Broadcasting*, p. 168.

37 Scannell and Cardiff, *British Broadcasting*, p. 168.

38 Scannell and Cardiff, *British Broadcasting*, p. 167.

39 Scannell and Cardiff, *British Broadcasting*, p. 66.

40 Nigel Balchin, 'The Unscripted Discussion', *The BBC Quarterly* (1953), 8:1, pp. 7–11.

41 Scannell and Cardiff, *British Broadcasting*, pp. 345–349.

42 Olive Shapley, *Broadcasting a Life* (London: Scarlet Press, 1996), p. 50.

43 Shapley, *Broadcasting a Life*, pp. 124–127.

44 Scannell and Cardiff, *British Broadcasting*, p. 173.

45 Scannell and Cardiff, *British Broadcasting*, p. 176.

46 Kate Lacey, *Feminine Frequencies: Gender, German Radio and the Public Sphere, 1923-1945* (Ann Arbor: University of Michigan Press, 1996), p. 17.

47 Lacey, *Feminine Frequencies*, p. 169.

48 BBC WAC R51/239, 18 September 1935.

49 BBC WAC R51/319, 13 February 1937.

50 BBC WAC R51/319, 13 February 1937.

51 BBC WAC R51/331, 11 May 1942.

52 BBC WAC R19/1460, 26 September 1941.

53 BBC WAC R19/1460, 19 September 1941.

54 BBC WAC R19/1460, 26 September 1941.

55 BBC WAC R19/1460, 29 November 1941. Also see Siân Nicholas, *The Echo of War: Home Front Propaganda and the Wartime BBC, 1939-1945* (Manchester: Manchester University Press, 1996), p. 118.

56 Nicholas, *The Echo of War*, 1 January 1942.

57 Nicholas, *The Echo of War*, 10 December 1941.

58 Nicholas, *The Echo of War*, 2 February 1942.

59 Nicholas, *The Echo of War*, 10 February 1942.

60 Nicholas, *The Echo of War*, 12 February 1942.

61 Nicholas, *The Echo of War*, 10 February 1942.

62 Nicholas, *The Echo of War*, 18 April 1942.

63 Nicholas, *The Echo of War*, 22 April 1942.

64 Nicholas, *The Echo of War*, 11 June 1942.

65 Nicholas, *The Echo of War*, pp. 122–123.

66 BBC WAC R51/645, 2 September 1943.

67 BBC WAC R51/645, 23 September 1943.

68 British Library Listening and Viewing Service, 1LP0167235, Track 2, 14 April 1944.

69 BBC WAC R51/331, 11 May 1942.

70 June Hannam and Karen Hunt, *Socialist Women: Britain, 1880s to 1920s* (London: Routledge, 2002), p. 47.

71 BBC WAC R51/645, 23 September 1943.

72 BBC WAC R51/645, 25 October 1943.

73 BBC WAC R51/645, 28 October 1943.

74 BBC WAC R51/645, 18 November 1943.

75 BBC WAC R51/645, 28 April 1944.

76 BBC WAC R51/645, 11 May 1944.

77 BBC WAC R51/645, 27 June 1944.

78 BBC WAC R51/645, 28 June 1944.

79 BBC WAC R51/645, 29 June 1944.

80 *Radio Times*, 15 September 1944, p. 1.

81 BBC WAC R51/645, 27 July 1944; 1 September 1944.

82 BBC WAC R51/645, 1 September 1944.

83 BBC WAC R51/645, various, late 1944–early 1945.

84 BBC WAC R51/645, 9 March 1945; 14 March 1945, 15 March 1945.

85 BBC WAC R51/645, 26 March 1945; 10 April 1945.

86 BBC WAC R51/645, 5 October 1945.

Chapter 8

1   James Curran, 'Media and the Making of British Society, c. 1700–2000', *Media History*, 8:2 (2000), pp. 135–154, p. 138.

2   Maria DiCenzo, 'Feminist Media and History: A Response to James Curran', *Media History*, 10:1 (2004), pp. 43–49, p. 45.

3   Sidney Tarrow, *Power in Movement: Social Movements and Contentious Politics* (Cambridge: Cambridge University Press, 1994) (3rd ed. 2011), p. 69.

4   Tarrow, *Power in Movement*, p. 67.

5   Winship, *Inside Women's Magazines*, p. 123.

6   Simone Murray, *Mixed Media: Feminist Presses and Publishing Politics* (London: Pluto, 2004), p. 2.

7   Alison Adburgham, *Women in Print: Writing Women and Women's Magazines from the Restoration to the Accession of Victoria* (London: George Allen Unwin, 1972), pp. 86–92.

8   David Doughan and Denise Sanchez, *Feminist Periodicals 1855–1984: An Annotated Critical Bibliography of British, Irish, Commonwealth and International Titles* (New York, NY: New York University Press, 1987), p. 1.

9   Doughan and Sanchez, *Feminist Periodicals*, pp. 1–2. This emanated from the Langham Palace Circle.

10 Cathy Hunt, 'Binding Women Together in Friendship and Unity?', *Media History*, 19:2 (2013), pp. 139–152.

11 Doughan and Sanchez, *Feminist Periodicals*, p. 13.

12 Matthew Beaumont, 'Influential Force: *Shafts* and the Diffusion of Knowledge at the *Fin de Siècle*', *19: Interdisciplinary Studies in the Long Nineteenth Century*, 3 (2006), p. 15. www.19.bbk.ac.uk [accessed 29 June 1920].

13 For a comparative discussion of varying opinion regarding women's suffrage see DiCenzo, *Feminist Media History*, pp. 76–119. For another range of journals at this time see Sheila Rowbotham, *Dreamers of a New Day: Women Who Invented the Twentieth Century* (London: Verso, 2011), pp. 14–15.

14 Constance Rover, *Women's Suffrage and Party Politics in Britain, 1866–1914* (London: Routledge & Kegan Paul, 1967), p. 177.

15 Angela K. Smith, 'The Pankhursts and the War: Suffrage Magazines and the First World War Propaganda', *Women's History Review*, 12:1 (2003), pp. 103–118, p. 104.

16 See, for instance, Brian Harrison, 'Press and Pressure Group in Modern Britain' in Joanne Shattock and Michael Wolff (eds), *The Victorian Periodical Press: Samples and Soundings* (Canada: Leicester University Press, 1982), pp. 261–295, p. 263; p. 275. for a summary and Elizabeth Crawford, *The Women's Suffrage Movement: A Reference Guide 1866–1928* (London: Taylor and Francis, 1999); *The Women's Suffrage Movement in Britain and Ireland; A Regional Survey* (London: Routledge, 2006).

17 Angela V. John, *Evelyn Sharp: Rebel Woman (1869–1955)* (Manchester: Manchester University Press, 2009), p. 67.

18 *Votes for Women*, October 1907, p. 1.

19 Maria DiCenzo, 'Militant Distribution: Votes for Women and the Public Sphere', *Media History*, 6:2 (2000), pp. 115–128.

20 John, *Evelyn Sharp*, pp. 73–75.

21 Flint, *The Woman Reader*, pp. 238–239.

22 Maria Di Cenzo, 'Gutter Politics: Women Newsies and the Suffrage Press', *Women's History Review*, 12:1 (2003), pp. 15–33.

23 The WLM had its own official mouthpiece, *W.I.R.E.S.*

24 Sheila Rowbotham, 'The Beginnings of Women's Liberation in Britain' in Michelene Wandor (ed.), *Once a Feminist: Interviews by Michelene Wandor* (London: Virago, 1990), pp. 14–27, pp. 19–21.

25 Doughan and Sanchez, *Feminist Periodicals*, p. 106; p. 105.

26 Murray, *Mixed Media*, pp. 2–3.

27 Winship, *Inside Women's Magazines*, p. 144.

28 *Spare Rib*, October 1972.

29 *Spare Rib*, November 1972.

30 *Spare Rib* also followed more conventional distribution patterns and was eventually sold through W. H. Smith, a national newsagent chain. It had a distribution

of between 20,000 and 40,000, with copies frequently passed on and read by many readers.

31 Laurel Forster, 'Printing Liberation: The Women's Movement and Magazines in the 1970s' in Laurel Forster and Sue Harper (eds), *British Culture and Society in the 1970s: The Lost Decade* (Newcastle, Cambridge Scholars Publishing, 2010), pp. 93–106.

32 *Spare Rib*, July 1972, p. 2.

33 *Spare Rib*, July 1972.

34 Set up by Erin Pizzey, life-long activist against domestic violence.

35 Winship, *Inside Women's Magazines*, pp. 140–147.

36 Shelley Budgeon, 'The Contradictions of Successful Femininity: Third-Wave Feminism, Postfeminism and "New" Femininities' in Rosalind Gill and Christina Scharff (eds), *New Femininities: Postfeminism, Neoliberalism and Subjectivity* (Basingstoke: Palgrave, 2011), pp. 279–292, p. 283.

37 Sometimes spelt 'mash' and refers to an aggressive form of dancing.

38 Chérie Turner, *The Riot Grrrl Movement: The Feminism of a New Generation* (New York, NY: Rosen, 2001), pp. 11–12.

39 Shelley Budgeon, *Third Wave Feminism and the Politics of Gender in Late Modernity* (Basingstoke: Macmillan, 2011), pp. 114–116.

40 Rosalind Gill, 'Postfeminist Media Culture: Elements of a Sensibility', *European Journal of Cultural Studies*, 10 (2007), pp. 147–166.

41 Women's Library Glasgow houses a good selection of these.

42 Budgeon, *Third Wave Feminism*, p. 37

43 Budgeon, *Third Wave Feminism*, p. 50.

44 Hyun Jung Yun, Monica Postelnicu, Nadia Ramoutar and Lynda Lee Kaid, 'Where Is She?', *Journalism Studies*, 8:6 (2007), pp. 930–947.

45 There are also mainstream offerings on the Internet of course, some broaden existing commercial magazines, http://www.goodhousekeeping.co.uk/ and http://www.menshealth.co.uk/ [accessed 20 June 2013], whilst others have invented a new social mode of communication for women such as Mumsnet, a web/club page for parents.

46 Jess Mc Cabe, 'Leading from the front page', *Guardian*, 13 June 2007.

47 http://knockback.co.uk/ Blog post 'Knockback Times' posted on 6 September 2012 [accessed 23 June 2013].

48 http://knockback.co.uk/ 'Knock knock Knockback' originally posted on 2 November 2011.

49 http://knockback.co.uk/ posted 19 May 2013.

50 http://www.upliftmagazine.com/uplift/ [accessed 23 June 2013].

51 *Verge*, a glossy feminist magazine, originally to be 'Vagina Magazine', also only had one print issue in June 2006. *Subtext* had a grassroots feel to its feminism

and its production values, was rooted in pop culture feminism and ran from 2006 to 2010.

52 Raven had previously been involved with *Modern Review* (1991–1995) and knew Julie Birchall, one of its founders.

53 Ben Dowell, *Guardian*, 26 April 2013.

54 *Guardian*, 30 April 2013.

55 Nina Power, *One Dimensional Woman* (Hampshire: Zero Books, 2009); Caitlin Moran, *How to Be a Woman* (London: Ebury, 2011).

56 *Guardian*, 26 April 2013.

57 *Guardian*, 8 May 2013.

58 *Guardian*, 13 June 2013.

59 Rowbotham, *Dreamers*, pp. 13–14.

60 DiCenzo, 'Feminist Media and History', p. 45.

61 Harrison, 'Press and Pressure Group in Modern Britain', p. 278.

62 Harrison, 'Press and Pressure Group in Modern Britain', p. 276.

63 Murray, *Mixed Media*, pp. 1–6.

64 *Votes for Women*, October 1907, p. 2.

65 *Votes for Women*, October 1907, p. 1.

66 John Mercer, 'Making the News: *Votes for Women* and the Mainstream Press', *Media History*, 10:3 (2004), pp. 187–199, p. 193.

67 Mercer, 'Making the News', p. 195.

68 *Votes for Women*, October 1907, p. 1.

69 *Votes for Women*, October 1907, p. 68.

70 *Votes for Women*, October 1907, pp. 52–53.

71 Evelyn Sharp, 'The Crank of All the Ages', pp. 68–74; 'Patrolling the Gutter', pp. 75–82; and 'Votes for Women – Forward!', pp. 92–100 in *Rebel Women* (New York, NY: John Lane, 1910) (Cheshire: Portrayer Publishers, 2003).

72 Angela V. John, '"Behind the Locked Door": Evelyn Sharp, Suffragette and Rebel Journalist', *Women's History Review*, 12:1 (2003), pp. 5–13.

73 Elizabeth Nelson, *The British Counter-Culture 1966–73: A Study of the Underground Press* (Basingstoke: Macmillan, 1989), p. 47.

74 From a different perspective, Elisabeth A. van Zoonen has discussed how the women's movement in the Netherlands was constructed in the general news in 'The Women's Movement and the Media: Constructing a Public Identity', *European Journal of Communications*, 7:4 (1992), pp. 453–476.

75 Interview posted on *the F-Word*, http://www.thefword.org.uk/features/2008/01/marsha_rowe [accessed 17 June 2013].

76 Joanne Hollows, 'Spare Rib, Second-Wave Feminism and the Politics of Consumption' *Feminist Media Studies*, 13:2 (2013), pp. 268–287.

77 *Guardian*, 25 April 2013 (online).

78 *Guardian*, 30 April 2013.

79 The website was announced as www.spare.rib.co.uk and the launch date as 27 May 2013, with a printed edition to follow in the autumn. It was to be run as a members' organisation.

80 *Times*, 11 May 2013.

81 *Guardian*, 8 May 2013.

82 *Telegraph*, 13 June 2013.

83 *Guardian*, 15 May 2013.

84 *Telegraph*, 24 June 2013.

85 This was produced as a weekly web magazine, with some monthly subscriptions for 'members'. It covered serious issues and offered an ironic take on patriarchy; it also offered meeting places, parties and quizzes for feminists to gather. There was no printed version and it ceased in July 2014.

86 *The Independent*, 15 June 2013.

87 From *SHEquality Matters*, a free online magazine set up by Northern working class women in July 2012, and established as a 'social enterprise with the aim of getting out and involving women in the magazine'. This post suggests that on the Internet, there is room for all and that there is a 'host of New AgeHERs doing their thing' such as 'the Fword, Feministing, Vagenda, The Women's Room', also mentioned in a later post is a new national magazine about to be launched called 'Brass Magazine'. http://www.independent.co.uk/voices/comment/spare-rib-whatever-happened-to-sisterhood-8658152.html [accessed 24 June 2013].

88 *Telegraph*, 24 June 2013.

89 Sheila Rowbotham has identified *La Femme Libra* (1832–?) a feminist magazine of the French revolution in Sheila Rowbotham, *Women in Movement: Feminism and Social Action* (London: Routledge, 1992), p. 59.

90 van Zoonen, *Feminist Media Studies*, p. 128.

91 Maria Mies, 'Towards a Methodology for Feminist Research' in Gloria Bowles and Renate Duelli Klein (eds), *Theories of Women's Studies* (London: Routledge, 1983), pp. 117–139.

92 Flint, *The Woman Reader*, p. 236.

93 Flint, *The Woman Reader*, p. 238.

94 *Votes for Women*, October 1907, p. 8.

95 *Votes for Women*, November 1907, p. 17.

96 *Votes for Women*, January 1908, p. 51.

97 *Spare Rib*, July 1972, p. 12.

98 *Spare Rib*, July 1972, p. 15

99 *Spare Rib*, August 1972, p. 8.

100 Spare Rib, Issue 70.

101 *Spare Rib*, May 1978, 70, pp. 20–23.

102 Marsha Rowe (ed.), *The Spare Rib Reader* (London: Penguin, 1982), pp. 604–605.

103 Rowe, *The Spare Rib Reader*, p. 604.

104 Dale Spender, *There's Always Been a Woman's Movement This Century* (London: Pandora, 1983), pp. 11–14.

105 Dated 3 February 2010 by Heather McIntosh.

106 http://www.thefword.org.uk/features/2010/02/bring_the_herst [accessed 22 July 2013].

107 *Guardian*, 10 December 2013.

108 *Guardian*, 10 December 2013, p. xi.

109 *Guardian*, 26 April 2013.

110 *Guardian*, 26 April 2013.

111 Elizabeth Groeneveld, 'Crafting Public Cultures in Feminist Periodicals' in Rachel Schreiber (ed.), *Modern Print Activism in the United States* (Farnham, Surrey: Ashgate, 2013), pp. 205–220.

112 *Guardian*, 30 April 2013.

113 http://www.mylatestobsession.org.uk/2013/04/controversy_in_feminism_nothing_new [accessed 24 June 2013].

114 Aronson, 'Still Reading Women's Magazines', pp. 31–61, p. 38.

Afterword

1 Marshall Berman, *All That Is Solid Melts into Air: The Experience of Modernity* (New York, NY: Simon and Schuster, 1982), p. 35.

Bibliography

Adams, R.G. and Allan, G. (eds), *Placing Friendship in Context*, Cambridge: Cambridge University Press, 1998.

Adburgham, A., *Women in Print: Writing Women and Women's Magazines from the Restoration to the Accession of Victoria*, London: George Allen and Unwin, 1972.

Adorno, T. and Horkheimer, M., *Dialectic of Enlightenment* (trans. J. Cumming), New York: Herder and Herder, 1972.

Andrews, M., *Domesticating the Airwaves: Broadcasting, Domesticity and Femininity*, London: Continuum, 2012.

Angelou, M., *'Ladies Please Don't Smash These Windows': Women's Writing, Feminist Consciousness and Social Change*, Oxford: Berg, 1995.

Aronson, A. 'Reading Women's Magazines', *Media History* 6:2 (2000), pp. 111–113.

———, 'Still Reading Women's Magazines: Reconsidering the Tradition a Half Century After *The Feminine Mystique*', *American Journalism* 27:2 (2010), pp. 31–61.

Atton, C., *Alternative Media*, London: Sage, 2002.

Bailey, J., *Can Any Mother Help Me?*, London: Faber and Faber, 2007.

Bailey, M. (ed.), *Narrating Media History*, London: Routledge, 2009.

———, 'The Angel in the Ether' in M. Bailey (ed.), *Narrating Media History*, London: Routledge, 2009.

Bakhtin, M.M., *The Dialogic Imagination: Four Essays* (trans. Caryl Emerson and Michael Holquist), Austen: University of Texas Press, 1981.

Balchin, N., 'The Unscripted Discussion', *The BBC Quarterly* 8:1 (1953), pp. 7–11.

Ballaster, R., Beetham, M., Frazer, E. and Hebron, S., *Women's Worlds: Ideology, Femininity and the Woman's Magazine*, Basingstoke: Macmillan, 1991.

Basu, S., 'The Blunt Cutting-Edge: The Construction of Sexuality in the Bengali "Feminist" Magazine *Sananda*', *Feminist Media Studies* 1:2 (2001), pp. 179–196.

Beaumont, C., *Housewives and Citizens: Domesticity and the Women's Movement in England, 1928–64*, Manchester: Manchester University Press, 2013.

Beaumont, M., 'Influential Force: *Shafts* and the Diffusion of Knowledge at the *Fin de Siècle*', *19: Interdisciplinary Studies in the Long Nineteenth Century* (2006), 3.

Beddoe, D., *Back to Home and Duty: Women Between the Wars 1918–1939*, London: Pandora, 1989.

Beetham, M., *A Magazine of Her Own?: Domesticity and Desire in the Woman's Magazine, 1800–1914*, London: Routledge, 1996.

Beetham, M. and Boardman, K. (eds), *Victorian Women's Magazines: An Anthology*, Manchester: Manchester University Press, 2001.

Bell, S. and Coleman, S. (eds), *The Anthropology of Friendship*, Oxford: Berg, 1999.

Berlant, L., 'Intimacy: A Special Issue' *Critical Enquiry* 24:2 (Winter 1998), pp. 281–288.

Berman, M., *All that Is Solid Melts in Air: The Experience of Modernity*, London, Verso, 1983.

Bingham, A., *Gender, Modernity, and the Popular Press in Inter-War Britain*, Oxford: Oxford University Press, 2004.

Bonner, F., *Ordinary Television: Analyzing Popular TV*, London: Sage, 2003.

Brah, A., 'Difference, Diversity and Differentiation' in J. Donald and A. Rattansi (eds), *'Race', Culture and Difference*, London: Sage, 1992.

Braithwaite, B., *Women's Magazines: The First 300 Years*, London: Peter Owen, 1995.

Braithwaite, B. and Barrell, J., *The Business of Women's Magazines: The Agonies and the Ecstasies*, London: Associated Business Press, 1979.

Brake, L., Bell, B. and Finkelstein, D. (eds), *Nineteenth-Century Media and the Construction of Identities*, Basingstoke: Palgrave, 2000.

Brooker, P. and Thacker, A. (eds), *The Oxford Critical and Cultural History of Modernist Magazines*, Oxford: Oxford University Press, 2009–2013.

Bruce, A., *Why Should I Be Dismayed?*, London: Faber and Faber, 1958.

Brunsdon, C., 'Identity in Feminist Television Criticism' in C. Brunsdon, J. D'Acci and L. Spigel (eds), *Feminist Television Criticism: A Reader*, Oxford: Oxford University Press, 1997.

——, *The Feminist, the Housewife, and the Soap Opera*, Oxford: Oxford University Press, 2000.

Brunsdon, C., D'Acci, J. and Spigel, L. (eds), *Feminist Television Criticism: A Reader*, Oxford: Oxford University Press, 1997.

Budgeon, S., 'The Contradictions of Successful Femininity: Third-Wave Feminism, Postfeminism and "New" Femininities' in R. Gill and C. Scharff (eds), *New Femininities: Postfeminism, Neoliberalism and Subjectivity*, Basingstoke: Palgrave, 2011.

——, *Third Wave Feminism and the Politics of Gender in Late Modernity*, Basingstoke: Macmillan, 2011.

Butler, J., *Gender Trouble: Feminism and the Subversion of Identity*, London: Routledge, 1990.

Cameron, D. and Scanlon, D., *The Trouble and Strife Reader*, London: Bloomsbury, 2010.

Cannadine, D., *The Rise and Fall of Class in Britain*, New York: Columbia, 1999.

Certeau, M. de, *The Practice of Everyday Life* (trans. S.F. Rendall), Berkley, University of California Press, 1984.

Chignell, H., *Public Issue Radio: Talks, News and Current Affairs in the Twentieth Century*, Basingstoke: Palgrave, 2011.

Combahee River Collective, 'A Black Feminist Statement' in L. Nicholson (ed.), *The Second Wave: A Reader in Feminist Theory*, London: Routledge, 1997.

Contractor, S., *Muslim Women in Britain: Demystifying the Muslimah*, Abingdon: Routledge, 2012.

Cooke, L., *British Television Drama: A History*, London: British Film Institute, 2003.

Corner, J., *Theorising Media: Power, Form and Subjectivity*, Manchester: Manchester University Press, 2011.

Crawford, E., *The Women's Suffrage Movement: A Reference Guide 1866–1928*, London: Taylor and Francis, 1999.

——, *The Women's Suffrage Movement in Britain and Ireland: A Regional Survey*, London: Routledge, 2006.

Curran, J., 'Media and the Making of British Society, c. 1700–2000', *Media History* 8:2 (2000), pp. 135–154.

Cutler, M., 'Educating the "Variant", Educating the Public: Gender and the Rhetoric of Legitimation in *The Ladder* Magazine for Lesbians', *Qualitative Sociology* 26:2 (Summer 2003), pp. 233–255.

D'Emilio, J., *Sexual Politics, Sexual Communities in the United States 1940–1970*, Chicago: University of Chicago Press, 1983.

Derrida, J., *Politics of Friendship* (trans. George Collins), London: Verso, 1997.

Dhaliwal, S. and Patel, P., 'Feminism in the Shadow of Multi-Faithism: Implications for South Asian Women in the UK' in Srila Roy (ed.), *New South Asian Feminisms: Paradoxes and Possibilities*, London: Zed, 2012.

DiCenzo, M., 'Militant Distribution: Votes for Women and the Public Sphere', *Media History* 6:2 (2000), pp. 115–128.

——, 'Gutter Politics: Women Newsies and the Suffrage Press', *Women's History Review* 12:1 (2003), pp. 15–33.

——, 'Feminist Media and History: A response to James Curran', *Media History* 10:1 (2004), pp. 43–49.

DiCenzo, M., Delap, L. and Ryan, L., *Feminist Media History: Suffrage, Periodicals and the Public Sphere*, Basingstoke: Palgrave, 2011.

Doan, L., *Fashioning Sapphism: The Origins of a Modern English Lesbian Culture*, New York: Columbia University Press, 2001.

Donald. J. and Rattansi, A. (eds), *'Race', Culture and Difference*, London: Sage, 1992.

Donnelly, M., *Britain in the Second World War*, London: Routledge, 1999.

Doughan, D. and Sanchez, D., *Feminist Periodicals 1855–1984: An Annotated Critical Bibliography of British, Irish, Commonwealth and International Titles*, New York: New York University Press, 1987.

Duberman, M., Vicinus, M. and Chauncey, G. (eds), *Hidden from History: Reclaiming the Gay and Lesbian Past*, London: Penguin, 1991.

Edwards, B. and McCarthy, J., 'Resources and social Movement Mobilisation' in D. Snow, S. Soule and H. Kriesi (eds), *The Blackwell Companion to Social Movements*, Oxford: Blackwell, 2004.

Ellis, J., *Seeing Things: Television in the Age of Uncertainty*, London: I.B. Tauris, 2000.

Eyles, L., *Cutting the Coat*, London: Hutchinson, 1941.

Faderman, L., *Surpassing the Love of Men: Romantic Friendship and Love Between Women from the Renaissance to the Present*, New York: Morrow, 1981.

Feasey, R., 'Reading Heat: The Meanings and Pleasures of Star Fashions and Celebrity Gossip' *Continuum: Journal of Media and Cultural Studies* 22:5 (2008), pp. 683–695.

Felski, R., *The Gender of Modernity*, Cambridge, MA: Harvard University Press, 1995.

Fergusson, M., 'Imagery and Ideology: The Cover Photographs of Traditional Women's Magazines' in G. Tuchman, A. Kaplan Daniels and J. Benet (eds), *Hearth and Home: Images of Women in the Mass Media*, New York: Oxford University Press, 1978.

——, *Forever Feminine: Women's Magazines and the Cult of Femininity*, London: Heinemann, 1983.

Finney, G., *Women in Modern Drama: Freud, Feminism and European Theater at the Turn of the Century*, Ithaca: Cornell University Press, 1989.

Fiske, J., *Television Culture*, London: Methuen, 1987.

Flint, K., *The Woman Reader 1837–1914*, Oxford: Clarendon Press, 1993.

Forster. L., 'Revealing the Inner Housewife: Housework and History in Domestic Lifestyle Television' in G. Palmer (ed.), *Exposing Lifestyle Television: The Big Reveal*, Aldershot: Ashgate, 2008.

——, 'Printing Liberation: The Women's Movement and Magazines in the 1970s' in L. Forster and S. Harper (eds), *British Culture and Society in the 1970s: The Lost Decade*, Newcastle: Cambridge Scholars Publishing, 2010.

——, ' "Everything That Makes Up a Woman's Life": Feminism and Femininity in Houseparty', *Critical Studies in Television*, 9:2 (2014), pp. 94–116.

Forster L. and Harper S. (eds), *British Culture and Society in the 1970s: The Lost Decade*, Newcastle: Cambridge Scholars Publishing, 2010.

Freedman, E., Gelpi, B., Johnson, S. and Watson, K. (eds), *The Lesbian Issue: Essays from Signs*, Chicago: University of Chicago Press, 1985.

Friedan, B., *The Feminine Mystique* (1963), London: Norton, 1997.

Gauntlett, D., *Media, Gender and Identity: An Introduction*, London: Routledge, 2002.

Geraghty, C., *Women and Soap Opera: A Study of Prime Time Soaps*, Oxford: Polity, 1991.

Giles, J., *Women, Identity and Private Life in Britain, 1900–50*, Basingstoke, Macmillan, 1995.

——, *The Parlour and the Suburb: Domestic Identities, Class, Femininity and Modernity*, Oxford: Berg, 2004.

Gill, R., *Gender and the Media*, Cambridge: Polity, 2007.

——, 'Postfeminist Media Culture: Elements of a Sensibility', *European Journal of Cultural Studies* 10 (2007), pp. 147–166.

Gill, R. and Scharff, C. (eds), *New Femininities: Postfeminism, Neoliberalism and Subjectivity*, Basingstoke: Palgrave, 2011.

Gledhill, C. and Swanson, G., *Nationalising Femininity: Culture, Sexuality and British Cinema in the Second World War*, Manchester: Manchester University Press, 1996.

Gough-Yates, A., *Understanding Women's Magazines: Publishing, Markets and Readerships*, London: Routledge, 2003.

Granovetta, M., 'The Strength of Weak Ties: A Network Theory Revisited', *Sociological Theory* 1 (1983), pp. 201–233.

Groeneveld, E., 'Crafting Public Cultures in Feminist Periodicals' in R. Schreiber (ed.), *Modern Print Activism in the United States*, Farnham: Ashgate, 2013.

Hacker, R., *Abraham's Daughter: The Life and Times of Rose Hacker*, London: Deptford Forum Publishing, 1996.

Hackney, F., ' "Use Your Hands for Happiness": Home Craft and Make-do-and-Mend in British Magazines in the 1920s and 1930s', *Journal of Design History* 19:1 (2006), pp. 23–38.

Hall, C., *White, Male and Middle Class: Explorations in Feminism and History*, Cambridge: Polity Press, 1992.

Hall, S., 'The Spectacle of the "Other" ' in S. Hall (ed.), *Representation: Cultural Representations and Signifying Practices*, London: Sage, 1997.

Hamer, E., *Britannia's Glory: A History of Twentieth-Century Lesbians*, London: Cassell, 1996.

Hannam, J. and Hunt, K., *Socialist Women: Britain, 1880s to 1920s*, London: Routledge, 2002.

Harrison, B., 'Press and Pressure Group in Modern Britain' in J. Shattock and M. Wolff (eds), *The Victorian Periodical Press: Samples and Soundings*, Canada: Leicester University Press, 1982.

Heaphy B., 'Situating Lesbian and Gay Cultures of Class Identification', *Cultural Sociology* 7 (2013), pp. 303–319.

Hennessy, B., *The Emergence of Broadcasting in Britain*, Lympstone: Southerleigh, 2005.

Hermes, J., *Reading Women's Magazines: An Analysis of Everyday Media Use*, Cambridge: Polity, 1995.

Higginbothan, E.B., 'African-American Women's History and the Metalanguage of Race' in Scott, J.W. (ed.), *Feminism and History*, Oxford: Oxford University Press, 1996.

Hobson, D., *Soap Opera*, Oxford: Polity, 2002.

Hof, K., 'Something You Can Actually Pick Up: Scrapbooking as a Form and Forum of Cultural Citizenship', *European Journal of Cultural Studies* 9 (2006), pp. 363–384.

Hollows, J., *Feminism, Femininity and Popular Culture*, Manchester: Manchester University Press, 2000.

——, 'Spare Rib, Second-Wave Feminism and the Politics of Consumption' *Feminist Media Studies*, 13:2 (2013), pp. 268–287.

hooks, b., *Ain't I a Woman: Black Women and Feminism*, London: Pluto, 1982.

Horowitz, D., 'Rethinking Betty Friedan and The Feminine Mystique; Labor Union Radicalism and Feminism in Cold War America', *American Quarterly* 48:1 (1996), pp. 1–42.

Hunt, C., 'Binding Women Together in Friendship and Unity?', *Media History* 19:2 (2013), pp. 139–152.

Irwin, M., 'What Women Want on Television: Doreen Stephens and BBC Television Programmes for Women, 1953–1964', *Westminster Papers* 8:3 (December 2011), pp. 99–122.

——, 'BBC's *Wednesday Magazine and* Arts Television for Women', *Media History*, forthcoming.

Jackson, J., *Living in Arcadia: Homosexuality, Politics, and Morality in France from the Liberation to Aids*, Chicago: University of Chicago Press, 2009.

Jenkins, J., 'Resource Mobilization Theory and the Study of Social Movements' in V. Ruggiero and N. Montagna (eds), *Social Movements: A Reader*, London: Routledge, 2008.

Jennings, R., *Tomboys and Bachelor Girls: A Lesbian History of Post-war Britain 1945–71*, Manchester: Manchester University Press, 2007.

——, *A Lesbian History of Britain: Love and Sex between Women Since 1500*, Oxford: Greenwood World Publishing, 2007.

John, A., *Evelyn Sharp: Rebel Woman (1869–1955)*, Manchester: Manchester University Press, 2009.

Johnson, L., '"As Housewives We Are Worms": Women, Modernity and the Home Question' in M. Shiach (ed.), *Feminism and Cultural Studies*, Oxford: Oxford University Press, 1999.

——, '"Revolutions Are Not Made by Down-trodden Housewives": Feminism and the Housewife', *Australian Feminist Studies* 15:32 (2000), pp. 237–248.

Johnson, L. and Lloyd, J., *Sentenced to Everyday Life: Feminism and the Housewife*, Oxford: Berg, 2004.

Jones, B., *The Practical Woodworker: A Complete Guide to the Art and Practice of Woodworking*, London: Cassell, 1920.

Jorgensen, K.W., 'Understanding the Conditions for Public Discourse: Four Rules for Selecting Letters to the Editor', *Journalism Studies* 3:1 (2002), pp. 69–81.

Kendall, D.E., *Sociology in Our Times: The Essentials*, London: Wadsworth, 2003.

Kimble, J., 'The Home as Battlefront: Femininity, Gendered Spheres, and the 1943 Women in National Service Campaign', *Women's Studies in Communication* 34 (2011), pp. 84–103.

King, A. and Plunkett, J., *Victorian Print Media: A Reader*, Oxford: Oxford University Press, 2005.

Kipling, R., 'The Ladies' in *Seven Seas* and *Barrack-Room Ballards*, London: Methuen, 1896 (13th edition, 1908).

Knowles, C. and Mercer, S., 'Feminism and Antiracism: An Exploration of the Political Possibilities' in J. Donald and A. Rattansi, *'Race', Culture and Difference*, London: Sage, 1992.

Lacey, K., *Feminine Frequencies: Gender, German Radio, and the Public Sphere, 1923–1945*, Ann Arbor: University of Michigan, 1996.

Laraña, E., Johnston, H. and Gusfield, J.R. (eds), *New Social Movements: From Ideology to Identity*, Philadelphia: Temple University Press, 1994.

Light, A., *Forever England: Femininity, Literature and Conservatism Between the Wars*, London: Routledge, 1991.

Livingstone, S., *Making Sense of Television: The Psychology of Audience Interpretation*, London: Routledge, 1998.

Mahrt, M., 'The Attractiveness of Magazines as "Open" and "Closed" Texts: Values of Women's Magazines and Their Readers', *Mass Communication and Society* 15 (2012), pp. 852–874.

Marshall, C., *The Cat-Walk*, London: Hutchinson, 1978.

Matheson, H., *Broadcasting*, London: Thornton Butterworth, 1933.

McCarthy, J. and Zald, M., 'Resource Mobilization and Social Movements: A Partial Theory' in V. Ruggiero and N. Montagna (eds), *Social Movements: A Reader*, London: Routledge, 2008.

McCracken, E., *Decoding Women's Magazines: From* Mademoiselle *to* Ms, New York: St Martin's Press, 1993.

McLaine, I., *Ministry of Morale: Home Front Morale and the Ministry of Information in World War II*, London, George Allen and Unwin, 1979.

McRobbie, A., *Feminism and Youth Culture: From* Jackie *to* Just Seventeen, London: Macmillan, 1991.

Melucci, M., *Challenging Codes: Collective Action in the Information Age*, Cambridge: Cambridge University Press, 1996.

Mercer, J., 'Making the News: *Votes for Women* and the Mainstream Press', *Media History* 10:3 (2004), pp. 187–199.

Mies, M., 'Towards a Methodology for Feminist Research' in G. Bowles and R. Klein (eds), *Theories of Women's Studies*, London: Routledge, 1983.

Millum, T., *Images of Woman: Advertising in Women's Magazines*, London: Chatto and Windus, 1975.

Mirza, H.S., (ed.), *Black British Feminism: A Reader*, London: Routledge, 1997.

Moran, C., *How to Be a Woman*, London: Ebury, 2011.

Morley, D., *The 'Nationwide' Audience*, London: BFI, 1980.

Morris A., and Mueller, C. (eds), *Frontiers in Social Movement Theory*, New Haven: Yale University Press, 1992.

Moseley, R., 'Makeover Takeover on British Television', *Screen* 41:3 (2000), pp. 299–314.

Moskowitz, E., ' "It's Good to Blow your Top": Women's Magazines and a Discourse of Discontent 1945–1965' *Journal of Women's History* 8:3 (Fall 1996), pp. 66–98.

Munt, S., *New Lesbian Criticism: Literary and Cultural Readings*, Hemel Hempstead: Harvester Wheatsheaf, 1992.

Murray, S., *Mixed Media: Feminist Presses and Publishing Politics*, London: Pluto, 2004.

Nasta, S., *Home Truths: Fictions of the South Asian Diaspora in Britain*, Basingstoke: Palgrave, 2002.

Nelson, E., *The British Counter-Culture 1966–1973: A Study of the Underground Press*, Basingstoke: Macmillan, 1989.

Newman Christy, 'Reader Letters to Women's Health Magazines', *Feminist Media Studies* 7:2 (2007), pp. 155–170.

Newton, E., 'The Mythic Mannish Lesbian: Radclyffe Hall and the New Woman' in E. Freedman, B. Gelpi, S. Johnson and K. Watson (eds), *The Lesbian Issue: Essays from Signs*, Chicago: University of Chicago Press, 1985.

Nicholas, S., *The Echo of War: Home Front Propaganda and the Wartime BBC, 1939–45*, Manchester: Manchester University Press, 1996.

Nicholson, L., *The Second Wave: A Reader in Feminist Theory*, London: Routledge, 1997.

Oakley, A., *Housewife*, Harmondsworth: Penguin, 1974.

Omi, M. and Winant, H., *Racial Formation in the United States: From the 1960s to the 1980s*, London: Routledge, 1989.

Oram, A., 'Feminism, Androgyny and Love between Women in Urania, 1916–1940', *Media History* 7:1 (2001), pp. 57–70.

O'Sullivan, T., 'Researching the Viewing Culture: Television and the Home, 1946–1960' in H. Wheatley (ed.), *Re-viewing Television History: Critical Issues in Television Historiography*, London: I.B. Taurus, 2007.

Palmer G. (ed.), *Exposing Lifestyle Television: The Big Reveal*, Aldershot: Ashgate, 2008.

Peach, A., 'What Goes Around Comes Around?: Craft Revival, the 1970s and Today', *Craft Research* 4:2 (2013), pp. 161–179.

Peacock, P., *Jack Hargreaves: A Portrait*, Preston: Farming Books and Videos, 2006.

Pederson, S., 'What's in a Name? The Revealing Use of noms de plume in Women's Correspondence to Daily Newspapers in Edwardian Scotland', *Media History* 10:3 (2004), pp. 175–185.

Power, N., *One Dimensional Woman*, Hampshire: Zero Books, 2009.

Pumphrey, M., 'The Flapper, the Housewife and the Making of Modernity', *Cultural Studies* 1:2 (1987), pp. 179–194.

Redfern, C. and Aune, K., *Reclaiming the F Word: The New Feminist Movement*, London: Zed Books, 2010.

Rooks, N., *Ladies' Pages: African American Women's Magazines and the Culture That Made Them*, New Jersey: Rutgers University Press, 2004.

Rose, S., *Which People's War?: National Identity and Citizenship in Wartime Britain 1939–1945*, Oxford: Oxford University Press, 2003.

Rover, C., *Women's Suffrage and Party Politics in Britain, 1866–1914*, London: Routledge and Kegan Paul, 1967.

Rowbotham, S., 'The Beginnings of Women's Liberation in Britain' in Michelene
    Wandor (ed.), *Once a Feminist: Interviews by Michelene Wandor*, London: Virago,
    1990.
——, *Women in Movement: Feminism and Social Action*, London: Routledge, 1992.
——, *Dreamers of a New Day: Women Who Invented the Twentieth Century*, London:
    Verso, 2011.
Rowe, D., 'A Quick Look at Lesbians', *Twentieth Century* 171 (Winter 1962–1963),
    pp. 67–72.
Rowe, M. (ed.), *The Spare Rib Reader*, London: Penguin, 1982.
Roy, S., *New South Asian Feminisms: Paradoxes and Possibilities*, London: Zed, 2012.
Ruggiero, V. and Montagna, N. (eds), *Social Movements: A Reader*, London: Routledge,
    2008.
Scannell, P. and Cardiff, D., A *Social History of British Broadcasting: Volume One
    1922–1939 Serving the Nation*, Oxford: Blackwell, 1991.
Schreiber R. (ed.), *Modern Print Activism in the United States*, Farnham, Surrey:
    Ashgate, 2013.
Scott, J.W. (ed.), *Feminism and History*, Oxford: Oxford University Press, 1996.
Shapley, O., *Broadcasting a Life*, London: Scarlet Press, 1996.
Sharp, E., *Rebel Women*, New York: John Lane, 1910.
Shattock, J. and Wolff, M. (eds), *The Victorian Periodical Press: Samples and Soundings*,
    Leicester: Leicester University Press, 1982.
Shaw, P., 'Changes in Female Roles in Taiwanese Women's Magazines 1970–1944', *Media
    History* 6:2 (2000), pp. 151–160.
Shiach, M., *Feminism and Cultural Studies*, Oxford: Oxford University Press, 1999.
Silverstone, R., *Television and Everyday Life*, London: Routledge, 1994.
——, (ed.), *Visions of Suburbia*, London: Routledge, 1997.
Skoog, K., 'The "Responsible" Woman: The BBC and Women's Radio 1945–1955'
    Unpublished PhD thesis, University of Westminster (2010).
Smith, A., 'The Pankhursts and the War: Suffrage Magazines and the First World War
    Propaganda', *Women's History Review* 12:1 (2003), pp. 103–118.
Smith, E., *Hard-Boiled: Working-Class Readers and Pulp Magazines*, Philadelphia:
    Temple University Press, 2000.
Smithells, R., *Make Yourself at Home*, London: Royle Publications, 1948.
—— (ed.), *News of the World Better Homes Book*, London: News of the World, 1954.
Snow, D.A., Soule, S.A. and Kriesi, H. (eds), *The Blackwell Companion to Social
    Movements*, Oxford: Blackwell, 2004.
Soares, M., 'The Purloined Ladder', *Journal of Homosexuality* 34:3–4 (1998),
    pp. 27–49.
Spender, D., *There's Always Been a Woman's Movement This Century*, London: Pandora,
    1983.

Summerfield, P., '"The Girl that Makes the Thing that Drills the Hole that Makes the Spring…"': Discourses of Women and Work in the Second World War' in C. Gledhill and G. Swanson (eds), *Nationalising Femininity: Culture, Sexuality and British Cinema in the Second World War*, Manchester: Manchester University Press, 1996.

Tarrow, S., *Power in Movement: Social Movements and Contentious Politics*, Cambridge: Cambridge University Press, 1994 (3rd edition, 2011).

Taylor V. and Whittier, N. 'Lesbian Feminist Mobilisation' in A. Morris and C. Mueller (eds), *Frontiers in Social Movement Theory*, New Haven: Yale University Press, 1992.

Tiernan, S., *Eva Gore-Booth: An Image of Such Politics*, Manchester: Manchester University Press, 2012.

Tinkler, P., *Constructing Girlhood: Popular Magazines for Girls Growing Up in England 1920–1950*, London: Taylor and Francis, 1995.

Tolson, A., '"Being Yourself": The Pursuit of Authentic Celebrity', *Discourse Studies* 3:4 (2001) pp. 443–457.

Tuchman, G., Daniels A.K. and Benet, J. (eds), *Hearth and Home: Images of Women in the Mass Media*, New York: Oxford University Press, 1978.

Turner, C., *The Riot Grrrl Movement: The Feminism of a New Generation*, New York: Rosen, 2001.

Turner, G., 'Catching the Wave: Britain's Lesbian Publishing goes Commercial', *Journalism Studies* 10:6 (2009), pp. 769–788.

Turney, J., 'Sex in the Sitting-Room: Renegotiating the Fashionable British Domestic Interior for the Post-permissive Generation' in L. Forster and S. Harper (eds), *British Culture and Society in the 1970s: The Lost Decade*, Newcastle: Cambridge Scholars Publishing, 2010.

van Zoonen, E., 'The Women's Movement and the Media: Constructing a Public Identity', *European Journal of Communications* 7:4 (1992), pp. 453–476.

van Zoonen, L., *Feminist Media Studies*, London: Sage, 1994.

Visram, R., *Asians in Britain: 400 years of History*, London: Pluto, 2002.

Waller, J. and Vaughan-Rees, M., *Women in Wartime: The Role of Women's Magazines 1939–1945*, London: Macdonald Optima, 1987.

Wandor, M. (ed.), *Once a Feminist: Interviews by Michelene Wandor*, London: Virago, 1990.

Wheatley, H., *Re-viewing Television History: Critical Issues in Television Historiography*, London: I.B. Taurus, 2007.

White, C., *Women's Magazines 1693–1968*, London: Michael Joseph, 1970.

Williamson, J., *Decoding Advertisements: Ideology and Meaning in Advertising*, London: Boyars, 1978.

Wilson, A., *Finding a Voice: Asian Women in Britain*, London: Virago, 1978.

Wilson, E., 'Forbidden Love', *Feminist Studies* 10:2 (1984), pp. 213–226.

Winship, J., *Inside Women's Magazines*, London: Pandora, 1987.

Wood, H., *Talking with Television: Women, Talk Shows and Modern Self-Reflexivity*, Chicago: University of Illinois Press, 2009.

Ytre-Arne, B., 'Women's Magazines and Their Readers: The Relationship Between Textual Features and Practices of Reading', *European Journal of Cultural Studies* 14 (2011), pp. 213–228.

———, 'Women's Magazines and the Public Sphere', *European Journal of Communication* 26:3 (2011), pp. 247–261.

Yun, H., Postelnicu, M., Ramoutar, N. and Kaid, L., 'Where Is She?', *Journalism Studies* 8:6 (2007), pp. 930–947.

Index

Ablaze! 218
About Women 74
Ack-Ack, Beer-Beer (BBC) 197
advertising 1, 3, 9–10, 10, 11, 12, 17, 25,
    33–35, 36, 37, 38, 39–41, 44, 52,
    55, 63, 90, 92, 119, 104–105, 119,
    149, 157, 180, 209, 214, 215, 225,
    226, 229
Aëthnic Union 84
agony aunts 158, 169, 201–202
Ain't I a Woman 113–114
Anderson, Marjorie 178
Andrews, Maggie 25, 62, 183–184
Anglia Television 52
Anti-Suffrage Review 212
Arcadie: Revue Littéraire et Scientifique 87
Arena Three 14, 79–109, 241
Asian women's advice centres 116

Bailey, Jenna 147–149, 156
Bailey, Michael 182–183
Bakewell, Joan 52
Bakhtin, Mikhail 116
Balchin, Nigel 191
Ballaster, Ros 7, 21
Barnes, Djuna 106
Barrell, Joan 9
Barringer, Claire 105–107
Baty, Thomas 84–85
Baudry, André 87
BBC 13, 52, 56, 62, 88, 94, 177, 179–180,
    183–188, 189, 191–192, 194,
    195–196, 199, 203
    Written Archive Centre (WAC) 177
BBC Household Talks 1928 186
BBC Quarterly, The 191
de Beauvoir, Simone 95, 105
Beetham, Margaret 7, 10, 36
Bell, Avril 58, 74
Bell, Jane 86
Berlant, Lauren 157

Berman, Marshall 239
Berry, Marie 219–220
Bingham, Adrian 21
birth control 47, 76, 156, 157
Bitch 218
Boardman, Kay 10
Bonner, Frances 53
Bowen, Elizabeth 106
Boycott, Rosie 215–216, 226–229
Braithwaite, Brian 9
Bread and Roses 215
Britannia 213
Britannia's Glory 82
Brittain, Vera 24
Budgeon, Shelley 217–218
Burgess, Anthony 107
Business of Women's Magazines, The 9
Bust 218

Campbell, Archie 194, 196
Cannadine, David 21
Cappon, Daniel 97
Cat Walk, The 57
Celebrity 8, 24
Chapman, Diane 80
Chignell, Hugh 191
childcare 13, 35, 38, 47, 49, 52, 56, 57, 76,
    118, 151, 157, 172, 182, 184, 192,
    203, 227
children 6, 26,33, 52, 76, 96, 97, 125, 133,
    134, 141, 156, 161, 163–165, 181,
    216
    evacuees 35, 38, 42, 44, 173
Children's Hour (BBC) 179, 180
Citizenship 24, 32, 33, 41, 126, 131–133,
    137
City of Night 106
class 11, 19, 21–22, 26–30, 33, 41, 44, 45,
    46, 75, 103, 114, 140–142, 150,
    162–165, 190
clothes 30, 56, 58–59, 103–104, 173, 202

Clothes that Count 56
COC 87, 98
Colette 106
Collins, Norman 178, 192
Combahee River Collective 113
Common Cause, The 212
community 8, 14, 46, 49, 79, 99–105,
     112, 120–125, 127–130, 131, 136,
     138–144, 216
consciousness-raising 15, 47, 54, 91–93,
     108, 113, 118, 122, 127, 130–131,
     221, 145, 151, 214–215, 221, 227,
     229, 230
Constructing Girlhood 11
Consumerism 2, 11, 20, 23, 38
     anti-consumerism 55, 58, 221, 226, 235
Contractor, Sariya 117
conversation 8, 53–56, 60–63, 65–67, 69,
     70, 72–73, 77, 104, 160, 165, 171,
     177, 179, 181, 183, 189–191, 193,
     214, 229, 241
cookery and food 30, 35, 38, 45, 54, 56,
     63, 67, 69, 70–72, 74, 179, 181, 184,
     186, 188, 215, 226
Cooperative Correspondence Club (CCC)
     147–175, 241
Corner, John 28
Cosmopolitan 8, 9, 216, 227
Country Woman 215
Craddock, Fanny 52
craft 29, 30, 45, 54, 55, 57–59, 65, 67, 70,
     76, 198, 215, 220, 226, 235–236
Curran, James 207
Cutler, Marianne 94

Daily Chronicle 223
Daily Mail 86
Daily Mirror 199
Dark Side of Venus, The 106
Daughters of Bilitis (DOB) 86, 94
Davidson, Emily Wilding 232, 235
Decoding Advertisements 10
Decoding Women's Magazine 10
Delap, Lucy 10
Denby, Elizabeth 46
Denman, Lady Gertrude 181
Der Kreis-Le Cercle-The Circle 87
Desai, Jayaben 129–130

Desert of the Heart, The 106
Dhaliwal, Sukhwant 112
Dhupa, Venu 123
dialogics 18
DiCenzo, Maria 10, 207, 222
Dickens, Monica 46
divorce 31, 62, 160–161, 174
Doan, Laura 82
domesticity 2, 6–7, 10, 13, 17–20, 24, 26,
     42, 49, 51–52, 53, 55, 150, 157, 169,
     178–179, 181, 184, 192, 200
domestic skills and roles 11, 30–31, 33, 44,
     45, 48, 70, 151, 156, 173, 182–183,
     190, 205
Doughan, David 211
dowry 125–126
Drew, Helena 101–102
Driberg, Tom 46
Duchein, Michel 87
Dusty Answer 107

Eagle 21
Economical Cookery 186
Eddo-Lodge, Reni 221, 236
editorship of magazines 6–7, 34, 44, 47,
     112
Edwards, B 81
Egan, George 55, 63, 68, 73–74
Elliot, Matty 86
emotions 38–39
English Woman's Journal, The 211
Englishwoman's Review, The 211
entertainment 29
ethnicity 11, 14, 111, 126
Eve's Weekly 115–116, 133, 134
Everyday Sexism Project, The 227
Eyles, Leonora 30–31

Faderman, Lillian 82
family income 21–22, 23, 25, 30, 31, 33,
     35, 188
family life 76, 124–125, 161 214
Farm Woman's Hour (BBC) 165
Farmer's Wives (BBC) 165
fashion 20, 30, 35, 57, 59–61, 64, 68,
     72–73, 104, 179, 226
Fawcett Society, The 220, 223
Fawlty Towers 52

Feasey, Rebecca 8
Felski, Rita 20
Feminine Mystique, The 6–7
femininity 2, 7, 10, 18–19, 21, 31, 49, 52,
    156, 169, 173–175, 215, 218, 226
feminism 12, 47, 49, 52, 55, 76, 113
    flappers 85
    and Marxism 136–137
    moderate feminism 55, 129–130
    and publishing 211–222, 223
    and race 113, 116–117
    suffragettes 85, 212–214, 225, 232–233,
        234, 235
    utopian feminism 55
    women's suffrage 5, 10, 12, 211–214,
        222, 231–234
feminist history 5–8, 11, 16, 18, 79–82, 85,
    105, 115–116, 128, 131, 147–148,
    178, 230–231, 237
Feminist Media History 10
Feminist Times 210, 228, 235
    as new 'Spare Rib' 220–221, 227–228,
        236
Fergusson, Marjorie 7
Finding a Voice: Asian Women in Britain
    116
Fitzgerald, Ella 180
Flint, Kate 10, 231
foreigners 44
Forever Feminine 7
Forster, Jackie 108
Forty, Michael 95
Foster, Jeanette 106
FOWAAD 114
Frazer, Elizabeth 7
Freewoman 212
Freundschaftsbanner 87
Friedan, Betty 6–7, 17–18
friendship 54, 69–72, 74, 174–175
Friendz 225
Furlong, Monica 86
F-Word, the 210, 219, 221, 227, 234

Garvey, Jane 178
Gender and the Media 10
Gender of Modernity, The 20
Geraghty, Tony 86
gifts 74, 76

Giles, Judy 20, 27
Gill, Rosalind 10
Girl 21
Gittings, Barbara 86, 97
Glamour 227
Good Housekeeping 21, 22, 32, 186
Good Life, The 52
Gore-Booth, Eva 84
Gough-Yates, Anna 9, 65
Government, local 111, 119–120, 143
Granovetter, Mark 149–151, 172–173
Grass Roots Books 116
Grazia 227
Grey, Anthony 80, 84
Griffiths, Joan 178
Groeneveld, Elizabeth 235–236
Group, The 107
Guardian, The 86, 219, 236

Hacker, Rose 147–148, 151, 156, 159, 165, 172
Hackney, Fiona 29
Hall, Catherine 18
Hall, Stuart 113
Hallinan, Hazel Hunkins 234
Hamer, Emily 82
*Hard-Boiled: Working Class Readers
    and Pulp Magazines* 11
Hargreaves, Jack 55, 68–69, 74
Harpers and Queen 9
Harrison, Brian 222
Hebron, Sandra 7
Hermes, Joke 8
Hidden from History 82
history of magazines 6–8, 9–11, 84–87,
    207–237
home
    as income 43
    post-war homes 46
    as television studio set 64–65
Home, Health and Garden 186
home front 21, 32–34, 41–43
Homes and Gardens 21
Homosexual Law Reform Society (HLRS)
    80, 84
homosexuality 14, 79–109
    in American history 86
    in European history 87
    'homophile' movement 86–87

Honey for the Bears 107
hooks, bell 113–114
Household Talks (BBC) 181–182, 183–188, 192
Houseparty 51–77, 240–241
housewife 13, 17–18, 24–25, 156
    inter-war 17–19
    medieval 18–19
    nineteenth century 19
    royal connections 32
    wartime 32–49, 203
Housewife 17–49, 240
housework 18–20, 46–47, 51, 137, 172, 182
How 125
How to Be a Woman 221
HTV (Harlech Television) 52
Hulton Press 21, 46, 55
humour 72, 93, 98, 107

Ideal Home 21
Images of Woman 10
immigration 14, 111, 115, 116, 131–133
In the News 90
Inglis, Lynne 58
Inside Women's Magazines 7
interior design 35
Internet 2, 13
ITV (Independent Television) 63
Ivimey, Alan 178

Jackie 11
Jennings, Rebecca 82
Johnson, Lesley 10, 41
Jones, Bernard. E 21, 22
Jones, Margot 21, 47

Karen Ablaze 218
Karimjee, Mumtaz 123
Kazi, Najma 141–142
Kenric 108
KnockBack 219–220

Lacey, Kate 192
Ladbury, Ann 56, 75
Ladder, The 86–87, 94, 97
Ladies' Pages 11
Lady's Companion 156

Langley, Esmé 79
Lawrence, D. H. 106
Lee, Daphne 58
Lehmann, Rosamond 106, 107
Lesbian History of Britain, A 82
lesbianism
    and Asian identity 128
    in British history 79, 102–103
    and 'cure' 95, 97, 98
    in European history 102
    lesbian novels 85, 105–107
    mannish lesbian 85
    and the media 88, 90
    and public appearance 94–95, 101, 103
    and transvestism 103–104
letters 4, 86, 115, 132, 147–175
    article-letters 165–168
    and expression 171–173
    as life writing 159–161
    from listeners 181, 195, 201, 203
    postcards 166–167
    from readers 4, 92–93, 98, 103–104, 144, 208, 236
    as reportage 162–165
    from viewers 53–54, 62–64, 66, 67, 69, 72–73, 77
Levensrecht 87
Light, Alison 19
Lilliput 21
Listener, The 24, 187, 189
Lloyd, Justine 10
Love Thy Neighbour 52
LWT (London Weekend Television) 52

MacGregor, Sue 178
MacLurg, William 197–200
Magazines and
    appearance 119, 147, 154–155, 215
    audience 3, 37, 67–68, 143, 145, 177, 200–201
    committees 112, 120–122, 131, 142–144, 181–182, 217
    communication style 1, 3, 4, 124, 131, 133, 142–143, 148, 195
    editorial role 7, 11, 17, 21, 30, 31, 32, 36, 44, 47–48, 53, 56–64, 66, 79, 82, 84–88, 97, 105–106, 116–121, 123, 129–134, 137–142, 147–149,

152–154, 158, 171, 209, 212–213, 216–217, 219, 225, 236
feedback 169–171, 195–197, 203, 205
feminism 2, 4–5, 15, 134, 207–209, 235
flexibility of form and format 1–2, 3, 4, 5, 15, 20, 54, 58, 121, 145, 175, 226, 237, 239
front covers 26–27, 119, 121, 154–155, 224
intimacy 15, 68, 105, 108, 151, 156–158, 165, 174
narrative 157, 169, 171
public sphere 8, 11, 229
publishing and printing 36, 83, 92, 99, 115–116, 119, 142–143, 187, 189, 211–212, 215, 222–223, 224, 236
War Departments 34–35, 37, 38, 180, 201
Magazine of her Own, A 10
Mainland 80
Maitreyi 134
Mansfield, Katherine 105
Manushi 121, 125, 134
Marchant, Hilde 199
marriage 31, 129, 132, 138, 151
Marshall, Cherry 57, 70–71
Marshall, Sylvia 'Marshie' 56–57, 70–71
Mass Observation Archive (MAO) 147–148
Matheson, Hilda 183–184, 190–192, 200
Mattachine 86
McCabe, Jess 219
McCarthy, John 80–82
McCarthy, Mary 107
McCracken, Ellen 10
McRobbie, Angela 11
Melucci, Alberto 99
Men's Hour (BBC) 179–180, 205
Men's Talks (BBC) 180
Men Talking (BBC) 193
Mercer, John 224
Mies, Maria 230
Militant Suffragettes, The 232
Millard, Rosie 229
Millum, Trevor 10
Ministry of Food 34, 38, 180, 201
Ministry of Fuel and Power 34
Ministry of Information 34

Minorities Research Group (MRG) 79, 80, 84, 87–88, 90, 93–94, 97–99, 103, 107–108, 111
Mirza, Heidi Safia 123
Modern Home 22
Modern Woman 191
modernity 20, 22, 29–30, 31, 39, 41, 45, 239–241
Montagu, Lady Mary Wortley 211
Moran, Caitlin 221
Morgan, Elaine 165
Morgan, Lucy 57
Morris, Mary 57
Mostly for Women (BBC) 193, 202
Mount, Ron 90
Move 215
Mueller, Carol 99–100
Mukti 111–145, 241
multifaithism 112
Munro, Margaret 38
Munt, Sally 105
Murdoch, Iris 94–95, 105
Murray, Jenni 178
Murray, Simone 211, 223
My Home 22

narrative 28
Nasta, Susheila 125–126
Nationwide 52
Nelson, Elizabeth 225–226
New Freewoman 212
new woman 85
News of the World 90
newspapers 2, 12
Newton, Esther 85
Nightwood 106
Nonsense of Commonsense 211
Nursery World, The 149–150, 156
Nursing Times 211

Observer 90
Odhams Press 21
ONE 86
One Dimensional Woman 221
oppression 111
Orba, Jean 57–59, 63–66, 68–70, 76
Organisation of Women of African and Asian Descent (OWAAD) 114

Orlando 106
Orwell, George 24
Outwrite 116, 134, 143
Oz 225

Paget, H. M. 232–233
Pankhurst, Christabel 212, 213–214
Pankhurst, Emmeline 212, 213–214
Pankhurst, Sylvia 212, 231
Parlour and the Suburb, The 20
Patel, Pragna 112
Pethick-Lawrence, Emmeline 213,
    231–232
Pethick-Lawrence, Frederick 213, 223–225
Picture Post 21, 46
Pirate Jenny 235
Play for Today 52
Power, Nina 221
pressure group periodical 81, 210, 222
privacy 19, 42
Private Eye 227
private sphere 20
propaganda 34, 40
Proust, Marcel 106
Pumphrey, Martin 20

Queen Elizabeth, consort to George VI
    32–33, 36
Quigley, Janet 193, 194, 199

race and
    consciousness 123–124, 130, 140–141,
        144–145
    discrimination 132–134, 135
    prejudice 14, 111, 116
    racism 113, 115, 138–140
Radclyffe Hall, Margeuritte 85, 96, 105
radio 2, 12, 15, 24–25, 46
    and gender 182–183
    and print media 184, 186, 189, 192,
        197–198, 205
    programmes for women 177–205
    talking style 189–193
    two-way communication 185
Radio Times 180, 184, 203
Raeburn, Antonia 232
Rainbow, The 106
rationing 36, 37, 41
Raven, Charlotte 220–222, 227–229, 235

Reading Women's Magazines 8
Rebel Women 233–234
Rechy, John 106
Reclaiming the F-Word 235
Redfern, Catherine 219, 235–236
Red Rag 215
Reid, Cynthia 80, 93, 108
Reith, John 73, 183
Reports Action 52
resource mobilisation 81, 92, 109
Rhondda, Lady 234
riot grrrl 217, 234–235
Rooks, Noliwe 11
Roper, Esther 84
Rose, Sonya 32
Rowbotham, Sheila 214, 222, 232
Rowe, Dilys 88, 94
Rowe, Marsha 215–216, 226–229, 234
Rule, Jane 106

Sackville-West, Vita 46
Sanchez 211
Sappho 108, 109
scrapbook 2
*Sentenced to Everyday Life: Feminism and
    the Housewife* 10
servants and domestic help 11, 19, 22,
    27–29, 33, 41, 42, 43, 47, 49,
    141–142, 182
Settle, Alison 46
sewing and dressmaking 29, 30, 56, 60,
    75, 154
Sex Variant Women in Literature 106
sexuality 11, 14, 82–84, 90, 93, 103–104,
    109, 119, 121, 127–129, 216
Shafts 212
Shapley, Olive 178, 191–192, 200
Sharp, Evelyn 213, 223, 225, 233–234
Sheba Feminist publishers 116
Shopping and Cooking 186, 188
Shrew 214–215
Shuttleworth, Marian 57
Silverstone, Roger 24
Singleton, Valerie 52
Sister Immaculate 58
Six Point Group, The 234
Smith, Delia 52
Smith, Erin A. 11
Smithells, Roger 35

soap opera 52, 77
Social Movement Organisation (SMO) 14, 80–83, 93, 104, 109
social work 46
Southall Black Sisters 112, 116, 220
Southern Television 52, 54, 55, 63–65
Spare Rib 8, 116, 121, 143, 144, 209, 210, 215–217, 220, 225–229, 232–236
Spare Rib Reader, The 234
Stone, Christopher 24–26
Struther, Jan 19–20
suburban neurosis 24
suburbia 23–25, 41
Suffrage periodicals 5, 10, 12, 212–214, 222
Summerfield, Penny 45–46
Sunday Times, The 90
Surpassing the Love of Men 82
Switsur, Julie 80, 93, 97

Tarrow, Sidney 208
Tate, Mavis 47
Taylor, Verta 84
television 2, 3, 13, 52, 53–77
   presenting 51–77
This Morning 53
thrift 30–31, 35, 37
Times, The 19
Tinkler, Penny 11
Today (BBC) 205
Toward an Understanding of Homosexuality 97
Turner, Georgina 99
Twentieth Century 88, 94

Understanding Women's Magazines 9
Uplift! 220
Urania 84–85

Vagenda 227
Vaughan-Rees, Michael 34
Verel, Shirley 106
Visram, Rosina 115
Vivien, Renee 107
Vogue 57
Votes for Women 210, 213–214, 223–225, 233

Waller, Jane 34
Waverley Journal, The 211

Well of Loneliness, The 96, 106
White, Antonia 107
White, Cynthia 9, 22, 44, 156, 157–158
Whittier, Nancy 84
Why Should I be Dismayed? 79–80
Wife and Home 22
Williamson, Judith 10
Wilson, Amrit 116, 122
Wilson, Elizabeth 109
Winship, Janice 7, 209, 215, 217, 235
Wise Penny, The 186, 188
Wolfe, Beran 95
Woman 21, 22
Woman and Home 22
Women and Work 211
Woman Worker, The 211
Woman's Dreadnought, The 212
Woman's Hour, BBC 13, 15, 148, 177, 178–179, 180–181, 192, 200, 205
Woman's Journal 23, 186
Woman's Own 8, 22, 46, 56, 216
Woman's Page (BBC) 200–205
Woman's Penny Paper 211
Women in Print 116
Women's Institute 181
Women's Liberation Movement (WLM) 13, 51, 86, 114, 127–128, 144, 214
Women's Library, The 235, 241
women's life-stories 116–118
Women's Magazines 1693–1968 9
Women's Magazines: The First 300 Years 9
Women's Talks (BBC) 181–182
Women's Worlds 7
Woolf, Virginia 106, 107
World War Two 13, 18, 21, 31–49, 156, 194–204
work for women
   outside the home 45
   poor pay 135–137
   professions 46, 159, 193
   television presenters 52, 53–59, 74
   war-time 46, 47, 194–195, 201–202

Yorkshire Television 52
Ytre-Arne, Brita 8, 148

Zald, Mayer 80, 82
zines 218–219, 235
Zoonen, Liesbet van 230